Healing at Work:

A Guide to Using Career Conflicts to Overcome Your Past and Build the Future You Deserve

by

Susan Schmitt Winchester
and
Martha I. Finney

TELEMACHUS PRESS

Cover art by Kostis Pavlou

Cover designed by MavroCreative

Photography by Ted Saunders

Published by Telemachus Press, LLC
7652 Sawmill Road
Suite 304
Dublin, Ohio 43016
http://www.telemachuspress.com

Visit the authors' websites:
www.susanjschmitt.com
www.marthafinney.global

ISBN: 978-1-951744-51-9 (eBook)
ISBN: 978-1-951744-52-6 (Paperback)
ISBN: 978-1-951744-73-1 (hardback)

Library of Congress Control Number: 2021900651

Category: SELF-HELP / Personal Growth / General

Version 2021.12.02

Disclaimer

Neither Susan Schmitt Winchester or Martha Finney are mental health or healthcare professionals. The material you will read in these pages is based on how our personal experiences as adult survivors of damaged pasts (ASDPs) intersect with our professional career lives, as well as research into published materials by other experts. The material offered in these pages is for information and inspiration purposes only. Neither the authors, the publisher, nor the publisher's associates, shall be liable for any loss or damage allegedly arising from the material you will read in this book.

Your physician and/or mental health counselor should be consulted for direct intervention for physical and mental health care concerns.

For more information, please visit my disclaimer statement at https://www.susanjschmitt.com/disclaimer/

Table of Contents

Healing at Work:

A Guide to Using Career Conflicts to
Overcome Your Past and Build the Future
You Deserve

Is This Book For You?
Here's How to Know ...

- You are an over-achiever who never rests to enjoy the successes because you feel like you constantly need to prove yourself.

- You feel that what you do isn't enough at work.

- You feel like it's your responsibility to make sure everyone else is happy. If they aren't, you're pretty sure it's your fault.

- You are a people pleaser, often at your own expense.

- Upsetting childhood memories and feelings about yourself often diminish your confidence and may even threaten your career potential.

- When workplace conflicts happen, you spiral into feelings of stress, anxiety, and worry.

- When things don't go well, you almost always assume that it's your fault.

- You feel personally responsible for your coworkers' moods, especially their anger. If someone is mad, it must be something you did.

- Your own anger sometimes gets in the way of healthy workplace relationships.

- You feel like you're almost always on the defensive; that others are negatively judging you.

- Your negative and limiting beliefs about yourself and others get in the way of career-building, trust-based collaborations and projects.

- You watch your teammates thrive inside a safe setting of belonging, but you feel like you're on the outside looking in.

- You're often afraid that you may say or do something that will reveal your fears, secrets, and self-doubt.

- You feel like you're constantly "braced for crazy," ready for another shoe to drop and for chaos to take over.

- You're exhausted at the end of the day because you spend a lot of energy keeping up a false, brave façade. Sometimes you feel like you're actually wearing a mask at work, hiding your true feelings.

- You use unhealthy habits to comfort yourself and relieve your stress.

- You want new, positive ways to build a meaningful life-long career that harnesses your gifts and passions to make the world glad you were here in this life.

So Is This Book For You?

You will run across the acronym, ASDP, many times in this book. It stands for Adult Survivor of a Damaged Past. According to U.S. statistics, at least 67 percent of Americans can consider themselves ASDPs because they have experienced at least one *adverse childhood event* before they turned 18. You'll learn more about what an adverse childhood event is later in this book.

The question is: Do you think you might be an ASDP? Did you have explicit memories of really bad things happening when you were a child, events that made you feel out of control, unsafe, judged, or ashamed? If yes, the chances are excellent that some of the ripple effects coming from those experiences are getting in the way of your being able to fully thrive as an adult today.

If you don't have any particular memories of traumatic events, but work and life just seem harder for you than they are for the people you know, you might be an ASDP.

Either way, if you identify with any of the above bullet points, we hope you will give yourself the gift of enjoying this book. We're not therapists. We're career experts who also happen to be ASDPs ourselves. And the research we're bringing to you in these pages has helped us immensely.

We hope that it will help you too.

Nine Things We Believe About You

Before we get started with the book itself, we'd like to introduce you to nine essential principles that created the foundation of our message to you. This is our vision for you and what you deserve. Let's all start from this shared vision together as we dive into the material. And we'll see you on the other side!

Damaged is not doomed.

Your past isn't permanent. No matter how bad your past is, there's hope that you can have a successful career and a joyful life. Focus on filling your life with positive, practical skills, compassionate interpretations of confusing and stressful events, supportive relationships, and meaning. You can build a life that's even better than your past.

Joy and self-acceptance are within your reach.

This is not a privilege reserved only for those who were lucky enough to start out life in a healthy, functional, positive family environment. Even though you may have started out life overloaded with shame, pain, or trauma, you can learn skills and ways of thinking to discover amazing joy for your life and love for the people in it. Starting with learning to love yourself.

While you can't change the past, you have everything it takes to grow a joyful future.

The pain from your past is your fuel for growth. The depth and vastness of your childhood difficulties give you the capacity for experiencing and deeply appreciating the same expansiveness of the joy that comes with self-acceptance.

You deserve to live a full, happy life in collaboration with people who respect and value you.

There's nobody else like you in the world, and the world needs you. You are worthy of a good life. The time has come to shift your harsh, critical self-talk that echoes the messages you received as a child into one that is compassionate and healing. Respect and value yourself first, and the world will follow your example.

You bring special gifts of resilience and empathy to your career and colleagues.

What you survived from your childhood has made you a survivor. You have insight, perspective, depth of experiences that enrich your relationships at work on a daily basis—and throughout your career over time. When your empathy comes from a place of deep hurt and pain, you're more able to accept and receive other people where they are in their own healing journey.

You can use *all* your career experiences—negative and positive—to build healthy relationships with yourself and others.

Your day-to-day work life is a wonderful lab for growth and learning how to relate to yourself and others in positive, effective, and inspiring ways. Every day you have the chance to practice how to become less reactive, less triggered by other people's behaviors, and more inspiring for your colleagues.

Healing your wounds will make you an extraordinary, inspiring leader.

As you continue on your journey to healing your wounds, you'll find that people are drawn to you. You are becoming increasingly comfortable in your own life and skin, which makes everyone feel safe to be themselves around you. In that setting of confidence and mutual acceptance, you can speak to the greatness of everyone in your life. Your teams and your family alike will see the potential of their best selves in your eyes.

You have precious opportunity to heal your family by taking home what you learn at work.

When you're at work, you have the chance, every day, to practice your belief in yourself, your self-acceptance, and your joy in discovering your value for the world. Learning how to confidently thrive at work, in a positive, collaborative, productive, hopeful way, gives you the methodology to teach your family at home. When you learn new ways to override the workplace triggers that stem from your past drama and trauma, you can take those exact skills home to positively shape and influence the relationships that are closest to you personally. You become the teacher. You become the healer.

The world needs you to heal, so you can help heal the world.

You're not alone. When you start to become more comfortable with who you are and when you start to claim the gift of your life as your birthright, you'll see that others are suffering in secret, just like you. With your new wisdom, you're in a position to help.

Praise for *Healing at Work*!

If you grew up in any kind of abusive or dysfunctional childhood, here is some good news for you: You don't have to be imprisoned by your past. In their new book, *Healing at Work*, authors and career experts Winchester and Finney show us how meaningful and fulfilling workplace experiences can free you from the self-doubt and give you permission to achieve all that you dreamed possible. I know this first-hand. Growing up, I went through the experiences that came with an alcoholic father, divorce, sexual abuse, a mentally ill sibling, and a violent death of a parent. The day I stopped the negative dialogue in my head about how I "wasn't worthy" was the day I began my new life—the one I deserved.

Kelley Steven-Waiss, Founder & CEO of Hitch Works, Inc. and Co-Author of *The Inside Gig*, with Edie Goldberg, PhD

Do yourself a favor. On the very first page of *Healing At Work* there's a list of bullet points entitled, "Is This Book For You? Here's How to Know." Read it. I did and was hooked. Come to find out I'm not alone—and neither are you. What Susan and Martha have created is more than a book—it's a roadmap—a way out of a darkness you didn't even know you were in.

John W. Quinn, Author, *Someone Like Me—An Unlikely Story of Challenge and Triumph Over Cerebral Palsy*

I cried from the very first page. Not from sadness—although that was part of it—but from the discovery that I am not the only one going through life still affected by a past that I thought I put behind me. Those of us who have become leaders in the workplace, once you've learned what I now know from having read *Healing at Work*, you will deepen your understanding and compassion for your teams and yourself. What a blessing it is to discover that you're not alone in this. We're literally all in this together.

Laurie Shakur, Head of People, Rakuten Advertising

I picked up this book and could not put it down. It captivated me. I have led in business for 40 years and have seen first-hand that there are many ways to express and experience love in the workplace. Yet, the best way to start is through self-love, which comes from self-acceptance. But that's not an easy task when you build a career with a wounded heart. *Healing at Work* shows adult survivors of a damaged past how to reclaim their lives and use their worklife experiences to build a life of love, starting with themselves. This is a must-read for anyone who struggles with their past while trying to build a better future.

Joel Manby, Author of *Love Works, 7 Timeless Principles of Effective Leaders.* Former CEO, SeaWorld Entertainment, Herschend Enterprises and Saab Automobiles USA

From the very first examples, through sharing personal stories, to assimilating thoughtful research, and to offering useful tips and tools, this book captures my head and heart. It is not just for those who have had damaged pasts (ASDPs), but for everyone wanting to live up to their full potential. There are an abundance of many specific, actionable ideas that will have personal impact.

Dave Ulrich, PhD, Co-Author, *The Why of Work: How Great Leaders Build Abundant Organizations that Win* Rensis Likert Professor, Ross School of Business, University of Michigan Partner, The RBL Group

In *Healing at Work*, Susan and Martha shine a light on unconscious fears and ingrained responses that trap us in the past, rob our joy in the present, and limit our growth in the future. This is a courageous book—one I wish I had read 20 years ago. For anyone with an ASDP story, it is a compelling invitation to confront the pain in our past in a new, constructive way and a wonderful encouragement to use the workplace as our everyday training ground to practice the awareness, healing, and growth that brings freedom and joy.

Thys DeBruyen, President, Advanced Resources & Consulting

Foreword

MY NAME IS Chris Traub. I am the founder of a global executive search firm. I was raised in Connecticut, but I have lived in Taiwan for 36 years. And I am an adult survivor of a damaged past—or, as you will read about in this book, an ASDP.

Through my executive search work, as well as my participation in global leadership communities, I discovered that many high-functioning founders, enterprise executives, investors, heirs and heiresses, and other leaders, carry their own pain and trauma, so invisible to others around them. These leaders are frequently too busy, high-profile, and generally inaccessible, to easily share their very personal challenges with others; or to avail themselves of support groups and other resources to help them to do the personal work. They may not even be aware of how their pasts continue to get in their way. Often, as ASDPs, we are so good at convincing others of our points of view, we are equally good at convincing ourselves of the validity of our stories and behaviors. And, consequently, we continue to engage in behaviors and practices that don't serve us.

When Susan asked me to review the manuscript for *Healing at Work*, I was both keen to support her work and interested to learn her insights. And when I finally had the opportunity to read through it, I was stunned at the power and clarity of the work. The lists of experiences and beliefs that would help readers discern whether they are ASDPs (particularly the "Laundry List") rang true. In addition, the insight that ASDP experiences could lead to unconscious denial of pain; separating a person from their actual emotions; addictive behaviors; explosive triggers; and a core belief of unworthiness that drive perfectionist and pleaser behaviors all caused me to connect past events, present unconscious belief systems, and their resulting habitual behaviors, with how I was experiencing my relationships at work. In some cases, I'd forgotten about my past experiences on a conscious level. And linking them together, from my standpoint at age 58, gave me much greater understanding of what had happened and how I'd reacted to it at that time; and how those events still stayed with me many decades later without my even realizing it.

Susan and Martha create a powerful invitation to readers to step into their honest and open truths about their painful childhood experiences, by bravely and openly sharing their own intense and dramatic experiences from their pasts right out of the gate.

They then help readers understand that the most powerful healing is found through forgiveness—of themselves, for their behavior patterns and belief systems arising from traumatic childhood situations which they could never have reasonably taken responsibility for—and for their detractors, most often parents and other loved ones, for the painful experiences that they (knowingly or not) inflicted on them as children.

And having focused on amplifying forgiveness, Susan and Martha move on to demonstrate how the corporate world provides an excellent opportunity to practice reframing one's response and reprogramming the mind—to catch oneself in toxic patterns that don't serve and replace them with much healthier patterns that do serve. To step in confidence and peace from isolation to connection; from conflict to harmony; and from avoidance to self-acceptance and joy.

The book ends with pragmatic clues and hacks about creating positive and mutually supportive relationships with bosses, colleagues, and other stakeholders, while navigating a career that helps readers achieve their full potential.

Readers come out of the journey with a sense of calm, optimism, and connectedness that entail a sense of hope. They can see that what were once seemingly intractable challenges and blocks to fulfillment are, in fact, opportunities for further growth, challenge, and abundance.

You know that you have great opportunities to be more joyful with your work, as well as the rest of your life. I'm confident that if you intuitively scan your organization, you would find that a much larger group of your leadership team would identify with—and benefit from—this work than you might otherwise have imagined.

And if you sit quietly and give yourself the space to reflect as you read, you will find that it yields surprising gifts. It certainly has for me.

Enjoy your journey.

Chris Traub
Chairman, Strategic Executive Search Group
Curator, Vortex,
Co-Curator, Co-Mastermind

ctraub@sesasia.com
www.sesasia.com
www.vortexglobal.net

Introduction

IT'S MID-SUMMER 2020 as I'm writing this. I am a newlywed, on a road trip, accompanying my husband on his own lifechanging adventure, as he moves from Oceanside, CA, to Gurnee, IL, to complete his last assignment after nearly 30 years in the U.S. Marines Corps. As we drive the 2,000 miles through America's farmlands, cities and towns, I can't ignore the fact that most of those homes and office buildings I can see through my car window hold hearts and lives undergoing massive upheaval. Lights are on at 4 a.m. as families worry and wonder what's in store for them and how their lives will be changing once the dust of 2020 settles. Lives are changing all over the world. And as this writing, none of us are really sure what we can count on. But really, it's always been this way. It's just more in our faces these days.

What life-changing threat or opportunity will be top of your mind by the time you hold this book? Will it still be Covid? Will it be political unrest? Will it be the weather? Will it be your family's health? Your financial situation? Will it be the chance to relocate to your dream hometown and take up a career that inspires your heart? Whatever it is, one variable is likely to be present: Your life is in the process of changing. Yet again. You're doing it like it's your job.

Come to think about it, we're all in the business of changing lives. And we do it through our work and careers. All the time, even in normal times. People pay us to help them realize their vision, solve a problem, fix a leak, remove a stain, turn around a global corporation, cure a disease, save their marriage, teach their children. Whatever you do for a living, someone believes in you and your ability to create an essential shift in their day, their life, their family, or business. Even the man I'm sitting next to in this car pointed northeastward is my husband because someone started a life-changing conversation in the middle of doing her job. She is my favorite hairstylist. Well, in fact, she is my only hairstylist. I have traveled across the country to keep my appointment with her every six weeks for nearly two years. It was one day, when I was in her chair, when she casually said to me, "Say, I know this guy ..." And in a singular moment in the most normal of mornings, she changed my life. While doing her job.

This is how I've been changing lives: For over 30 years, I've been in corporate HR, helping hundreds of thousands of individuals build their careers, fulfill their potential and achieve their dreams through their relationship with the global companies we work for. For many years, I have cherished my roles in HR as an opportunity to help individuals while I add value to the corporations that hire them. It has been a challenging and rewarding *career* path, one where I see how I make a difference in people's lives every day.

I have also been on a *healing* path for many years, recovering from deep-seated emotional wounds from the past. When my coauthor, Martha Finney, and I came together, her brilliance focused us on workplace conflict as a catalyst for even greater healing at work. I have come to fully appreciate that I'm not the only one coming from a dysfunctional past that has ways to show up in my career. At least two thirds of the people in any workplace—assuming it reflects all the demographic characteristics of society—are on the same healing path I'm on. Or, rather, they could be. There are thousands of people in my workplace community who are just like me on a fundamental level—but one that we just don't talk about. And whether we know it or not, the workplace is providing us with tremendous opportunities to learn, grow, heal, and practice what it means to be our healing selves in an environment where our colleagues sincerely want us to succeed.

To meet me in the halls or watch me on stage, you would see a corporate executive who is on her game and knows her stuff. Hopefully you would come away thinking that you've just met a warm, kind, authentic, accessible person who makes you feel deeply cared about. My demonstrated business acumen and posture tell you that you're in excellent hands. My ready, open smile tells you that you can trust me and that working with me will be an enjoyable, rewarding experience that would likely move your own career along your chosen success path.

But, until you discovered this book, you probably wouldn't have known that I've come to this place in my career after a long journey of overcoming a traumatic early start in life. It left me with an overarching belief that I wasn't good enough. Behind my confident demeanor, I carried a tremendous amount of heartache, stress, anxiety, worry. I didn't have healthy coping skills. And so I used alcohol to numb the pain.

I am what I have come to call an ASDP—or *adult survivor of a damaged past.* You'll read more about my story later in this book. But for now, let's just say that my childhood was marked with fear, shame, neglect, the feeling of being completely helpless and at the mercy of a father who was a rage-a-holic. He was a victim of generations of abuse that preceded me, and he suffered a heavy load of self-loathing that drove him to unspeakable acts. I grew up thinking I somehow deserved his treatment, and that only if I was a very, very good girl with excellent grades, and did everything I could to please him, it would make him stop. But it didn't. And I unconsciously brought those beliefs into my adulthood with me. They came very close to devastating my life.

To be honest with you, it was decades before I fully appreciated how my damaged childhood damaged my adulthood and career. I knew I had it rough. "But that was then," I'd tell myself. I didn't connect my past beliefs about myself and life with how *hard* my adult life was on a daily basis, especially at work. I didn't connect the fact that I grew up with a father who was subject to unpredictable rages to the fact that I exhausted myself physically and emotionally with a constant drive to overachieve and people please. I didn't connect the fact that, growing up, I was always on hyper-alert for doing things wrong with the fact that as an adult I believed that I wasn't good enough, that I had to win people's approval and acceptance over and over and over again. I was constantly braced for attack. That hypervigilance not only exhausted me, but it also signaled to the outside world that, yes, here was someone who was attackable. I somehow came to the unconscious belief that only perfectionism would protect me. But I didn't realize that I had come to allow my perfectionism to turn against me like an autoimmune disease.

It wasn't until very recently in my career that I began to connect the dots. I finally came to grips with the fact that there was actual trauma in my childhood, and it still followed me around like Peter Pan's shadow. As much as I tried to will myself to get beyond these haunted feelings, I eventually learned that healing was never simply a matter of "I just have to get over it." Or "mind over matter." "It wasn't that bad, other people had it worse than I did." Or even, as many experts would advise, "act as if" I was confident and on my game. I may have successfully managed stressful high-level challenges, one at a time, with the help of professional and personal counselors and executive coaches. But the stress, anxiety, and worry persistently followed me up the career path of ever-more rewarding promotions.

I was actually having very normal experiences that came as a result of a very abnormal start in life! And there were actual tools within anyone's reach to override those effects of those childhood experiences on my career and on the rest of my life.

And those tools can be learned in the workplace!

Damaged is Not Doomed

Over the years, as I have worked on this book (and, believe me, its many drafts!), I have always wondered how other professionals and corporate executives like me would receive the reassuring, but annoyingly alliterative, message that "damaged is not doomed." No, I thought, high performers resist that idea that they might be damaged; that somehow carrying wounds from their damaged childhood means that they failed one of life's first resilience tests.

Fifteen years ago, if someone looked kindly into my eyes and said, "Damaged is not doomed," I would have bristled at the implication that not only was there something wrong with me, but also others could see my damage. That my mask was slipping. This is how I would have responded: "I'm not damaged, maybe you're projecting. I'm fine. And I don't appreciate the insinuation that there's something wrong with me. *I'm fine!* Now, if you will excuse me, I have to run to the wine shop before it closes. And, oh by the way, *I'm fine!*"

High performers like me, and maybe you, have a very hard time just accepting the fact that the legacy of a damaging childhood would be carried into even the most ambitious, over-achiever's adult life and career. "I'm not *damaged*," we think. "Some things are just harder for me than they are for others. I'll just work a little harder, later into the night, quadruple-check the quality of my work, book another appointment with my executive coach, tweak my behaviors, and everything will be fine. The family will understand if I have to spend the nights working—I haven't been that much fun to be around lately anyway. And I'll skip the gym—that extra hour a day will be just what I need to take my performance to the next level."

Here's the thing to know: If you grew up exposed to traumatic childhood experiences that left you feeling unsafe, unworthy, unloved, unnecessary, or unwelcome, you very likely experienced a damaged past. And you probably walked away from that past with some damaging beliefs about yourself. *This is a normal outcome of an abnormal set of experiences.* You may have heard—like so many children do when they're being abused by their parents or caretakers—"Children are resilient, they'll get over it." Or you may have been simply told, either by the behaviors or the explicit messages of the adults in your life, that what happened was no big deal. And that you're just being a baby. Or, "You need to grow a thicker skin." Or, "Stop crying or I'll give you something to really cry about." Or, "Stop trying to be the center of attention." No matter what the messages might have been, if you grew up under such circumstances, you were expected to absorb the physical and/or emotional assaults (overt or subtle), without letting anyone see that there was something wrong. That you weren't getting something that you needed.

So when you hit the high-achievement career superhighway, you're surprised or distracted by lingering feelings of self-doubt, being over-exposed, being vulnerable in ways that feel almost life-threatening at times. No matter how hard you try to rise above your past and the memories you bring to work with you, you're frustrated with yourself that your past keeps getting in your way. Or maybe like I was before I began my own journey of healing at work, you are completely unconscious of how much your past is showing up in your career today. It's almost like it's another failing, with the soundtrack of repeated, "I should be able to …" "I should be able to just get over it." "I should be able to settle down and concentrate." "I should be able to have a sensitive, high-stakes conversation without having people blow up at me." "I should inspire my direct reports to even better performance." "I should be able to influence my CEO in a graceful way." "I should be able to take this criticism for what it is, just performance evaluation." Whatever your own personal "list of shoulds" might be—those benchmarks of perfect performance that you always seem to fall short of (at least in your eyes)—if you think about it long enough, you will likely connect the dots yourself. And tie them to beliefs you created about yourself and life as a child just trying to get through another day. And then you'll start to see that those beliefs just aren't true anymore. If they ever were.

The Rest of Your Life Is Yours

So, yes, if you are an ASDP like me, and there is something about life that hurts or is harder than it needs to be, there is likely some damage from the past that you're carrying with you. But remember that I said, "Damaged is not doomed?"

In the decades since you were a child struggling to survive in the day-to-day of a devastating childhood, psychologists, neuroscientists, therapists, and other researchers have been learning about positive psychology and the principles of *neuroplasticity*—the idea that we can actually heal our physical brain by consciously rewiring it to serve us, instead of attack us from within. Our hyper-vigilant self-talk and braced-for-crazy coping mechanisms may have helped us survive a childhood where we had very little control over our day-to-day life experiences, even personal safety. But we are adults now, with more control over how we experience our lives, starting with how we choose to interpret those experiences. With each active choice to select the most self-empowering ways to interpret what happens to us (psychologists call that our *explanatory style*), we are mending our brains by minding our minds. And bit by bit, like the slowly growing coral reef that builds up one cell at a time, the life we build up for ourselves based on our commitment to healing is the one we truly choose.

Then the rest of your life really is yours. Will the painful memories, and maybe even some triggers, continue to present themselves to you at times? Sure. They're part of your past, and you can't change that. But what you can change is the way you respond to them in the now. Your triggers will lose their mastery over your emotions. And you will be so busy building up that coral reef of new, positive, meaningful life experiences and stories, your past will lose its immediacy and urgency.

What It's Like to Be You is Different Than What It Has Been Like to Be Me

Back in the spring of 2018, I had completed the second version of my manuscript and sent it around to experts and friends whose opinions I respect. But then I got this inner prompting to hop on LinkedIn and see what author and employee engagement expert Martha Finney was up to those days. For no special reason, at least not one that I could put my finger on. This urge was followed by an early morning prompting of her own that Martha followed to check out LinkedIn to see what was new (and if you know Martha you know that *early* is, like, 1 a.m.). And she saw that I had been updating myself on her. So, she reached out to say hi. No special reason, just hi.

We had collaborated on a project before, so we had had a professional relationship. But since that project had been long over, it's fair to say looking back that our relationship was at that point one of warm acquaintances. And here's the first thing to know about Martha: She doesn't read friends'—or even warm acquaintances'—manuscripts. Not even if you ask nicely. But, in this case, she made an exception. For some unknown reason ignited by that darn inner prompting. I even offered to pay her to review it. "Nope," she said, "just send it over. I'll take a look." I didn't know it then, but she was actually on vacation in West Palm Beach. And yet I heard back from her inside 24 hours. With commentary, insights, and advice I had heard from no one else. And, with that exchange, we both embarked on another two years of research, writing, banging our heads against our respective walls. What you have in your hands is the product of that time— which has changed our own lives as much as we hope will change yours.

Here's the other thing to know about Martha, at least for the purposes of this book and what we can help you with: She's an ASDP too. She grew up in a household of constant upheaval, moving at least once a year as her father took one CIA assignment after another that took the family around the world. But what makes her an ASDP is the fact that she grew up with a violently alcoholic mother who was so lost to her addiction that she died when Martha was just 12. Her mother was just 42.

Martha's life beginnings were similar in some ways—a troubled family dominated by a violently unpredictable parent. But our adult life's paths couldn't be more different. While my career skyrocketed inside the corporate world, she decided to hop off the corporate track altogether. She never felt safe inside the corporate setting. She could never trust or feel trusted inside any community of other people. In the habit of keeping secrets (both her mother's and her father's), she felt exposed and at risk in the day-to-day workplace. So she opted out. But she dedicated her life's work to building the body of knowledge around what she wanted to know most: What does it take to create a workplace culture where employees feel safe, welcome, and free to be their most authentic selves in order to give their best?

"So, Susan," she said to me the next day from poolside at her rented West Palm house, "Even with your devastating start in life and all the struggles you suffered to endure and prevail, you have achieved immense career success inside the corporate setting. This is what I would want to know if I was your reader: *How did you do that?*"

As we worked together on a nearly brand-new manuscript that would eventually become this book, Martha would weave into the copy her own experiences and reactions to those experiences. And then I would comment in the margins: "I didn't experience that." And then Martha would comment back: "Yes but others have." That's when I came to fully understand how gigantic the ASDP world is. We're raised to believe that we're all alone in this nightmare, largely because our parents or caretakers desperately needed to keep their secret secret. As children, most of us could turn to no one. Not our teachers. Not our pediatricians. Not our religious counselors (my father was the minister, so that would have been out of the question anyway). The police would be called. Jobs would be lost. Careers wrecked.

Community reputations destroyed. And then there would really be some trouble, possibly even involving jails or hospitals.

As a result, we grew up not fully grasping how universal our nightmare experience was—only the details might be different. According to U.S. national statistics, 64 to 67 percent of Americans experienced at least one of 10 officially identified traumatizing events by the time they're 18. (Look around at work. At least two thirds of your colleagues, the ones who seem to have it all together, experienced at least one life-shattering experience when they were a kid.)

As you read our stories in this book, you may react the way I initially reacted, "Well, I didn't experience *that*." Okay. So maybe you didn't. And maybe you don't associate with being from a damaged past at all, but one or both of your parents were overly critical, harsh, judgmental, or overbearing, leaving you with some negative self-beliefs. In any case, if you are an ASDP or do not think you're an ASDP, if you have even the vaguest inkling that what you experienced as a child has negatively influenced how you experience your adult life, stick with us. And if you are like me, you will discover how much your past unconsciously and negatively affects you in your career. You may see yourself in the pages after all. In either case, you will learn insights, tools, and perspectives that will support you as you emerge out of the protective shell you grew to encase your growing spirit into the full adult that you already are. Ready to take on the world in a new, empowering way.

The rest of your life really is yours, you know.

So, Why the Workplace as the Focus for This Book?

In today's society, the common opinion about the workplace is that it's a toxic, unhealthy, and dangerous place to be—both emotionally and physically. If you wanted to read up on all the different ways the workplace can suck the life out of you, you could max out your credit cards buying all the books on the subject that are available on Amazon.

So the idea of the workplace as a venue for emotional healing is a little bit out there, huh? We'll go into the details later in this book but let's set the stage for how you might want to look at things a little differently from here on out. Assuming that your workplace culture is a moderately healthy one, here's what you have going for you:

- You can count on reasonable, predictable behavior from most people you work with and for.

- You're there because of all the people who applied for your job, your colleagues picked *you*. You're wanted.

- You are evaluated on your performance, much of which is objectively measurable. No one is looking deep into your heart and judging your unworthiness as a human being.

- You are surrounded by people who want you to succeed. Maybe not everyone—there is that competitive nature in so many workplace cultures—but, overall, there are people who are actively invested in making sure you have what you need to do a great job for your community of colleagues.

- You have the chance to collect stories of how you played an active role in individual and team successes—making a significant, positive difference in desired results.

- You spend the most productive hours of your days working shoulder-to-shoulder with people who are equally committed to goals that are attainable.

- You learn through experience that it's safe to count on people to keep their promises.

- You receive training you need to improve your performance and interpersonal skills.

- You give your brain those actively positive examples of how your life has meaning, how you can make a real difference in the world in collaboration with people you respect and who are inspired by you too.

- You can create your own identity using the accumulating experiences and stories that support your belief that you are a valuable person with essential contributions to make to a mission or cause that are important to you.

- You can infuse your life with meaning. The smallest of us in the worst of circumstances, as children who were suffering at the hands of cruel caretakers, would think, "If my life starts out this badly, this must mean that I'm meant for something equally important in life." Meaning can come from a variety of sources: Our relationships, our causes and passions, our own children. But it can also come from the work we do, in collaboration with others, all focused together on the same goal to make the world a better place through their shared effort.

- Finally, you experience what I call Bumper Car Moments, those moments of interpersonal conflict that leave you mystified by *what just happened here?* We'll get into Bumper Car Moments in greater depth later on in the book. But for now, it's enough to just bear in mind that these moments—as uncomfortable as they are as they occur—are actually great opportunities for deep healing and discovery. You learn insights into yourself and the world around you that help you build healthier relationships and peace of mind going forward in life. Both at work and at home. That's a lot of meaning to be had on the job right there.

Wendy and Dave Ulrich, in their book *The Why of Work: How Great Leaders Build Abundant Organizations That Win* write: "The meaning we create can make life feel rich and full regardless of our external circumstances or give us the courage to change our external circumstances. When we find meaning in our work, we find meaning in life."

And no one has to know you're an ASDP. That experience that used to be the most important fact of your childhood life loses its power increasingly over time when you're able to displace it with examples and stories of who you are becoming as an adult. That too-heavy-to-carry truth that you may have kept secret while growing up loses its power over you. You are consciously displacing it with new positive facts and stories about who you are becoming. And life is offering new meaning and rewards as you set goals that help you build the career you desire. And attain them. (Which is a big deal if you grew up surrounded by adults who resolved to change, who promised promises but then broke them, or who managed their own pain and frustration by denying the damage they were doing.)

You may not be able to leave your past behind entirely. But you can put it in its place. And you can make it sit down, shut up and watch while you blow right through its limitations and warnings. And become the person you were born to be.

Why I Risked Everything to Bring You This Book

I am the chief HR officer of a Fortune 200 global technology company with more than 23,000 employees counting on me to provide them excellent leadership (not to mention the expectations of investors). So I have obligations. One of which is to have my act together at all times. My CEO, certainly, deserves to be able to depend on me for clear-headed, unemotional, uncomplicated judgment, perspective, and advice. What would the business world think when it discovers I'm an ASDP? What mistaken conclusions about my abilities will it draw?

It's been said that we're as sick as our secrets. And, yes, there's some truth to that. Really. Does the corporate world really need to hear about my past? I don't think so. Throughout the years, as I worked on developing my message of hope for ASDPs, my trusted advisors who cared about my career prospects urged me, *"Don't do it! Don't expose the truth about yourself!"*

If you are an ASDP struggling to thrive to your potential in the work world, I'm guessing you have secrets too. Your team members certainly don't need to know about that time when … Your admin doesn't need to know about your sensitivity around a certain emotional trigger. And heaven help you, does your CEO really need to know all the gory details behind why you would prefer to skip the annual winter party altogether? Nope.

There's a tremendous amount of risk that comes with telling one's truth and past. Especially when you're an ASDP. As I said before, we're in the habit of keeping secrets about ourselves. And many of us still hold this belief that those secrets would be devastating if we told them. Many of those secrets also involve others, such as our parents, whose own lives could be ruined if those stories are uttered aloud. (Some of those people are long dead, but we still worry about what ramifications they might suffer if word got out.) We've long built up the habit of keeping our selves to ourselves. It's safer that way. And the higher up the corporate ranks our successful careers take us, the more risk there is in exposing the sadnesses, fears, memories that threaten to undermine our effectiveness at work.

So, yes. There's some risk in going public with my story. But I'm both proud and reassured to know that I have a supportive CEO and colleagues all over the world who, after hearing my story, come to me to say, "When is your book coming out? I need to read that!"

When Martha wrote her first book, *Find Your Calling, Love Your Life*, she spent some time defining what a calling is—especially in a context that didn't necessarily depend on a religious interpretation. This is what she came up with:

"A calling is the thing that will not allow itself to go undone."

Bringing you this book feels like answering the call. For both Martha and me.

And it's been work. And because it's been work, it's been healing.

What to Look For Inside This Book

Every life has its own unique path to ultimate self-understanding, awareness, acceptance, and ultimately discovering a joyful way to live. ASDPs are also on their unique paths to understanding how their pasts influence the way they experience the rest of their lives. Martha, for instance, knew while she was enduring her childhood years that they would influence the rest of her life. And she was in her early 20s when she started studying what the psychologists had to say about what it meant to be an adult child of an alcoholic (ACOA). In contrast, I was already solidly on a super-achieving career track, handling the stresses, anxieties, and worries as they came flying at me like tennis balls out of one of those relentless serving machines. It wasn't until I was 53 that a counselor kindly looked at a timeline I had drawn as part of a group discovery exercise, and observed, "You have experienced a lot of trauma in your life." I realized in a thunderstruck kind of way how much the traumatic events of my childhood really did have a direct impact on the way I was living my life as an adult, who by all outward appearances, was extremely successful. With that single, simple, kind observation, I collapsed in a heap on the floor, sustained by the embracing, comforting arms of the others in my group.

All of which is to say that as we developed the content for this book, we held in mind that you could be anywhere along the path of self-discovery and healing. We're assuming nothing about you, other than the fact that you are ready to step out of a life of recurring pain and frustration. And that you are open to learning how the workplace can help you build that life that you know is within your reach.

So we've laid out the content of *Healing at Work* in two main parts:

Part I: Foundational Concepts

Chapter 1: My Story

This is where you'll meet me and learn more about my background. Fair warning: You might find the stories to be a grueling read. If you find yourself reading the words through splayed fingers, feel free to skip this part. My intention for sharing my story with you is to show how common and universal ASDP experiences are. You may see yourself in my story. Or you may see someone you know.

Chapter 2: Martha's Story

As I have already mentioned, Martha and I grew up in such different ways. And we entered our adult lives with different coping mechanisms and approaches to our day-to-day experiences. We thought you'd like to hear from her as well.

Chapter 3: What the Heck is an ASDP (And Am I One)?

In this chapter we introduce you to the emotional vestiges of the past that you might be bringing with you to work. You will see how what you're experiencing is actually a normal outcome from your abnormal past. We'll introduce you to the work done by therapists and psychological researchers on *adverse childhood events* (ACEs), and how they have shown to affect the way your brain and nervous system physically developed as you were growing up. You'll learn how workplace dynamics often echo entrenched family roles and how the coping strategies that you might have learned as a child can become maladaptive as an adult.

Chapter 4: Damaged is Not Doomed

This is where you'll start building up hope for yourself, your life, and your career. We will discuss the discoveries around positive psychology, neuro-plasticity, optimism, resilience, and how actively managing the way you talk to yourself about your experiences can rewrite your brain's neuro-pathways. We'll conclude this chapter by introducing you to PERMA, which then brings us into the next chapter on how the workplace is your next great step for healing.

Chapter 5: Why the Workplace is a Lab for Emotional Healing

In this chapter we look at modern workplace trends and research and discoveries that make the workplace a wonderful laboratory for healing. You can use workplace experiences to build up positive narratives and evidence to override the ways you talk to yourself about life that no longer serve you. Naturally, no workplace culture is perfect, but we can shed light on how the more progressive companies are investing their own energies into being emotionally supportive cultures.

Chapter 6: Self-Acceptance: The First Person You Hire is Yourself

Here we help you understand the concept of self-acceptance and how it can set you free to fully achieve your potential at work—and throughout other areas of your life.

Chapter 7: Joy is Within Your Reach

This chapter unleashes your ability to thoroughly enjoy your life and work by replacing your previous limiting beliefs with an image that supports your best vision and version of yourself.

Part II: Bumper Car Moments in Action

Chapter 8: What is a Bumper Car Moment?

In this chapter we introduce you to three main concepts that will support you as you claim control over the rest of your life: The Bumper Car Moment, the Rapid Power Reclaim process, and the Conscious Healing Career Path thinking process versus the Unconscious Wounded Career Path thinking process. Master these concepts, and start putting them into action right away, and you will see immediate results.

Chapter 9: Bumper Car Moments You Might Run Into

This final chapter gives you nine examples of how Bumper Car Moments present themselves to you at work. And how each one is an opportunity to build your skills and give your life story (through your changing *explanatory style*) new, fresh, positive, supportive material.

Epilogue: The Rest of Your Life is Yours

Notice we say "healing at work," not "healed at work." The bad news is that healing at work is an ongoing process. The good news is that there is always a new, wonderful opportunity to continue on that ongoing process. There is always something fresh to learn, either from a new book or a hard knock. You're invited to join us on our next journey, if you'd like to come! It will be more fun if you do.

"If I Read This Book Do I Get to Stop Therapy?"

Uhm. No. If I gifted you with a socket wrench set, you wouldn't say, "Does this mean I get to stop taking my vitamins?" It's like that.

Healing At Work is a valuable tool in your kit for thriving as a joyful adult for the rest of your life. It's not meant to replace any therapeutic program you have going right now or take on in the future. We aren't therapists or mental health experts. We are workplace and career experts, with personal stories and shared passion for the research that we bring you in this book.

Take our tools and use them to build something wonderful, sturdy, beautiful for yourself! Your life. Because the rest of your life is yours.

Part I
Foundational Concepts

Chapter 1
My Story

August 16, 1991

THE CALL CAME on a Friday afternoon. It was my mom. "Hurry home," she said with fear in her voice. "Nancy stopped breathing today, and we don't know if she is going to make it through the weekend."

I quickly packed a few things and left my apartment in Chicago to make the three-and-a-half hour drive back to my mother's home in Michigan.

My little sister, Nancy, had been battling cancer for 10 years, diagnosed when she was only 16 with Stage 4 Hodgkin's disease. She had fought valiantly through chemotherapy, radiation, and eventually endured a bone marrow transplant. Sadly, eight months before this call from my mom, in January 1991, the cancer had reappeared.

I was about to take a long and treacherous dive into a swamp of ugliness. It was the beginning of the darkest storm of my life. The storm would rage on for a very long time.

August 17, 1991

She was lying in a hospital bed in the middle of the family room in my mom's old farmhouse. She was ghostlike. Small, white and almost invisible in her white pajamas disappearing into the white sheets of her bed. She weighed no more than 85 pounds. Fighting her cancer had been a battle with a dragon, and now the dragon was devouring its victim. Nancy was being eaten alive in front of our eyes.

About 5:00 in the afternoon, she asked us to call our dad to come see her. She said she wanted everyone to be there. She had something important she wanted to say.

We gathered around her bed a little while later. She seemed so small and wise as she spoke.

She whispered softly saying, "I want every member of my family to have a part of me. And when I die, I want my ashes divided into three separate parts. I want you each to have a part of me. I don't want you to have to interact with regards to what you do with my ashes. That is why I want my ashes split into three parts. This is because I know that you will each have different relationships and thoughts of me based on our life together at this moment and in the past. I do not want you to use my request to separate my ashes as a reason that creates anger or conflict amongst you. My ashes are not meant to be used as a way to hurt one another."

Dad was furious. "This is not right. We have been separated too long." He and our mom had been divorced for 10 years already. He continued, "We should all hug and pray together as we dispose of your ashes. We need to do this as a family."

"No," said Nancy. "This is not my wish. Sue, I want you to write my words down on a sheet of paper. I want each of us to sign it in agreement that this is how you will take care of the ashes."

I did as she asked. I'm not sure how she did it, but she even managed to sign her own name as well, even though she could hardly hold the pen. It seemed the pen weighed two tons as she labored to sign her name to the document. She went on to repeat: "I represent different memories for each of you."

Then she turned to Dad and said, "Dad, you are a very angry man, and you need help. You need to heal. I want you to have Morey. He will help heal you."

Nancy had often sent Morey, a sweet stuffed mouse, to her friends and even to me when she thought we were sick or sad and needed cheering up. In fact, I would even say that Morey was her prized dear friend. After all, he had been with her through her entire ordeal with cancer.

I had no idea what she was talking about when she addressed Dad that night and told him that he needed to heal. I assumed it was in reference to his rage fits. So did my mom. He was like a volcano for so many years, ready to erupt at the slightest provocation. We never knew when he would blow, but when he did, it was never good. His words were loud, hurtful and furious. And he often threw things at my mom and me. He would rage toward us like an angry bull. But never at Nancy.

Nancy continued, in her soft small muffled voice, "I do not want anything to be used as weapons at my funeral. I don't want any outbursts of anger at my celebration. Mom and Sue, I want you to heal too."

I listened intently. I had no idea what she was really talking about. I assumed that she was talking about our need to heal after she died. She knew she was going to die. Earlier that same day, she had gotten mad at me because I wouldn't let her have ice water in bed because she kept spilling it. I overheard her whisper to my mom that she felt bad because she didn't want to yell at me on her last day.

My dad left around 6:00 pm. At 8:00 pm, it was time for Nancy's medications.

"Stop!" She declared when mom tried to give her the Demerol. "Stop it Dad! Go away! Just leave!" she exclaimed. She kept yelling at my dad.

"Nancy," I said, "Dad isn't here. He left a while ago. Just mom and I are here."

I struggled to help my mom give her the meds. Nancy fought us. I tried to hold her arms down with a large amount of force so Mom could administer the drugs.

But Nancy shouted, "*No!*" So my mom stopped.

About 11:00 pm, Mom tried to give Nancy a sedative because her little body was jerking so much.

"No, Mom," said Nancy calmly. "Please just give me half a dose."

Mom did as Nancy asked.

"Call Dad to come back," requested Nancy.

Mom did as she asked. He arrived about 11:30 pm, as he only lived a short distance from my mom's farm.

Nancy yelled at him for about 45 minutes. She was upset and angry. Mom and I only watched. He left shortly after midnight. He was mad too. It was all very strange and made no sense.

About 1:00 am, my mom and I were sitting on the couch at the end of Nancy's bed. I closed my eyes to try and get some sleep. As I relaxed on the couch, I could hear Nancy still screaming at our dad, even though he wasn't there anymore. The intensity of her screams and shouts were superhuman. It seemed so weird. She could hardly speak clearly the previous several weeks, and here she was just yelling and yelling.

"Take him out of here!" Nancy yelled, as if speaking to us.

But it was clear she wasn't addressing us.

My mom and I sat watching Nancy. Mom was leaning her head on Nancy's bed, just listening as the screams continued. It was such a helpless feeling. Nancy was lost in another world, and we were not part of it.

"I guess that she is going through something that is very deep and personal," said Mom. "I can't seem to comfort her at all," she continued with tears in her eyes. "I don't know what is happening, but I can't break into it. I guess she just needs to work this out herself."

At 2:00 am, I got up to use the bathroom. While I was in the bathroom, I heard Nancy scream, "Daddy, don't touch me there!"

"What did she just say?" I asked myself. She didn't just say what I thought she said, did she? I must have misunderstood her. No way did she just say what I thought she did.

I went back out to the couch and sat with my mom for a little while longer.

"Mom, do you think that Nancy was sexually abused?" I asked.

Mom began to cry. "I think so," she choked, gasping back the tears.

From this point on, it seemed as though Nancy was peeling back years of repressed childhood buried memories of sexual abuse by our dad. Watching her agony before us was worse than anything I had ever seen.

Mom kept saying, "How could this have happened to her? When could it have happened? How could I have missed this happening in my own home?"

Nancy was all alone caught in the nightmare of her memories. She began to act out what had happened to her, as if it were happening to her at that very moment. Here was this poor fragile, cancer-ridden, broken body with broken hips and fractured shoulder blades. She couldn't even turn herself in bed, violently trying to fight the ghost of my dad off of her body. She kicked at him with her hands covering her groin, and she screamed and screamed, yelling at him to get off of her. We could hear fragile, cancer-ridden bones in her body breaking as she fought the ghost of her abuser before us.

The torture we watched was sickening. I was disgusted and horrified over what she revealed to us that night. She never shared anything like this to either of us while she was growing up. Somehow, it felt as though she had pushed it so deep inside to ease the pain of what had happened that it was all coming to the surface as she prepared to return to God's loving arms.

"Daddy, you never listened to me," she sobbed. "Just go. Just go. Daddy, you hit Sue, you hit Mom in the heart, but you hit me in the crotch. Daddy, I'm bleeding. Daddy, that's not your hand. I don't want to play this game anymore!" she shrieked. "I see you by the bed Daddy! Daddy, I hate you. Daddy, I love you. Sweet Jesus, I don't want to go to hell."

The torture continued for another hour and a half. Mom and I just held each other crying and grieving over what we were witnessing. Nancy was confronting the ghost of her past, and there was nothing we could do to help her or comfort her.

Finally, at about 3:30 in the morning, she started to calm down and the violence of her past began to subside, like the tide going back out to the ocean. Mom and I got on each side of her bed and I said to her, "Nancy, Mom and Sue are with you. We love you. What Dad did to you was not your fault. God loves you too. You are not going to hell."

Then she opened her eyes and looked up at each of us. She held her hands up. Mom and I each took one. Her eyes were bulging, and the look in them was panicky as if she were still trying to escape from her horrific memories.

I kept talking to her, holding her hand. After a minute or so, the look in her eyes changed. She seemed to know we were there with her. She relaxed.

"Can you see God yet?" I whispered to her.

Then she smiled the most beautiful angelic sweet smile I have ever seen. The room seemed to glow with warm light.

I said to her, "Your suffering is finally over. You are finally free."

She smiled again with her tiny hands still in ours. There was a white light all around her. I knew she could see God's face. And then she stopped breathing. She was in the arms of God now.

My mom and I wept.

We cried for a long time near her body on the bed. This wasn't real. It couldn't be happening. After a while, as I sat, unable to move, Mom cleaned everything up. Nancy and the bed were totally soaked from her sweat and urine. She had just relived the sexual abuse by my dad for over two hours. Her body was broken and spent. Her soul was now in heaven.

Then came the moment we both dreaded. We had to call my dad and let him know what had happened. It was 4:10 in the morning.

I watched nervously as Mom dialed his number.

"Jim, I am calling to let you know that Nancy has passed away," she said. There was a short pause. She continued, "And," she sighed, "you need to know something else."

She went on to tell him what had happened before Nancy died. I couldn't tell what he was saying, but within seconds, he hung up on her.

"What did he say?" I asked.

"He denied everything, of course," replied Mom with a long sigh.

"What do you think he is going to do now?" I asked.

"I have no idea."

"Do you think he is going to come over here and try to hurt us?" I asked.

"I don't know."

I had visions of him coming over and either setting the house on fire or perhaps trying to kill us another way. He had always scared me. Visions of him coming at me as a child quickly entered my thoughts like a heavy sinking weight on my chest. When he was mad, which was a lot, he would run at me with his chest puffed out, his fat cheeks flushed with anger and his lips pursed tight as he yelled at me for some wrong-doing. I never had figured out why he was so angry. It always seemed like it was my fault because no matter what I did, *nothing* was ever good enough!

A million thoughts raced through my mind.

Mom was quiet too. I guess she may have been wondering too what he was really capable of in light of this horrible accusation. Working in our favor was that he was a minister and had a reputation to maintain. A minister, with a serious rage issue, who had sexually abused my sister when she was little.

Twenty minutes later, the crunching sound of a car on the gravel of the driveway pressed against the stillness of the breaking night.

He stomped into the family room and without a glance at Nancy's body, which was lying on the bed, he demanded, with his hands on his hips, face red and angry, "So what's this about? Molestation?"

"That's ridiculous" he snapped sharply after Mom told him what had happened before she died. "I didn't do that to her! She must have been hallucinating. It must have been the drugs."

Dad jerked in my direction, "Well, I never touched you, did I? You are evidence that I didn't do this. How dare you accuse me of this horrible thing? How dare you ruin my life on this beautiful night?"

I felt like throwing up again. "The fucking bastard," I thought.

He continued, "I never treated you any differently from each other."

"That's not true" I shouted back. "You *never* yelled at Nancy! She was your 'little Nanny.' You treated her so well it was sickening! You yelled at me all of the time!" I screamed back at him.

He reeled back. All I could say finally was, "I know what I saw tonight. And you've said you didn't do it. Now I have to deal with both of these things."

There was silence in the room. No one said a word while we waited for the funeral home to get to the farm. It was the longest 45 minutes of my life.

Suddenly mom whispered in my ear, "I know when it happened."

Then she turned to Dad and stated evenly, "Jim, when did I start working the night shift at the hospital?"

He stared blankly and said nothing.

Mom worked from 11 pm – 7 am for nine years as a nurse beginning when Nancy was seven.

"Kiss me," demanded my dad, as he was getting ready to leave.

"I can't kiss you," I responded coldly.

"I'm going home to shoot myself," he exclaimed.

"You do what you have to do," I replied as I wiped the sweat off my forehead.

Thank God he stormed out, leaving her little farmhouse with the feeling that a devastating tsunami had just swallowed up our hearts.

Finally, the funeral home team came to pick up Nancy's body. Mom and I followed the hearse in our own car. On the way back home, we stopped at a diner for coffee and toast.

"You know, the way this happened was a gift in so many ways," said Mom.

"I guess so," I replied, feeling the exhaustion of the trauma we had witnessed, plus the deep sadness of her death.

"Think about it," said Mom. "First of all, Nancy rewrote the rest of our lives so that we would know this had happened. Your dad was held accountable for his actions. And Nancy was able to let go of and conquer what happened to her before going on to the next life."

"And she waited until I could get here from Chicago to witness it," I said. "I think that is why she didn't die on Friday even though she probably could have."

Coming home from breakfast, we saw the most beautiful blazing fireball sunrise you could possibly imagine. The fog was lifting over the meadows near the farm. It felt peaceful and comforting, like the mist of sadness was being washed away. God was very close. We could feel his presence. So many things happened after her death to indicate that God wanted us to know His love for us and that Nancy was with Him.

Her funeral was a celebration of her life. The church was packed. A bagpiper played *Amazing Grace* as her casket was brought down the aisle just like she wanted. Nancy had planned the entire service.

"Leave it to Nancy to rewrite the whole book," I thought as the service carried on. God, she was so amazing. So small and yet so strong and wise in limitless ways. Little did I know how much she would rewrite my understanding of my life for years to come.

And then I went back to Chicago and resumed my work as if nothing had happened. No one was the wiser. No one knew my secret.

You Can Come From Really Bad Shit and Still Be Okay

My memories of my childhood are vague. My sister Nancy was the one with the crystal-clear clarity about everything that happened. I didn't know for many years that when you grow up in a family where there are adverse childhood experiences (ACEs, which we'll discuss in greater detail later in the book), it's normal to have a fuzzy memory of what was happening. God, how I miss Nancy and her ability to help me fill the holes of the lost memories.

But here goes.

My dad was the minister of a church in a small town with 300 members. I thought it was normal to have 300 family members. My dad wasn't the kind of minister dad who forced religion down his daughters' throats. I didn't even realize I was a preacher's kid for many years. My dad was a gifted speaker. Very smart and in command. A force of energy. He believed in equality for all, and he fought for social justice. The members of the church looked forward to his inspiring sermons. My dad had big ideas and lived a full life. He was 10 years older than my mom and had served in the United States Air Force, living in different places of the world. He had a global mindset. He was a big picture guy.

My mom was the perfect minister's wife. She sang in the choir, was active in the women's church group, and was a stay-at-home mom. Everyone at church loved her. She walked Nancy and me to school and often had homemade chocolate chip cookies waiting for us when we came home. My mom was a very loving mom.

When I was small, my life felt secure. My mom was always there for my sister and me. And my dad provided for the family. We enjoyed our church family. And all was good.

And then it wasn't. A slow decline of feeling safe occurred in our home. It was if I had been walking down a well-lit busy street at night but had somehow veered off without paying attention. And now I found myself in a dark, lonely alley, with only shadows of the night as my companions.

I honestly don't recall when I became aware that this once-safe house now seemed filled with eggshells, covering every floor in every room. Maybe it was as I grew older, I began to have a voice. Maybe the stress my dad was dealing with in his life became more intense. I'm not really sure. But the home had become unpredictable.

Dinner time became terrible. This was the time when my dad unleashed his venomous words, directed at either my mom or me or both of us. But never at Nancy. She would sit quietly with her head down, as my dad's bellows became louder and more aggressive. I can't remember his words or why he was angry all the time. All I remember was fist slamming, intense anger quickly igniting into rage, and myself feeling terribly afraid.

The frequency of his explosions increased over time. So did the intensity. Nancy and I would race upstairs and hide under our beds, holding our dog Dodger, crying as we could hear him yelling at my mom downstairs.

There were times when he would come storming fast at me, waving his arms, face bright red, chest puffed out, hair messed up, yelling at me for some infraction or another. I felt cornered like a small rabbit being chased by a coyote. I cowered down, covering my head waiting for a verbal attack as he towered over me shouting. I felt so small. So vulnerable. So afraid. I felt at times that I might die, killed by the sheer force of his rage.

I learned to be hypervigilant. Always tiptoeing around hoping to keep the jaws of anger at bay. The last thing I wanted was to "get into trouble." That was way too scary. Somewhere along the childhood way, I learned that if I could just do everything *just right,* maybe my dad wouldn't get so mad, and I wouldn't get in trouble so much.

I poured my energy into getting good grades. I got a high from excelling in school. Teachers liked me. My GPA kept creeping up. I pushed and pushed and pushed to get the best possible grades. If I wasn't performing at the highest levels, I felt that I had not done enough. The drive to prove myself created stress and exhaustion. This drive to excel stayed with me through high school, then college, then grad school.

I remember cramming for an exam one night while in graduate school. My roommate Becky listened to my worries for a while and then said, "Sue, it seems like you are always in a storm shelter riding out a tornado. But it's okay. You can come up from the storm shelter. There is no tornado. In fact, there is sunshine everywhere."

She then said, "Sue, you can only get a 4.0 on the exam, and you are studying like you want a 5.0."

One night, around that same time, I was at a party. But I was upset about something. A bad grade, or maybe it was about a boyfriend I was dating. I'm not even sure what it was. But I remember I was worried, stressed, and feeling small. I drank a lot that night. I ended up lying on the lawn of the house where the party was. Lying there, I looked up into the dark sky and the twinkling stars. The sky seemed to be spinning with the stars getting all jumbled together.

Later that night, I called my sister, who was fighting her first round with cancer. After she listened to my troubles, she said, "I think you have a drinking problem. You need to get help."

I hung up on her.

We never spoke about this ever again as I focused my attention on starting my professional life during the day and easing my feelings of not being good enough with Chardonnay during the evenings.

My Own Unconscious Wounded Career Path

I had a deep, but naïve, idea that when I grew up and left my childhood home, and earned my own money, all this pain and dysfunction would be behind me. I felt so grown up that cold blustery Chicago January morning in 1988 when I began my official adulthood with my first corporate job in human resources.

For the first several months, I sat in my cubicle learning the basics of compensation. My number one objective from the minute I walked through that formidable corporate door to the minute I walked out each night was to please, please, please. And if that wasn't enough, to keep pleasing more. Do more than anyone expected. Treat everyone as if their issue, problem, or project was the only one that mattered, even if it meant long hours for me or weekend work.

If someone looked at me with what I thought was even a hint of judgment, I would work even harder. Using the walk-on-eggshells coping skills I had learned at home, I was good at reading the psychological geography around me.

My new boss and his boss seemed pleased with my performance. I liked math and was good at building relationships—both attributes are important when you are a compensation analyst. The first two years there were all about learning the basics: How to be a good employee, how to navigate a company of 2,000 employees, how to stay out of trouble, how to establish rapport with co-workers, and an introduction to corporate politics, in which I was only a bystander.

Most of all, how to look normal. No one had a clue what storms, fears, and memories I carried around with me in my head and heart and how hard I worked to prove to them that I was, indeed, good enough.

Carrying My Past Into My Professional Life

A few years later, I was recruited to take my first people management role with a different organization. This assignment would bring with it an authority figure who would rival my dad in her intense and unpredictable anger.

This is when I began to discover how much my underlying perfectionism and people-pleasing tendencies would eventually undermine the quality of my life, my career, and relationships with others and even myself. In the early days of my professional life, I was totally unaware that I was skipping along on the Unconscious Wounded Career Path, completely blind to how my past was still damaging my health, my peace of mind, even my career. Would it have mattered anyway to this young career woman on her way? My career was "skyrocketing," as a colleague once put it. My performance record was the professional equivalent of that impossible 5.0 GPA I was shooting for in school. The pressure that I put on myself was intolerable and unhealthy. But it was a familiar old friend.

My second corporate job was off to a good start. I had developed a good working relationship with my new team and my new boss. Or so it seemed. I liked her, and she seemed pleased with my work. But there was something a bit strange that should have been a clue to be on alert. She had a figurine on her office desk of a two-sided witch. One side showed Glinda the Good Witch from *The Wizard of Oz*. The other side was the Wicked Witch. My new boss liked to flip the statuette every day on her desk, depending on her mood—signaling to her team whether they could relax around her or walk on eggshells. (Not a leadership behavior I recommend, by the way.)

One day, she assigned me to lead a major overhaul of a talent management process. My team completed the project on time and within the budget. It was a big win for me and my team. Shortly afterward, my boss told me that the team members would receive the President's Award of Excellence. All members, that is, except me. When I asked her why I was being left out, she gave me a vague, dismissive response that left me feeling undervalued, unfairly treated, confused, and angry.

One thing was clear to me though: I could no longer trust my boss to treat me fairly. And so I decided to take matters to *her* boss and get his advice. Within a week of my meeting with him, I received the award and a check for $3,000.

Then all hell broke loose. The Wicked Witch summoned me to her office. As soon as I sat down, she began screaming and spewing angry, vicious words at me like lava exploding from a volcano. She was in a full-on rage. She transformed into my father before my eyes. And I became the little girl still under the bed. I completely froze. I couldn't speak, I couldn't move. I only sat there with tears streaming down my face. One of my greatest fears was getting into trouble. And there I was, getting into full-fledged trouble.

I fled her office in tears, feeling as if I had just been beaten up. I was frightened and shaken. I was a professional, with a Master's degree and two undergraduate degrees. I wasn't a child. I was an adult. And yet, here I was watching a great big vice president in a prestigious organization losing her, well, shit, and I was 100 percent sure it was entirely my fault. I had screwed up. I was to blame. I was the stupid one. How dare I stand up for myself? I had unleashed this raging beast. I was so debilitated with fear, it never dawned on me how monstrous and wrong her behavior was. I was the one who had displeased. I was the one who was wrong.

I knew when I walked out of her office, I better start looking for a new job. It was time for flight.

Trying to Please The Unpleasable "Pirates"

I had been working for a different company for several years, and my career was going really well. My hard work and commitment to great work brought me bigger titles and more responsibility nearly every year. I was eventually promoted to Vice President of Human Resources for a large multi-billion dollar business unit.

Sounds great, right? Well, in the beginning, it wasn't so great at all. My predecessor had left the company under a cloud of rumors that she may have been asked to leave. Generally, the leadership team didn't respect the HR function. And so, by association, that team didn't have much use for me either. I was HR. And the only woman on the team of nine men, who called themselves the Pirates.

My first meeting with this new leadership team didn't go well. Just as the four-hour meeting was about to wrap up, I took the floor to share updates from my department. About a minute into my update, one leader, a tall intimidating guy who was known to be a corporate bully, slowly stood up, looked directly at me, slammed his notebook shut, and walked out of the room without a word. One of the other guys followed his lead and left, too.

Devastated, I wanted to burst into tears. But I didn't.

My next 11 months were grueling. I never felt good enough with these guys. I had never been in such a large role before. It seemed to me that they were doing everything they could to rattle me. And it was working. One leader would walk past my office and slam his fist on my glass wall just to watch me jump in surprise, especially early in the mornings. Any time I would schedule meetings with him, he wouldn't show up.

Another one of these guys enjoyed doing everything he could think to do to be every HR leader's nightmare. This ranged from making inappropriate comments at work to not giving a rat's ass about following corporate protocol, because he knew he was invaluable to the company. Which he was. This was a company culture that didn't fire troublemakers who were essential to the bottom line.

I did everything I could to be "one of the guys," to be accepted. I wanted them to officially anoint me as being "good enough." I would show them. I worked often 12 hours or more a day and many hours on the weekends. I also learned how to play golf, as this seemed to be a favorite company activity after long off-site meetings. They could tell any inappropriate joke they wanted in front of me. After all, I had given them amnesty. And I could drink with the best of them. I held my own with them every time alcohol was involved—which was often. Interestingly, our boss didn't drink, and one other leader was a recovering alcoholic. But the others organized their lives around when they could have their next drink. And so I did too.

And I was in the middle of this working environment, every day for four-and-a-half years.

One day, we were in a leadership team meeting that wasn't going well. One leader was feeling the pressure of low sales. He attacked the leader of Research and Development, stating it was his fault that we had nothing to sell. Before too long, the Marketing leader jumped into the fight as reasons for the dropped revenue were being blamed on each of them.

Our boss, one of the nicest guys you will ever meet, sat quietly as the three ratcheted up the heat of the argument. I knew I had to intervene or they might start throwing real punches.

I decided to get their attention.

I yelled and waved my arms, "Hey you guys, we are all on the same team, and we all want to win in the market!"

They instantly stopped yelling at each other and stared at me with surprise and irritation. It was like six daggers being thrown from around the room directly at me. As if they suddenly became a chorus, they opened their mouths and yelled, *"Shut up Susan!"*

And then they went right back into their argument.

It was my first year with the Pirates that I got to know my good friend Chardonnay even better than before. A bottle every other night. I should have been alarmed by the fact that the liquor store owner practically already had my bottle wrapped up and ready to go for me by the time I got there. But as skilled as I might have been at reading the room around me, I was out of touch with what was going on inside me.

The Aha's

I was ready to quit this vice president role inside the first year. I felt un-appreciated. Not accepted. Disrespected. Miserable. Defeated. Sad. The more I did to get this team's approval, the more they dismissed me. Everything that had worked for me throughout my entire life—getting people to like me—was no longer working. In fact, it was working against me. I was climbing an icy mountain and constantly slipping backwards.

As I was trying to figure things out, my executive coach, Toni Chinoy, led me through a life-changing intuitive exercise to help me figure out what I was doing that was getting in my own way.

"If your boss were seeing you in the form of animal, what animal would he see you as?"

At first, it was kind of weird to imagine myself in my boss's body and looking out of his eyes at me. But all of a sudden, I burst out laughing.

"Oh my gosh!" I shouted, "He sees me as a golden retriever puppy dog! I'm wagging my tail and wanting him to pat me and tell me what a good girl I am!"

I couldn't stop laughing.

"So how is that working out for you?"

"Not so well!"

We talked about how annoying puppies can be when they want too much attention. How people want them to leave them alone. Hmmmmm. I was beginning to get some interesting insight about how some of these guys were behaving toward me and why.

She then led me around the leadership team, one Pirate at a time, to get inside of his eyes and look at me in the form of an animal. She also asked me to go back into my own eyes and tell her what animal I saw the worst of the crew as. Here was the result:

	My view of him	His view of me
Matt	Wildcat	Deer
Bob	Gorilla	Puppy
Greg	Hyena	Bunny
Kyle	Wolf (with fangs)	Little bird
Brit	Grizzly Bear	Kitten

It was obvious that I was being devoured by these guys and I wasn't going to last long if I kept doing what I was doing. As much as I wanted to blame them, the real issue was me. Yes, my approval-seeking nature was no longer working for me. It was clearly time to rethink how much to weigh others' views of me. I needed to be the one to define me.

All of the animals they viewed me as were sweet and cuddly. Not intimidating, not powerful. All seeking others' love, attention and approval. Weak in many respects. Worse: At the bottom of the food chain.

This was not working for me professionally.

Experiencing Uncommon Kindness

I was on maternity leave when Gary Goberville came to be our new head of HR. He called me at home and asked me if I would be willing to come in for lunch so we could meet. Even though he was interrupting my maternity leave, I said yes. I had to. Otherwise, I would be the one at fault if we got off on the wrong foot. Bad things would result. And it would be my fault. My fault.

"So, Susan," he began. "What are your dreams? And how can I help you achieve them?"

I nearly fell out of my chair. I had just come off 10 years with 10 different HR bosses. I had been feeling all alone, with limited leadership support. And now here comes this new guy asking me how he could help *me*? His servant leadership came with strength. Within a few months of joining the company, he was successfully taking on the corporate bullies. I came to love and trust this new leader who modeled how strength, fight, grace, kindness could co-exist. I would have followed him anywhere because the learning would never stop.

About four months into our work together, we were gathered at my home, with Ken Wright, a consultant, eating a late dinner and hashing out leadership capability ideas. Gary stared at his sandwich, and said, "The food doesn't taste right. Is anyone else feeling sick?"

Ken and I looked at each other and then back at Gary and in unison, said "No." We shrugged and continued our conversation.

A few weeks later, he was diagnosed with a recurrence of melanoma. He died two months later.

Before he left work for good, we saw each other near his office. I couldn't stop crying. He hugged me with such acceptance and kindness. He was saying goodbye and I knew it. His soul had touched my heart and I would be forever changed. He valued me. He challenged me. He pushed me. He stretched me. He respected me. He accepted me. I grew as a leader and as a human.

He taught me through his example that power could be a safe, kind, nurturing thing. It doesn't have to be a raging bear.

Pathways to Successful Living

Because I had become close to Gary and his wife Patty, she asked me to speak at Gary's two memorial services. During the service in Lake Forest, IL, there was woman who sang beautiful opera in Gary's honor. Her voice was angelic. The sound was straight from God Himself.

After the service, I asked her if she was a professional singer. She laughed.

"No," she said, "This is the first time I have sung in front of people in 20 years."

"What?" I exclaimed, "You're kidding, right?"

"What inspired you to do it?" I asked.

Marla got a big smile on her face and said, "Pathways to Successful Living."

I asked her, "What is that?"

Marla smiled again and said, "Ask Patty."

Patty also got a big smile on her face and said, "The Gary Goberville you knew and loved was the way he was because of Pathways."

That was all it took. I signed up for Pathways' Basic program the very next day.

On the second day of the seminar, I stood up to share a thought. When I did, Sue Paige, the founder and owner of the company, said, "Everything about you says you are seeking approval from all of us.

Your facial expressions, your hair, your clothes, how you hold yourself. You wear Approval Seeker as if it were your clothes!"

"Oh my God! Ouch! Was it that obvious? Really? What was she saying? Why was she being so hurtful?" I thought. Her words and tone stung. I sat down feeling humiliated and embarrassed, certain everyone was staring at me. As the sting subsided, and the more I thought about it, the more I realized she was right.

Being a pleaser all of my life had taken a lot of effort. Wanting everyone to like me, to approve of me, to fill me up took a lot of energy. And it had finally worn me down. All of those years of trying to get my Dad's attention and acceptance. All of those years, trying to prove myself to my teachers, authority figures, and bosses.

This is not healthy for anyone! The impact can be profound. But I was doing this to myself. This is not about blaming anyone. My stress, anxiety, and worry were all self-inflicted. In the end, it is *my* responsibility to own the job of determining my worthiness and level of acceptance. My own self-acceptance is my job. No one else's. My workplace conflicts were way more challenging and painful than they needed to be because I had given up all duty of self-acceptance to everyone else, indiscriminately. This wasn't about anyone else. This was about me. I was finally beginning to see that if I continued to blame others for not approving of me, I would stay stuck needing others to validate me. If I wanted different outcomes and professional experiences in life, it was up to me to figure out what is missing inside me, so that I can address it, and not look to others for the magic experience of complete acceptance.

Diffusing Intimidation

For the longest time, I believed that I was responsible for other people's negative moods and emotions. And I attached my sense of self-worth and self-acceptance to what others thought of me. Therefore, if someone was angry, then, I was sure it was my fault.

The very first day after my Pathways to Successful Living Advanced class, I boarded the corporate jet with the Pirates to head to a meeting in Arizona. One of the most challenging men stood up in front of me blocking my way onto the plane and began yelling at me. He was furious that it was taking too long for new ideas for products to get to market so his team could sell and drive revenue for the company.

Before Pathways, I would have personalized his anger and blamed myself for him being so mad. It would be up to me to fix it. But this time, as he was standing there yelling at me, I looked up at him and calmly said, "What are you so pissed about?" And then I just looked at him and waited. I remained grounded. Calm. Detached.

Instead of cowering and getting defensive, I simply said, "You seem upset. This is between you and Shannon. Now go sit down, we're about to take off."

He immediately calmed down and actually apologized, saying that he was frustrated with another part of the organization. He didn't realize he was taking it out on me. With that, his mouth clapped shut, and he obediently took his seat. And that was the end of my inner puppy dog.

"I'm a bad ass!" That thought put a smile on my face as I took my seat and buckled up.

I had never done that before. Before that day, every time he would get mad, I would revert to approval-seeking mode, trying to figure out what I needed to do differently to get him to stop yelling at me. But this time, I knew his anger had nothing to do with me. Breakthrough! It was time for me to stop blaming myself for everyone else being unhappy. Their unhappiness was about them. *Not me*!

Perfectionism and Addiction

I was slowly building up a skill set for dealing with the external pressures of corporate life. But the secret pressure I held within was relentless. Addictions often medicate a critical view of self. If I felt I wasn't good enough, I set unrealistic goals and standards of perfectionism that I couldn't ever meet. That pressure drove me to seek ways to numb my thoughts and memories. Like the memory of Nancy warning me about a growing alcohol problem.

In the early 2000s, I would often come home craving a glass of Chardonnay. As time went on, the nightly glass would become a near nightly bottle.

I had also convinced myself that in order to fit in with the Pirates, I would have to prove I could drink with the best of them. And I did. Shots all around? Sure. That corporate jet where I so proudly stood my ground? We knew where catering kept the onboard booze stash, and we merrily helped ourselves. Business meetings always ended in the hotel bar. Luckily, no major negative issues arose with my drinking with "the guys."

Chardonnay was my good friend back then. She seemed to know just how to make me relax and forget all of the worries of the day. Was I good enough? Did my boss think I was adding enough value? What should I have done or not done differently in the meeting? Was my team on my side with this new initiative that I had proposed? The inner critic ready to eviscerate me for my day's behavior didn't have a chance when face-to-face with my bottle. But neither did I. Chardonnay had taken the controls. Well, almost.

It was April 2004. I was at an HR conference in Phoenix. The meeting was scheduled to start on Monday, so I had Sunday night to socialize. Someone I knew from a major consulting firm invited me to join a private dinner with several of his colleagues. It was a nice dinner. At least I assume it was. I don't remember much from that night. Except that Merlot had been served; not my customary Chardonnay.

I woke up the next morning with a terrible headache. It felt like six bulls were fighting in my brain, snorting and stomping the ground. I wasn't used to red wine and it had hit me hard. How many glasses did I drink? I could only remember that the glasses were the really big goblets for red wine, not the smaller white wine ones that I was accustomed to. I vaguely remembered something about spilling an entire goblet of red wine. The image that came flooding into the raging bull fight in my head was the crimson liquid cascading over the white tablecloth as if a dam of blood had been released onto a white glacier of snow. With everyone at the table staring at me, appalled. Slow motion, of course. On a loop, of course. Over and over again, the humiliation washed over me.

Had I done anything else embarrassing? Was there more? Did I need to call my host colleague and apologize? What was wrong with me?

Why couldn't I control how much I drank? Why did others seem to be able to do so, but I never could?

I rationalized my drinking. I didn't have a problem. No sir. I never missed a day of work due to being too hung over. I never drank at work. I always seemed to manage, perform and excel. No one, except my sister, had ever said, "Hey Susan, I think you have a problem with drinking."

I sat in my bed a little while longer, watching the mental video loop again and again in mounting shame.

All of sudden, I had the most overwhelming feeling that God was sitting right in the chair in my room looking at me.

I heard Him say this: "Susan, it's time. You must stop drinking or you will hurt yourself or someone else."

I started to weep. I knew it was true. I was scared.

It was that day that I decided Chardonnay and Merlot were liars. They really weren't my good friends, like I had believed they were for so many years. No, in fact, they were conspiring to bring me down and keep me from knowing true joy and acceptance. They were all about numbing me so I wouldn't feel pain. And if I wasn't careful, they were going to get me into very serious trouble.

I decided to reach out to Chris Lapak, whom I had met at a Pathways seminar. I knew Chris had been sober for 20 years. He would help me figure out what I would do next. Chris picked right up when I called that morning. I told him I was scared, and I didn't know what to do. He said, "It is simple Susan. I want you to make an agreement with me. Any time you want to take a drink, you have to call me first. Deal?"

"Yes."

I knew the power of making agreements and holding others accountable. When you make an agreement with someone else, your word is everything. And you hold each other accountable to the agreement because you care about each other. When I told Chris I would call him before taking a drink, I never had a doubt that I would keep the agreement.

Every time I called Chris, he always picked up the call and he always talked me out of taking a drink. Poor Chris, I bet I called him a thousand times in the first month. I didn't realize how Chardonnay had taken over my life. Many nights I called him because I had just had a difficult day at work.

Or someone had gotten mad at me and I wanted the alcohol to take the edge off of me feeling badly about doing something wrong or that it should have been done differently. The worry that would play over and over in my head until I could get relief. Before Chris, my relief came from Chardonnay. With Chris's commitment to being there for me, my relief came from Chris.

Chris never gave up on me. Those first nine months were really hard. Chardonnay had weaseled her way into life in ways I didn't even realize. Like one Christmas when I was preparing to sit down and wrap presents. I wanted a glass so badly. Chardonnay was such a habit. She had twisted herself into all aspects of my life, like a snake wrapping itself around a tree and then beginning to squeeze to hold on.

The last most serious time I called Chris, I was standing in the parking lot of a restaurant in Florida. All of my work colleagues were inside bemoaning the fact that we had recently been given a new HR leader. No one was happy. But they were drinking margaritas. I wanted one terribly. So I called Chris for about the millionth time.

And it worked. To this day, I call Chris every April 26 to thank him for saving my life.

Even though it has been many years since I have taken a drink, I may not have always lived my life in sobriety. I wasn't drinking but I was substituting work, horseback riding, exercise, and dancing as my drink. Busyness became the driver of my life. No longer alcohol. When a friend, John Quinn, pointed that out to me, I decided to attend my first 12 Step program. Fellow recovering alcoholics told me in my first meeting that recovery will be much easier and softer following the 12 steps.

Here's the thing I've learned about alcohol. If you are someone with an "alcoholic brain," as described in *Alcoholics Anonymous: The Big Book*, if you don't stop drinking, you either die, end up in jail, or in a hospital. These may be extreme outcomes, and don't always happen, but I have come to believe that alcohol for me is a poison.

A conclusion of watching my life of drinking is that I was numbing myself from my feelings of not being good enough at work. This was despite many successes, promotions and recognitions. It never felt like enough. My performance was never quite enough. My thinking was broken. I was completely unconscious of how much the limiting beliefs I took away from my childhood were negatively affecting my inner story about how I was doing in my career. When my own view of measuring up at work was not met, I had to fill the hole somehow. That is what the Chardonnay did for me.

Thank you, God, for saving me. Thank you, Chris Lapak, for making sure I followed through on God's clear direction for me that night. Thank you to John Quinn for taking me further down the path to sobriety by introducing me to the 12 Step program.

Putting a Name to the Past

My 19-year marriage had been slowing unraveling and was coming to an end. I told my husband in the summer of 2016 that I wanted a divorce. It was a very tumultuous time for both of us. Ask him what he remembers from this time and he would describe it as coming out of a coma into a nightmare. Over time we had become more and more distant. I used work to avoid the issues that weren't working in the relationship. And he used his passion of restoring vintage cars as his escape.

Like many couples in this situation, we began seeing a therapist. The more I talked in those sessions, the more I realized I still had some major work to do on myself. And so, I started working with a different therapist in the same office. Pam P. helped me realize that so much of what had happened in my marriage was a repeating pattern that I had adopted from my childhood—people pleasing. When I was stuck in people pleasing mode, my true feelings and concerns stayed buried deep. And so, while I thought I was letting my husband know how things weren't working, I never truly said it as clearly as he needed to fully understand how we were growing apart. I stuffed my increasing frustration and anger into a vault buried deep inside my heart. Then one day, the vault burst and the overwhelming sense of being done overcame me. We were well and truly done.

Pam helped me evaluate all significant relationships I had had with men over my lifetime. And yes, there was a pattern, starting, of course, with my father. Throughout my childhood, I tried to be the perfect daughter, and then maybe Dad wouldn't blow up. In that dynamic, every word I spoke was measured with the desire to not set off the explosion. Any hint of anger from him and I would go running to my bedroom. And it seemed that even to that point, I was still trying. Only this time with the people in my adult life, including my husband. I was allowing other people's anger to keep my voice quiet. That was my choice, mine and mine alone.

In one of our sessions, Pam told me that she thought I would benefit from attending a program called Healing Trauma, offered by a place outside of Nashville, called Onsite. I looked them up on their website and read these words: "*Our life-changing therapeutic framework combined with our healing hospitality will enable you to find the emotional healing you need to thrive in the future.*"

And so I signed up for the April 2017 program. The setting is a charmingly renovated farm home, complete with cabins for guests, horses in the grassy fields, and a facility for their programs.

And yet, even though I was out of control over my life during seven days with total strangers, I felt safe. Upon arrival, the staff gave us time to settle into our cabins and get ready for the first evening's orientation and program. First on the agenda: Turn in all cell phones. What? Are you kidding me??? Is this for real? I had read about this requirement but didn't really believe it. For how long? All seven days? We had been instructed to let loved ones and work know we could be reached only in an emergency by calling their 24-hour office line. Okay. Breathe. "Oh my. What have I gotten myself into?" I asked myself.

We were told we would meet as a big group for lectures, meals, and evening "fun time." The rest of the time we would work in small groups of eight, each group led by a therapist. Carlos was assigned to lead my group. Carlos changed my life.

Every day included a healthy breakfast, lunch, and dinner served family style in the old farmhouse. We had time to be outside in nature; naturally I sought out the horses. After dinner, we had games and movie nights, which were a welcome relief from the hard, healing work we did during the day. We learned that healing includes taking care of our body, mind, and heart. We learned that having fun is a part of healing. We were told to have lights out every night by 10:00 pm. We were there to do real and meaningful work. And we needed that sleep.

To be honest with you, I wasn't really sure why I was there, other than the fact that Pam recommended it. I hadn't experienced trauma in my life.

I hadn't been abused, gone to fight a war, or was raped. Nothing like that. The word trauma didn't resonate for me. Sure, my dad had anger issues, but he was human. He did his best. So many other people had a much harder childhood and life than I had had. I had no right to claim trauma as part of my background.

All in all, my life was really great. Just a few bumps here and there. Still Pam suggested it. And I respected her opinion. So I was there. And I'd see what I might learn. Maybe I could use the insights I learned to help someone else at work. Or even my husband.

One day, Carlos asked us to sit quietly with a large poster board and draw a timeline of our life from birth to the current date. On the timeline, he said, we had to plot our life according to what traumas we experienced—both big "T" traumas and little "t" traumas. Little "t" traumas might be ongoing yelling in the home or being picked on the playground by someone. A big "T" trauma might be sexual abuse or a divorce. It was up to us to decide whether these experiences were big "T" traumas or little "t" traumas. Carlos also told us that experiencing lots of little "t" traumas over time actually equate to a big "T" trauma.

After several hours of intense quiet, focus, and reflection, we each had to share our timelines with the group. As accustomed as I was to dismissing all the negative things that I had experienced or had done myself throughout my life, I felt nervous and exposed, to the point that I was shaking by the time my turn came up. My small group would judge me and my life. And I would no longer be safe in this Tennessee countryside with these strangers who were becoming friends. And I wouldn't be able to grab my cell phone, pack my stuff, and get out of there.

When I finished telling my life story by referring to my little "t's" and big "T's," I turned to Carlos. He looked deep into my eyes and with the gentleness of an angel, said to me, "Susan, you have had a lot of trauma in your life."

With that, I burst into tears. No one had ever validated that what had happened to me as a little girl was indeed trauma. I wept and wept. My fellow group mates surrounded me in love and support.

I was 53 years old when I finally realized that I had experienced significant trauma and it was affecting my present-day life. My marriage, my career, my happiness.

And, thanks to Onsite and Carlos, I had taken a huge step in healing my life. I had a word for what had happened to me. And that word was trauma.

I had spent my life minimizing the negative things of my past, rationalizing traumatic events as being not really that big of a deal. I even compared my life to others' lives and decided I had it easy compared to many. How dare I think I had a bad childhood, when others had it so much worse?

All of this denial came crashing down when he said those eleven simple words to me. I had never acknowledged the significance of all of the things that had happened or had been able to see the patterns in my life until we did that exercise. I had never truly understood the significance of what I had survived until that moment.

And just like we had for all of my small group members, they surrounded me and comforted me.

Through all of these experiences and because of many key relationships along my life journey, I have come to a place of understanding and appreciation about the ongoing influences of my childhood on my career and adult life. I've also seen how significantly my career has been influenced by trauma, fear, the self-limiting belief that I am not good enough, people pleasing, and perfectionism.

And, especially in my leadership role in HR, I have a front row seat to seeing the ghosts of peoples' traumatic pasts following them around, influencing their behaviors, haunting their potential, getting in their way. Every day. Believe it or not, everyone has some degree of issues they are navigating, including those in the most executive levels of our companies. And that is why I have dedicated my life to teaching self-acceptance to create a more joyful world.

Chapter 2
Martha's Story

(A note from Susan: ASDPs experience life and work in unique ways—as individual as our fingerprints. All our life circumstances, how we were raised to believe about ourselves and what to believe about others, influence the career paths we end up on. My career path has been an international corporate one, where my success path continued to climb, despite the emotional turmoil I worked hard to overcome. In contrast, Martha decided to hop off the corporate career path altogether and build a self-employed life of writing, consulting, and publishing. Since our professional success stories are at opposite ends of the employment spectrum, we thought you might like to read about her experiences too. Here is Martha, in her own words.)

WHILE SUSAN AND I were wrapping up the final chapters of *Healing at Work*, I had a houseguest for an extended stay. After decades of solitary living, it was pleasant sharing my space with someone who is also a smart, self-employed, ambitious, idea-driven professional. Especially at the end of the day, when we would kick back and watch some TV together. She introduced me to some programs I would never have watched on my own—primarily competitive reality TV shows.

Competitive shows make me tense; everyone is so mean. If I'm going to watch a cooking show, for instance, I would naturally go for *The Barefoot Contessa* or *The Pioneer Woman*, where nice, smiling ladies cook yummy meals for loving friends and family. Everyone is welcome to sit down at the same table, eat the same thing, and smile some more. But my guest loves the cutthroat shows like *Chopped* and *Top Chef.* In these shows, there is only one winner at the end of the season. And everyone else disappears one by one, heartbroken and disappointed. Every night I would identify with the loser of the evening and feel demoralized by the zero-sum game aspect of storyline.

Things were a little different with the 2019 season of *Top Chef,* though. Everyone was so nice to each other. Sure, they were competitors, with only one clear winner at the end of the last episode. But there were many challenges where they were still expected to work in teams. By the time the last episode revealed the winner, she won the final challenge with the support of the others—the previous shows' losers who returned to support her as sous chefs. If there is a codependent node in our brains, that aspect of the show lit up in my head like an arcade light.

"You know," I mused aloud as the final credits rolled, "If I won this show, I wouldn't feel right taking the prize money all for myself. I'd want to split it evenly among everyone. They all helped her get there."

To which my guest—who has no trouble with the competitive spirit—looked at me aghast and said exactly this, "WTF, ASDP?"

Which was only my latest reminder that I'm not cut out for organizational life—especially if my getting the job meant that all the other applicants would lose out. My friend's reaction to my out-loud thoughts also gave me some insight into what it must be like to work with *me,* when the occasion calls for group effort. How awkward would it be, for instance, for the other chefs on *Top Chef* to be told that the winner was divvying up her $250,000 prize so that everyone would get an equal share of the prize money? Would they all be thinking to themselves, "WTF?" And reluctantly take the money anyway? (In thinking this scenario all the way through, if I was one of the losers, would I have accepted my share like everyone else? It's not entirely out of the question that I would divvy up even my share among my peers, willing to settle for bus fare home. With everyone, the chef competitors, the producers, the advertisers, the suppliers, the TV watchers in living rooms the world over going, "WTF?")

Yes, I'm an adult survivor of a damaged past. My mother was a violent alcoholic who drank so much she died of cirrhosis at age 42. She used her little girl as the scapegoat on whom she futilely tried to purge her own self-loathing. I was her "mini-me," and it was easier to take her pain out on me than it was to look in the mirror. She was also a neglected wife of a man who had huge fish to fry. My father had a high-stress job with the CIA, which required secrecy and hypervigilance for the sake of national security. We moved once a year until I was 13; we were always afraid of being "discovered." There were fights, police cars in the driveway with lights flashing red and blue in the night, hospital stays, broken bones, lies, and denials. The family motto seemed to be, "Kids are resilient, she'll get over it." When my mother died, my father and I went into a different kind of dysfunction—I spent my teenage years keeping him company night after night, quietly reading, both of us grateful for the serenity. Finally. In my relief, I had decided to take an emotional vacation from life. My only job was to be no trouble for my father. Which made it easy for him to overlook whatever duties he might have had as the father to a young girl, and take care of his preferences first.

"Don't hug me, I don't like it," he once told me when I reached out for some rare physical attention. I make a point of not thinking about that moment now, decades later because the memory of the rejection still makes my eyes sting. And what's the use of that, today?

And so I had stopped growing ... all those teenage years when kids are supposed to be at least a little annoying as part of the natural maturing process, I was the ideal companion to a man who just wanted to take a breather from life as well. Kind of like his surrogate wife, secretly sacrificing my own needs out of awareness of the fact that he'd had enough family turmoil over the last couple of decades. No muss no fuss.

I grew up with this constant sense of being in hiding. Hiding the fact that I was still growing up and needed at least one parent who was aware enough to teach me how to move through life with confidence and self-regard, not shame. But, emotionally, I was still on the run. Traveling incognito. I was an escapee from my own life and the truth about what it was to be me. That fear of being discovered? I took that fear with me into my adult life. And more than once I noticed my feelings and impulses and asked myself, "Why am I reacting to this situation like a fugitive?"

I carried this fear of discovery with me when I tried to join the world in a series of jobs. This was in the years before the world began to study and understand the common characteristics of adults who survived abused childhoods. All I knew was that I was weird, and my number one job was to hide the fact that I was freaking out inside. The day-to-day expectation of showing up at work looking relatively sane and competent made me feel at risk of being exposed. How long could I keep up the mask?

Being an ASDP brings a level of awkwardness to the workplace. We're trying to figure out what simple normal behavior is in an entirely different community of people that has dysfunctions of its own—company politics; leaders with personal problems of their own, who may not be the most talented *people* people; being expected to do more with less; and that bugaboo that gets most of us at one time or another: Competing with people we like for the one promotion opportunity that's currently available. Non-ASDPs and ASDP colleagues alike are working out their own personal and professional challenges. And then we bring into the mix our own beliefs, behaviors, and anxieties. And we ASDPs tend to confuse others with bizarre behaviors that no one can predict—like my imaginary impulse to divvy up the hypothetical prize money. On a regular day-to-day basis, the overall vibe is just weird.

There is another aspect to being an ASDP that often gets overlooked because the horror stories tend to grab the spotlight: We often don't get the fundamental life skills and healthy coping training that others get at home while growing up. Not everyone in non-abusive families are raised by Mr. Rogers, I get that. Few families—even the healthiest ones—are perfect when it comes to giving children what they need to thrive as adults. But when you stop to think about it, parents who are struggling with themselves and their beliefs about the world are not great teachers around these kinds of life lessons that we all need:

- How to ask for what you want and need with confidence, calm, and grace.
- How to say no and still keep the friendship intact.
- How to know when others are trying to manipulate or control you.

- How to authentically apologize with dignity.
- How to have a difficult conversation that brings understanding to both of you.
- How to take rejection in stride.
- How to handle stress without heading for the bottle, needle, or candy jar.
- How to comfort yourself through a low mood and encourage yourself during a run of depressing, helpless thinking.
- How to set healthy goals and achieve them by methodically pursuing them, with step-by-step self-discipline.
- How to ask for help; how to offer help.
- How to responsibly and confidently commit to stretch goals while saying no to unreasonable demands.
- How to take responsibility for your own emotional reactions so that others feel safe around you.
- How to be confident, proud, and optimistic in all aspects of your life.

These are just a few examples of the many life lessons that are typically taught in emotionally healthy families. ASDPs, on the other hand, learn from our parents who are in their own painful struggles. We just don't get many of those lessons. So that's something else we are hiding—the simple fact that we're just trying to learn what it means to be normal. Or at least behave like a normal person. And our colleagues can sense it. Which can make us even harder to know, like and trust.

How Being an ASDP Affected My Own Workplace Experience

With zero negotiation skills, I would routinely accept the initial rock-bottom salary offer, grateful that someone saw value in me, having no clue that some haggling back-and-forth was expected. I took everything way too personally, routinely crying in the ladies room stall because someone looked sideways at me, or spoke with a slight edge in their voice. I always felt that when my boss was in a bad mood, it was about me and I was going to be fired. I wouldn't have a clue exactly why but there was always this feeling of an axe hanging over my head on a fraying rope. Psychologists have noted that that's a common feeling among traumatized people. They even have a name for it: *Cherophobia* (*chero* in Greek means *rejoice; phobia* is one you already know. Put them together and you have the *fear of rejoicing*—which basically means, "knowing you had better not let your guard down for a single second because that's when the axe will drop").

I couldn't say "no," or "I don't understand the assignment," or "I've never done this before, can you tell me how to do this?" because I didn't want to show people that I was stupid or unqualified for the workload. I would take on assignments that were over my head, and the anxiety or confusion would slow me down. I hoped that acting "as if" (as if I was confident, as if I belonged, as if I was carefree, as if I was optimistic, as if I wasn't frozen in fear) would build up an impression among my coworkers that I was competent, talented, valuable, dependable, etc. And that I'd just figure out the puzzle along the way. But instead, in retrospect, I think I just broadcasted a signal that I wasn't being entirely authentic or maybe even, at times, sane. I developed a habit of changing jobs once a year, duplicating the rhythm of moving once a year as a child. My internal clock said, "Get out now before you're found out." (What being "found out" meant was anyone's guess. The fugitive spirit inside me just said, "Time to split.")

Because the therapy world was only just beginning to discover the long-term psychological and behavioral impacts of starting out life as abused children (and because of my own go-to habit of making my choices without benefit of the advice of others), I was finally exhausted by my string of failed attempts to fit in and function inside an organization setting. My few futile attempts to seek counseling make me cringe today when I remember how destructive they were—because, like me, the counselors didn't have the confidence to say, "This is out of my range of competence."

My decision: To be a self-employed writer and ultimately an expert on—ironically—career success inside corporate cultures. The thing that eluded me personally became the question that has driven my entire career: How do people achieve fulfillment and reach their potential inside the work aspect of their lives?

Do I still travel incognito? To a certain degree, yes. But here's what I learned along my own healing path: Everyone does to some extent. Whether we're ASDPs or not, we edit what we reveal about our true natures and pasts with the people we work with. That's what keeps the organizational mechanism moving relatively friction-free. And that is, word has it, what makes us grown-ups.

What Working *With* an ASDP Must Be Like for Others

When my houseguest reacted so strongly to my musings about sharing the hypothetical *Top Chef* prize money, I started to think about how confusing it must be for others to have worked with *me* over the many jobs I had before I decided to jump off that career path altogether. What's it like to work with ASDPs in general, for that matter?

Here are some characteristics generally associated with ASDPs. And how they might be experienced by their coworkers:

Many ASDPs feel constant pressure to be perfect. It's challenging to relax with someone who isn't comfortable in their own skin. So, as ASDPs tend to be hypervigilant about work, their colleagues pick up on that tension. Commonly, coworkers also interpret that ASDP drive for perfection as being competitive against *them*—therefore even untrustworthy. In reality, though, ASDPs are only competing against themselves and the voices in their heads telling them that they are unworthy unless they deliver flawless work.

Many ASDPs have trouble letting loose in a spirit of fun. When the family of origin is constantly in some kind of fugitive, survival mode, fun isn't something that comes naturally. I remember as a pre-schooler standing apart from the rest of the kids playing on the playground, and thinking, "I don't get it." Today, as an adult, I look at photos on LinkedIn of workplace teams joyfully celebrating some off-site retreat and "goofball" team-building game, and I think, "I'm so glad I don't have to do that." I really can't get excited about standing on the top of a telephone pole. I don't even like breakout sessions in conferences; they make me feel too exposed.

Many ASDPs don't openly share personal stories. I can stand in an office kitchen and listen to a colleague complain about his or her bossy mother. And not share a word about my own. My thinking: "If you knew even a smidgeon about my past, it would ruin your whole day." Sharing personal stories is a culturally acceptable bonding ritual, the more reciprocal the better. But ASDPs whose pasts are so horrible that they believe that the movie *Carrie* has a happy ending, just don't want to go there over the office coffee pot. They're actually doing their non-ASDP colleagues a favor. But their colleagues can misinterpret the ASDP's silence as being judging, secretive (in a bad way), stand-offish.

Many ASDPs have boundary issues. This is actually the opposite of being secretive. Some ASDPs don't realize that their colleagues feel like they're being held responsible for the ASDP's feelings or triggers. Some ASDPs identify so thoroughly with their pasts still, not embracing the positive belief that the rest of their life is theirs to create what they want of it, that they over-burden their colleagues with their stories and feelings. Their coworkers discover that they have to modify their own behaviors to prevent emotional outbursts. And before long the workplace culture has a walking-on-eggshells feeling. And when the ASDP goes to the kitchen for a fresh cup of coffee, everyone clears out.

Many ASDPs accidentally offend and hurt feelings. Sometimes, as an ASDP, it feels like you were raised by wolves. Overly strict caretakers compensate for their own personal shame by taking it out on the children— even in their facial expressions and their tone of voice. A coworker once said to me, "You know, you could have said that much more nicely and gotten an even better reaction from people." And I thought I was being nice. More than once I've had people say to me, "Don't look at me that way!" and I realize I'd been scowling. (In contrast, there's a lovely young woman who works the drive-thru window at the café where I buy my stress-eating, comfort muffins. And the first time I saw her, I thought to myself, "Now here's someone who has been smiled at since she was a baby." You can just tell by her overall warmth and positive demeanor that smiling is her resting, "hello" face.) Harsh words and stern expressions are "normal" to many ASDPs. And we learn very quickly in the workplace that what comes naturally to us is the very thing that gives others the wrong idea about who we are.

"Did I Say Too Much?"

As I write this, I wonder if I might have over-shared. But then I remember that the purpose of this piece is to let others know that they're not alone in their experiences as ASDPs. If 100 people were to be crammed into the office kitchen, statistically speaking, 67 of them would stick around and whisper in my ear, asking me if there's a secret handshake we can all agree upon. It's an isolating life, this business of trying to look like we've got it all together when we're all just trying to get on with things and do the best we can.

A few years ago, I was having lunch at an elegant Washington, DC, place to see and be seen (the kind of high-quality, lifestyle moment that would have been completely beyond my mother's imaginings). My lunch-mate is also an ASDP. Because of the very upsetting breaking news of that particular day, we had the following conversation:

Me: "Do you think that having been ASDPs might uniquely equip us to handle the chaos that might be coming our way as a nation?"

Him: "Maybe so. Or maybe we'll be the first to break. And there will be pictures of us in *The Washington Post* yelling at taxi cabs and shaking our umbrellas at pigeons."

We laughed sardonically and resumed eating our salads. The choice to eat a healthy lunch, I thought, is a vote for the future. All hell might break loose, but our arteries will be in great shape. And sardonic humor is another one of those common coping mechanisms.

I look back on that day, and I consider the amazing collection of coincidences that brought Susan and me together on this project, and I am grateful for how our respective paths brought us to this place where we're working together.

When I think about Susan's courage and determination to thrive on the successful corporate career trajectory, I ask myself repeatedly, "How did she *do* that?" And I both admire and envy the fact that she has built a world-class niche and reputation.

When I think about my earliest decision to jump the career tracks, I know that I was both following my heart and my fears. And yet my life has given me gifts. For example, as a result of my career decision, I live in a beautiful resort mountain town where many people would love to live. But they can't because towns like this aren't good for growing corporate careers. So they can only come on vacation. I can live and work anywhere, and so I live and work here. I am comfortable in chaos and uncertainty—in my chosen lifestyle, workstyle, and addiction to following the news, there is plenty of both.

My history and my father's example, especially, have equipped me to establish intimate rapport with strangers quickly. And almost every conversation is deep with meaning. My life is varied, interesting, and I am led with a strong sense of purpose. True, it might take me longer to lose myself into the concentrated joys of creative flow than others because I have to settle down the PTSD drive to run away from my desk. But, thanks to this work, I know that I'm not the only one who has to tell the negative thoughts and urgings to simmer down so I can get some work done.

And the work itself? I have the freedom to choose the main theme of my professional life: Positive experiences in the workplace.

I have learned so much in the research of this book. My only wish is that I could have passed this knowledge on to my mother before it was too late for her.

Chapter 3
What The Heck is an ASDP
(And Am I One)?

IF YOU HAD asked me a week before my Onsite experience if my past was negatively affecting my future, I would have been mystified by the question. Of course not, I would have said. Look at my career path. Wasn't my resume proof enough that I had it all together?

But then a week later, I was on the floor crying in the arms of people who just days prior were total strangers.

We each come to our life's hardest truths when the time is right. Everyone is different. (Martha knew that her life was going to be emotionally complicated as young as 6 when she experienced the First Bad Day with her alcoholic mother. Of course, at that age she didn't have the knowledge, vocabulary, or understanding about life that would have enabled her to predict the ways being an ASDP would affect her life. But she never had that breakthrough a-ha moment I did. She never needed it.)

For many ASDPs, the key to functioning in a fundamentally dysfunctional environment is denial. Denial starts with parents who refuse to address what happened last night ("we don't talk about such things in this family"), who tell their children that they'll get over that bad thing ("children are resilient, you'll land on your feet"), or that the parents only did what they did because their needs were more important than the children's or that their kids somehow "deserved" the maltreatment.

There's a meme in circulation throughout social media that says something to the effect of, "When an abusive parent rages at a child, the child doesn't learn to separate from the parent. The child separates from himself." Part of that separation is separating from the truth of what happened. The truth about how you really didn't get what you needed to feel safe and thrive in your most formative years. The truth about how your needs were real and legitimate. That you weren't just being spoiled, self-centered, demanding, selfish in a family situation where other needs were more "important" than your own. For many children growing up in environments where they experienced neglect or abuse as a chronic characteristic of their family life, the only way to endure those early years was to deny their own needs.

Then the denial becomes a habit that they take with them into adulthood. And then they're mystified as to why and how life seems to be so much harder and complicated for them than it is for others. And then someone kindly and gently suggests to us that we read the Laundry List, just to see if there might be something there that resonates with us.

Oh My God, That's Me!

"Have you ever seen the Laundry List?" This is the question that friends have asked friends for decades, hoping to gently lead them into a self-discovery that will set them on the path to healing. The Laundry List was written by Tony A. and published in 1978 in the book, *Adult Children of Alcoholics/Dysfunctional Families*. This book, lovingly referred to as the Big Red Book by millions of adult children of alcoholics (ACOAs), lists 14 common life experiences and emotions that ASDPs endure—often in silence and isolation. Even if your parents weren't alcoholics, if you experienced some negative dynamic growing up (a neglectful parent, an overbearing or controlling parent, a very judgmental parent, etc.), my guess is that the Laundry List will resonate for you.

When shown this List, they often realize for the first time that they're not alone in these feelings. And how they've grown up is actually a very normal outcome of a very abnormal childhood. These 14 common life experiences and emotions stemmed from a set of coping mechanisms that

ASDPs needed to survive. But now those same mechanisms are *maladaptive*, meaning that they're getting in the way of living a life of happiness, healthy relationships, and successful careers.

Since my message to you is strictly focused on how to use the workplace as a venue for healing from the past, let's just focus on your on-the-job experiences as we look at the Laundry List below. If you're an ASDP, you will likely recognize yourself here (and if you know ASDPs, this would be a good list to show them):

1. We become isolated and afraid of people and authority figures. You may feel uncomfortable working in teams where you have to rely on others to honor their commitments. And you experience anxiety when dealing with your boss—a feeling that is reminiscent of the way you used to feel with your parents.

2. We became approval seekers and lost our identity in the process. You are so eager to please people, you see yourself behaving like a puppy dog, as I discovered. Your coworkers don't know what to make of you. And if asked if they respect and value you, they might even say no.

3. We are frightened by angry people and any personal criticism. You feel judged, small, and overpowered when your coworkers or boss lose their temper, raise their voice, or blame you. You dread performance appraisals because negative observations make you feel like you're being personally destroyed. No one really enjoys annual reviews. But where others might take a criticism as an isolated invitation to improve in that one area, you may feel as though your worthiness as a human being has just been called into question.

4. We either become addicts, marry them, or find another compulsive personality trait such as workaholism to fulfill our sick abandonment needs. As an ASDP, you commonly find yourself either working for other ASDPs or addicts (Cassandra's story later in the book will show you what that looks like). Or you discover that you've hired them. And suddenly, company objectives are interwoven with people unconsciously trying to work out their childhood issues with their colleagues. And you're all caught up in the drama.

5. We live life from the viewpoint of victims and are attracted by that weakness in our love and friendship relationships. You may be drawn to personal friendships with colleagues who focus only on negative stories of victimhood or who routinely let down their teams. Just as importantly, you shy away from building personal relationships with empowered, successful coworkers who can be your true role models for building success.

6. We have an overdeveloped sense of responsibility, and it is easier for us to be concerned with others rather than ourselves; this enables us to avoid looking too closely at our own faults, etc. It's said that ASDPs don't have friendships (or healthy working relationships), they have *case loads*. Of course, we have real friendships. But we seem to be very susceptible to assuming responsibility for other people's personal problems. Taking these problems on helps us feel strong, even sane, and stable. But, in truth, we're just putting off the real hard work on ourselves.

7. We get guilt feelings when we stand up for ourselves instead of giving in to others. If you grew up in a dysfunctional household, you remember how dangerous it was (and still can be) to stand up for yourself—especially to authority figures. Standing up for oneself is hard enough for anyone. But you never learned the skills of calmly establishing boundaries and saying no in a safe way. It has always been much easier to capitulate yet again, promising yourself that you'll draw the line the next time when you're feeling more confident. But that time never seems to come.

8. We became addicted to excitement. Do you say, "I work best under pressure?" Do you let things go neglected so long that by the time you get around to focusing on them you're in a panic? Do people routinely come to you because you can reliably keep a cool head when chaos reigns?

9. We confuse love and pity and tend to love people we can pity and rescue. This is closely related to #6 above. This scenario might show up for you in that ASDPs confuse coaching with codependency when dealing with our coworkers. You find that you're the one who always "has time" for a meeting from someone who just wants to vent. Hours go by, you haven't done your own work, and the coworker is going over the same problem from the umpteenth time. This behavior intrudes on your home life as well, when you find yourself hanging on the phone listening to hours of the same unresolved dramas from coworkers who have your home phone number but no will to fix their own problems.

10. We have stuffed our feelings from our traumatic childhoods and have lost the ability to feel or express our feelings because it hurts so much—denial. If you are an ASDP, you probably grew up being told that many of your basic needs, preferences, wants were selfish—especially when compared with the magnitude of your parents' requirements, worries, tragedies, addictions, moods, and other kinds of drama. If that was the case in your childhood, you grew the habit of telling yourself that you were insignificant, especially as compared with the larger issues swirling around you. Consequently, today you can talk yourself out of letting people know what you want—whether it's a promotion, a raise, a new assignment, or even a desk chair that rolls smoothly. Someone else's issues always take priority.

11. We judge ourselves harshly and have a very low sense of self-esteem. When we were children who depended utterly on our damaged parents or guardians, we came to our own conclusions as to why we weren't getting what we needed to thrive emotionally and physically. The adults in our lives couldn't be wrong—we needed them too much. So the only conclusion we came to is that we must have been bad and unworthy. Even as we grow into adults and can give ourselves what we need, that belief is still deeply ingrained for many. It touches every aspect of our lives, including our workdays and career. As a result, we overcompensate with perfectionism, we beat ourselves up for saying what we think is the wrong thing. We blow small mistakes out of proportion. We subconsciously signal to others that we volunteer to be the scapegoat, and it's okay for them to take out their frustrations on us or use us as a pawn in office politics.

12. We are dependent personalities who are terrified of abandonment and will do anything to hold onto a relationship. We all know that it's typically not cool to say to a coworker or boss, "It's not my job." But still there comes a time when someone at work pushes your boundaries, and you're brought face-to-face with your will to say "no." Do you have what it takes to be willing to lose a workplace relationship, a promotion, or even a job, if it means taking a stand for your professional reputation when someone demands just way too much?

13. Addiction is a family disease. We become para-addicts who took on the characteristics even though we don't use the addictive substance ourselves. If you grew up with damaged parents, they taught you behaviors and dysfunctional ways of interacting with the world. Maybe you didn't take on their addiction or foundational dysfunctional nature. But maybe you learned that it was okay to break your promises. That eating too much sugar is great for stress relief. That people will take advantage of you the second you let your guard down. That the best way to deal with a problem is to simply ignore it and it will eventually go away. That the best way to get someone's attention or obedience is to yell at them. How do those old childhood lessons show up in the way you behave at work?

14. Para-addicts are reactors, rather than actors. Many ASDPs grow up believing that they are powerless to improve their situation. They've seen the adults in their lives make promises, try to keep them and give up at the first hint of struggle. These ASDPs grow up to believe that will power alone won't enable them to create the change and improvement they dream of. Many simply become passive in the face of challenges that might be seen as opportunities by someone else. Instead of being the captain of their own ship sailing to the destination of their dreams, they're bailing water constantly struggling to keep that ship from sinking.

Do any of the characteristics of the Laundry List sound like you? If you're an ASDP, you probably identify with at least a few of them. How do they show up at work for you?

The gift is that the workplace is a great opportunity for you to learn new behaviors and beliefs that will help you not only thrive in your career but also benefit your private life as well. The workplace is where you will learn so much more about people and the way the world works beyond the tight confines of the troubled home of your childhood.

The workplace is also where you will meet other ASDPs (you didn't think you're the only one, did you?), who are struggling with the same issues you are. And then, when the moment is right, you can kindly and gently ask:

"Do you know about the Laundry List?" And then continue to sit with them as they realize, "Oh my gosh, that's *me!*"

Science Gets Involved in a Big Way

Up until the 1990s, the conversations around what it means to thrive as an adult survivor of a dysfunctional or damaged past were mostly the wheelhouse of psychologists, psychiatrists, social workers, and other kinds of therapists trying their best to make sense of the common behaviors and struggles their patients were reporting from their day-to-day lives. Some groundbreaking books were published (*Healing the Shame That Binds You, Adult Children of Alcoholics*, etc.) that helped us ASDPs at least realize that we weren't alone in our experiences.

Some of us grew up to be impressively successful in our careers, but at the expense of our family lives and personal relationships. Others of us, in our attempts to ease our internal torment, did things that we thought would work, but only landed us in jail, in hospitals, or in the cemetery. Our collective thrashing around, in search of the thing (the insight, the guru, the beverage, the drug, the money) that would be the answer attracted cultural backlash as some of our friends and families got tired of the cycles of our own resolve and struggles. Even The Eagles, that rock band that made its fortune encouraging non-stop rumination and self-pity with its songs, got sick of us. And so they wrote the song, *Get Over It.*

Other than ACOA and other 12 Step group meetings, and therapy, there wasn't much effort to scientifically validate who we were and support any kind of recovery. Then came two threads of discovery that have begun to change everything for us: The discovery and codification of *adverse childhood experiences* (ACEs). And neuroscience discoveries that show how traumatic childhood experiences have real and demonstrable physical effects on the developing brain.

Let's start with the story of ACEs first. This is just a brief overview. If you're interested in the more complete, complex story, the two books *The Deepest Well: Healing the Long-Term Effects of Childhood Adversity* and *Childhood Disrupted: How Your Biography Becomes Your Biology, and How You Can Heal* are excellent reading.

A long story short: Back in 1985, physician and researcher Vincent J. Felitti, was conducting a preventative care survey for the San Diego Kaiser Permanente Medical Program. And, without really looking for it, he discovered a trend that the obese patients he was interviewing reported having had at least one traumatic experience as children. Eating had become their coping mechanism to help with the anxiety and depression they were secretly coping with as adults. When he made presentations on his discoveries, Felitti's peers dismissed the correlations he was describing as patients just making excuses for their "failed lives." And they ridiculed him in the process. (This professional reaction, by the way, was an indication of the general health care attitude of "just get over it," causing ASDP patients to find other ways to relieve their anguish than turn to their doctors.)

Felitti refused to be discouraged, so he and Kaiser Permanente teamed with the Centers for Disease Control and one of its medical epidemiologists, Robert Anda, who had already been looking into the connections between heart disease and depression.

First they had to identify experiences that would capture all the different possible kinds of traumatic events a child might be exposed to in an ongoing way—not just one isolated incident in what would otherwise be a stable childhood. And they developed what would be eventually known as the Adverse Childhood Experiences (ACEs) survey, which included these 10 questions:

Before your 18th birthday,

1. Did a parent or another adult in the household often or very often swear, insult you, put you down, or humiliate you? Or act in a way that made you afraid you might be physically hurt?
2. Did a parent or another adult in the household often or very often push, grab, slap, or throw something at you? Or ever hit you so hard that you had marks or were injured?
3. Did an adult or person at least five years older than you ever touch or fondle you or have you touch their body in a sexual way? Or attempt to touch you or touch you inappropriately or sexually abuse you?

4. Did you often or very often feel that no one in your family loved you or thought you were important or special? Or feel that your family members didn't look out for one another, feel close to one another, or support one another?

5. Did you often or very often feel that you didn't have enough to eat, had to wear dirty clothes, or had no one to protect you? Or that your parents were too drunk or high to take care of you or take you to the doctor if you needed it?

6. Was a biological parent ever lost to you through divorce, abandonment, or another reason?

7. Was your mother or stepmother often or very often pushed, grabbed, slapped, or have something thrown at her? Or was she sometimes, often or very often kicked, bitten, hit with a fist, or hit with something hard? Or ever repeatedly hit over the course of at least a few minutes or threatened with a gun or knife?

8. Did you live with anyone who was a problem drinker or alcoholic, or who used street drugs?

9. Was a household member depressed or mentally ill, or did a household member attempt suicide?

10. Did a household member go to prison?

The affirmative answers—and the percentage of them as compared with the general American population—were eye-opening. Here are just a few of the top line figures:

- 67 percent of all Americans had experienced at least one ACE.
- 40 percent had two or more ACEs.
- 25 percent of those with one or more ACEs had a parent who was addicted to alcohol.

So many diseases are associated with adverse childhood experiences. Cardiovascular disease; diabetes; multiple sclerosis; chronic fatigue syndrome; autoimmune diseases; bowel disorders; migraines; alcoholism and other substance abuse; eating disorders, as Felitti had discovered; and notably major clinical depression. Those numbers are staggering. According to Donna Jackson Nakazawa, in her book, *Childhood Disrupted*, of those who had ACE scores of just 1, 19 percent of men and 24 percent of women also had clinical depression. Of those with ACE scores of 4 or more, 35 percent of the men and 60 percent of the women had clinical depression.

Patients with ACE scores of 4 or more were 460 percent more likely to face depression than anyone with a score of 0. They were also twice as likely to be diagnosed with cancer. Patients with ACE scores of 6 or more could expect a lifespan shortened by 20 years.

And even those who didn't smoke, who weren't overweight, who didn't have high cholesterol or diabetes, but had an ACE score of 7 or more, still had a 360 percent higher risk of heart diseases than those with an ACE score of 0. So clearly, Felitti's critics were wrong. So were The Eagles. Surviving a childhood riddled with adverse childhood experiences has never been just a matter of getting over it.

(In case you're wondering, my ACE score is 5. Martha's is 8. We'll see what the future brings. But so far so good in the physical health department for both of us.)

A Lot of It Really Is in Our Heads (But Not the Way You Might Think)

I like to say, "Damaged is not doomed," which is true. And you'll discover why and how as you progress through this book. But we owe it to our brains to understand at least somewhat how traumatic childhoods really do affect the way our brain physically develops.

A childhood filled with chronic and unpredictable, traumatic stresses attacks our brains, our synapses, the way we respond to unpredictable stressful events as adults (even the sudden sound of a slamming door). The child who grows up always on the lookout for the unexpected slap, punch, insult, raging episode, unwelcome touch, or ringing doorbell, with police car lights flashing in the driveway, grows up to be the adult who is hypervigilant about almost everything almost all the time. It's not because we like being scaredy cats or nervous Nellies. It's because our brains make us this way. Because our childhoods made our brains that way.

Here are a few ways how:

Simply having an ACE score of 1 puts us at higher risk of having a brain that shrank in size and volume as a child.

Chronic adversities and stressors literally break our stress response mechanism, lowering its setpoint so that we hit alert mode more easily and have more difficulty returning to a relaxed mode—if we ever do thoroughly. The stress response mechanism—the hypothalamus, pituitary, and adrenal glands—are constantly releasing a toxic cocktail of stress hormones that keep us in a state of hyperarousal.

Those same stress hormones cause *neuroinflammation* in our brain, which puts the brain at risk in multiple ways. We have what's known as *microglian cells* in our brain which are basically housekeepers. Think of someone constantly on the move, reliably dumping out ash trays, throwing away old newspapers, cleaning the cat hair off the sofa. That's our microglian cells at work. We need them to keep our brain functioning in great working order. But when we are chronically stressed, the housekeepers start throwing away the good stuff in your brain, too. That great book you were in the middle of reading. Your grandmother's china. The diamond ring you inherited from an aunt. The vintage Lamborghini in the garage? Say bye bye.

In the case of microglian cells, they are not only pruning away unneeded neurons, they're also destroying that neuron you needed for keeping your spirits up while preparing for your critical test. Or coming up with that one great idea that will turn your company around. Or prevailing over your brain's impulses to really speak your mind to the boss and burn all your bridges. Microglian cells run amok will attack the neurons you actually had plans for. Chronic stress will do that to you.

But wait, there's more: Unpredictable and chronic stressors (for instance, all those terrible events described in the ACE survey) attack the way the hippocampus and the amygdala communicate with each other. The amygdala is the fear and emotion center, which tells us to get the hell out of there. The hippocampus combines that impulse with memories of similar situations and analyzes our levels of safety or peril. It neutralizes the false alarms. When these two aren't communicating well, that sets the adult up for being triggered. Post-traumatic stress disorder (PTSD) sufferers call those experiences *flashbacks*. And we're only just coming to terms with the fact that children who have experienced ACEs are at risk for suffering PTSD—in this case, what is known as complex PTSD.

There is also scientific research that shows that those moments when we feel suddenly triggered emotionally are actually our brains at work to protect us from threats that we perceive as immediate and real—even though they're memories of a long-gone past still held in current mode. We'll get into the science behind triggers in the section on *Bumper Car Moments*, when we'll talk about how workplace conflicts can actually be healing moments. But just know for now that those moments when you are emotionally responsive in a way that even you might intellectually see is probably out of proportion given the immediate circumstance, those reactions are likely due to your brain trying to protect you from a past emotional assault. However, in relation to the present-day moment, your out-of-proportion emotional response can negatively affect you in many ways—including hurting your work relationships and long-term career prospects.

But wait, there's even more: The stressed-out brain hits our DNA; most notably the telomeres that protect the tips of our DNA (like those caps on the end of our sneaker shoelaces). When the telomeres are compromised, our DNA is attacked. And that leads to disease and rapid aging.

There is good news to be had here, though. Through discoveries in the field of interpersonal neurobiology and positive psychology, we are learning that the brain is *plastic*, which means that it can be healed—or rewired—to give us a more fulfilling life, with joys and rewarding experiences and relationships—especially the one with ourselves. This is why I say, "Damaged is not doomed." Those healing joys and experiences can be had at work!

If you're an ASDP, you have had a childhood that haunts you to some degree to this day. Maybe it takes you by surprise, when, like me, you're so practiced at denying your trauma. Or maybe it follows you around every moment—awake or asleep—getting in the way of a joyful life.

You can start the journey of rebuilding your brain, through the process of learning how to create what I call the *Conscious Healing Career Path*. All those moments of tension and conflict that you have in your everyday work life can be used to your advantage. Here you can learn to trust yourself and others. Stand up for what you want and deserve. Respond differently when you get triggered and upset. Attract the people who will respect and support you as you use your newfound healthy mindset to create new ideas of what your future can bring you. You can turn your traumas into building blocks that will benefit you and inspire generations to come.

Frequently Uttered Yeah-Buts

Every ASDP experience is different. We have some common traits, but as individuals we learn to cope with them differently. When you combine the many variables that factor into what can be identified as an adverse childhood experience with the many variables that go into how you learned to find your way in life, the combinations are beyond counting.

Again, I'm not here to tell you who you are. You've already have had enough of that kind of input over your lifetime. But you're still here in this conversation with me, with this book in your hand. So there must be something here that resonates as relevant to your life experience in some way. With that in mind, let's review some of the "yeah buts" I've encountered over the years. Maybe you'll see yourself here as well.

"Other people had it a lot worse than I did." Maybe some did. So what? We're talking about *you* here and what you might not have received that *you* needed—and deserved—simply by the fact that you were a child whose well-being was completely in the hands of other people. Recognizing the very real possibility that the way you live your life today has been negatively affected by the way you grew up as a child is simply taking stock of reality, not indulging in setting yourself up as a victim of why-did-it-have-to-be-me circumstances.

"I'm a super achiever. I remember every detail of my horrible past, and it actually was the thing that inspired me to be successful. Just to show them they were wrong." Many ASDPs are extraordinarily successful, that's true. But at what expense? Peace of mind? Family balance? Physical health? Being an ASDP doesn't doom you to failure, necessarily. It can fuel amazing achievements. But imagine what life could be like for you if you could achieve that success without those haunting memories or learning how to stop the voice inside your head that keeps repeating: "You must keep proving yourself. What you have accomplished is not enough. You are not enough." Those thoughts leave you exhausted and not fully present to areas of your life outside of work.

"Everybody has bad things happen to them in life. The last thing I want to do is wallow in self-pity. That's what losers do." It's unrealistic to expect life to be an easy ride, free of worries, pain, and sadnesses. But what we're talking about here is the legacy of a childhood of chronic and unpredictable stressors that kept you feeling unsafe and on high alert for a sustained amount of time. It's those experiences that create the lasting impacts that make adult life especially difficult, stressful and complicated. I'm not encouraging self-pity. But I am encouraging you to gently review your life, and all the childhood events that you can remember that influenced what you believe about your place in the world, as data points. Then you can determine whether you're an ASDP and what kind of support you need to neutralize the negative impacts of adverse childhood experiences that are influencing your life even today.

"My parents weren't alcoholics, and I was never abused. None of these examples apply to me." Okay. Fair enough. But you've come this far in this book. There must be a reason why. I've found that many people in the workplace do not believe they are ASDPs. But they relate to what I am saying anyway. When they talk to me, it comes out that they may have had an overly critical parent, or a parent who wasn't present. (All I have to do is show them the ACE questionnaire, and a whole new conversation starts.) It doesn't matter what you experienced. If you walked away from your childhood with negative beliefs about yourself that affect how you feel at work, this book is for you. Or, maybe you know someone this book can help. If so, please come along.

"If I look too closely at my past, I'm going to end up blaming my parents. And I don't want to do that. Their lives were hard enough as it was." I don't want you to blame your parents either. The chances are excellent that they were ASDPs themselves. Their behaviors and beliefs about themselves and the world were based on how their parents treated them. And so on and so on going back generations. It's also possible that they actually gave you a better life than they had them-selves. The best gift that you can give to your parents and ancestors go-ing all the way back into their damaged pasts is to look compassionately at what you have needed and didn't get while growing up, make sure you continue on the healing path so that you enjoy the life you've been given, and contribute that learning to future generations, so that the healing journey continues deep into the future. This isn't about blame; this is about healing.

"I'm not an ASDP, but my partner is, and it's affecting our kids." This book is one tool in your toolkit for helping your partner and raising your children to be empowered, optimistic, confident adults. It's not meant to take the place of mental health counseling. But you can use it to understand—and help your partner understand—ways to replace limiting beliefs about yourselves and the world with empowering, posi-tive ways to move through life that has less stress, anxiety and worry.

There's A Better Way Within Your Reach

In closing this chapter, I would like to introduce you to the word, *eudaimonia.* In short, it means a general sense of well-being and positivity. But most recently, positive psychology researchers and thought leaders have gotten more granular in identifying the six elements that create the uplifting feeling of eudaimonia:

- Self-discovery
- Perceived development on one's best potentials
- A sense of purpose and meaning in life
- Investment of significant effort in the pursuit of excellence
- Intense involvement in activities
- Enjoyment of activities as personally expressive

If you're an ASDP, you may not have had many of those experiences while growing up and struggling with adverse childhood events. (In fact, you don't have to have been an ASDP to have missed out on some of these elements. But in the context of what we've defined as an ASDP childhood, you can be pretty sure that what you learned about yourself and what the world has to offer you in your life may have fallen short of at least some of these six elements.)

But you're an adult now. You actually deserve to be congratulated. The mere fact that you're reading this book shows that you not only survived your childhood (which is big right there), but you also have sheltered a place in your heart that still hopes for a better way to move through life from this point forward.

So where does your work life fit into your healing journey? Look at all these above six elements, starting with self-discovery. Assuming your current job aligns with your values, and the workplace culture is relatively humane and non-toxic (I say relatively because no workplace is perfect), you can see at a glance all the possibilities that the workplace brings you to discover your best self. The version of you that is able to fulfill your potential; find a purpose and meaning beyond what your wounded parents might have told you about you and life; able to do work you're proud of; thoroughly engage your focus in activities and goals that reflect your own personal priorities and dreams.

Nobody ever said that valuable gifts are only wrapped in pretty boxes and feel-good experiences. Some of the most valuable gifts of life hurt. And they hurt a lot because they force you to look unblinkingly at some fact of your life that is standing in the way of your growth and your ability to achieve your full potential. I think of this as "dark storms—great gifts."

This is the gift of the workplace as a powerful venue for healing from your damaged childhood. For many ASDPs, like me, the workplace is our first opportunity to realize just how much healing needs to be done. Up until our first job, we had been living inside the context of our damaged family, using all the powerful coping mechanisms that we had developed over time to help us survive the abuse, neglect, rage, unrelenting judgment, lies, narcissism of those who were supposed to take care of us. As we grew up, those coping mechanisms have turned into behaviors that were our "normal." And they were normal at home.

But maybe not so much in the workplace. We may bring those old be-haviors of surviving, succeeding, protecting ourselves and relationship-building into a relatively intimate culture (these people see you every day; some count on you to perform; others are judging your performance). And you're suddenly feeling over-exposed and vulnerable all over again. It's hard to hide your struggle and suffering.

But then we come to work where people are happy to see us; where we have the satisfaction and joy of accomplishing work that is meaningful to us. We have a support system that truly wants the best for us and is committed to encouraging our development. Some of us may even feel praised and acknowledged for our gifts and contributions for the first time in our lives. We also discover the power we have in helping others experience positive, rewarding days when we praise them.

Your work life can bring those experiences to you, in ways that your family of origin couldn't. I'm not saying it will be easy. But it will definitely be rewarding. And it will be healing.

Chapter 4
Damaged is Not Doomed

THERE ARE SO many ways we ASDPs inadvertently hurt ourselves by perpetuating the stories and beliefs that we carry with us from our childhood. One of the best gifts we can give ourselves is to fully understand that we are not necessarily the victims of other people's mistreatment. Our interpretations of events and the way others treat us might be driven more by the beliefs we created during our wounded past than what's really going on at the moment. And maybe, just maybe, the person we believe is harming us in some way is actually coping with overwhelm, pressure, unkindnesses, politics, you name it. And that the best thing you can do for both of you is step onto the Conscious Healing Career Path, and handle the situation with compassion. This is one way you can reclaim power over your own life's experience, while giving the other person much-needed emotional support. And this is an opportunity where you can proclaim to your own spirit, "I am not doomed to live out the damaged past for the rest of my life."

These opportunities for big a-has that lift us up onto the Conscious Healing Career Path come toward us in waves—some gently rolling swells that lift us up and set us down again, some crashing over our heads that make us feel as powerless as rag dolls. But they come. And we can take advantage of all of them to ultimately step up to a more fulfilling presence in life, with fresh understanding that other people are struggling as much as we are. And that we all deserve compassion.

I know this because it is a revelation that happens to me, continuously, just as I need the reminder. But one of the major life-changing, perspective-shifts happened to me over 15 years ago when I learned the lesson of how a manager needed my understanding and compassion as much, if not more, as she needed my work product. She was my new manager at a job that I had turned my life upside down to take. This new job required a life-changing move that left me feeling like I was thousands of miles away from all those support systems that I had built up over my lifetime. So the pressure was on to make sure she was consistently happy with me and my work. I was still going after that 5.0 GPA! Understandably, she had no way of really knowing what kind of pressure I was under. She didn't know me and my nature at all. And she had her own pressures she was focused on.

All was marching along well. And then it wasn't. A major project was due in a very short amount of time for her manager. Because I was still new, I didn't have the full background or context around this project. And, wouldn't you know it, the internal subject matter expert I normally would have asked for help had decided to take a new role at a different company. Right when I was coming into the company.

So, I did what I always do. I jumped right in, trying to fast forward my learning as quickly as possible. I worked day and night, reaching out to others who might know the nuances around this assignment and how best to approach it.

To make matters worse, she called often as we were finalizing the project's presentation. I was worried. What if I didn't meet her expectations? What if her boss felt the work was mediocre? I felt like the walls were closing in. I felt like I was trapped. I couldn't breathe. My limiting beliefs felt like an elephant standing on my chest. My desire to please my new manager was kicked into major overdrive, but all the while, I was feeling very sad. Depressed. I missed my home. I missed my friends and family. I missed the old familiar ways that my life had been a few months prior. I cried. Was I up to this new job? Was my new manager pleased with her choice to bring me in? I felt uncomfortable. Yes, I was triggered. I wanted to show her she had made a good decision to hire me. The harder I tried, the more I felt like I was missing the mark.

(It's not completely out of the question that my own anxieties might have been adding to her own sense of pressure, even if subconsciously. My issues weren't helping either of us.)

But then, amid the darkness, sadness, anxiety and regret, something magical happened. My executive coach said, "I hear you judging your new manager. What I want you to do is to shift the judgment to compassion."

"*What?*" I exclaimed! I hadn't realized that in my worry about meeting my new boss's expectations, I was unconsciously redirecting my energy and putting the blame on her for how I was feeling. How unfair! My coach helped me realize that people in leadership roles often feel judged. Maybe if I flipped my focus from myself to my manager and what she might be experiencing in a higher-level role I might see things differently. "The bigger the job, the bigger the bull's eye," my coach reminded me.

I had nothing to lose by trying a little dose of compassion on her and in doing so, taking my foot off the unconscious blame pedal I was pressing all the way to the floor. The time was perfect too. It was the night before the big meeting. My boss was still undecided which direction we were going to take in the presentation. (In retrospect, I could only imagine what kind of stress she was under that night for other important reasons unrelated to our project.) I decided to create two sets of slides. I was ready for whichever path she selected.

She had to take a last-minute business trip and would not be getting back till very late on the night before the big meeting. So, I decided to send her a message of compassion. My email said that I was sorry, that I knew she would be getting back late and would likely be tired and would need to read both decks. I told her I wanted to do everything I could in the future to avoid a last-minute experience. I told her I looked forward to hearing her direction the next morning. And then I let go. There was no point in beating myself up anymore.

As soon as I sent my compassion message, I had the chance to reflect. All the stress, anxiety, and worry I had been feeling was all mine. It was all self-inflicted. I had been unconsciously triggered by my perception of not meeting her expectations and by the sense of feeling concerned by her calls, which I interpreted as her being unhappy with my performance. My reaction belonged to me, not her. The stories I was telling myself about how badly I felt were just that. Stories. Based on my past relationship with my dad. My boss was an innocent bystander who I had unconsciously dragged into the story in my own head. *Wow.*

I was becoming aware of the fact that I didn't have to feel this way. I could choose a different response to what was happening. I had no idea what she thought about her decision to hire me, but I certainly didn't have to conclude that she was regretting it. I mentally, physically, and emotionally stepped back from the unproductive messaging going on in my head about my not being good enough. I was seeing clearly that it is no one's duty to approve of me. That is my job.

I breathed a sigh of clarity and calm after I sent the compassion email. And then the next day, I was amazed by the outcome. In the meeting, she told her boss that she loved many things about me and then went on and on about what those things were. I was blown away!

This compassion thing worked! Or, maybe, just maybe, she had never been disappointed in me or felt judged at all! Of course, she had her own major priorities and pressures to manage and assumed that she had hired a capable leader. Regardless of what was happening and as crazy stressful as those two months were, I felt like the skies were opening after a dark storm and the sun was blazing through a gorgeous rainbow! I was blessed by the power of becoming conscious of my own trauma-filled past colliding with my current career reality. And the realization that I could make very different choices in the future when the old triggers of not being good enough would kick in.

I had officially stepped off the Unconscious Wounded Career Path full of stress, anxiety, and worry, onto the Conscious Healing Career Path by leveraging the Bumper Car Moment of not feeling good enough in the context of a new work assignment. And the beautiful part of this story is that my relationship with that manager was forever positively changed because of the act of becoming conscious and practicing a different response. In doing so, I consciously released her from being an actor in my mind's story and took back responsibility for my reactions, unconscious old scripts and reactions that had been kicked into gear in a new situation. Being compassionate toward another was key to seeing the possibilities of responding consciously to stressful workplace moments that threaten our confidence.

"Why Does It Have to Be So Hard to Be Me?"

Before we dive deeply into the main content of this chapter, let's take a moment to look at the word "damaged." Before I started my own healing journey, I would have resisted that word as a label in my life. In fact, it would have offended me. *Damaged* is a bent fender in the supermarket parking lot. *Damaged* is a cracked glass on the cell phone that dropped on the bathroom floor. *Damaged* is not a human being. And it most certainly was not me. Or so I thought. A thought I clung on to for dear life. With or without the comforting companionship of Chardonnay.

"I'm not damaged," I would have said in a huff. "Take a look at my resume. Look at what I've accomplished. Take a look at my happy, healthy family and homelife. I'm successful. Take a look at my ballroom dancing and equestrian competitions. Look at all those ribbons and awards. I'm successful in all of these activities because I'm disciplined. I strive for performance excellence in everything I do. There's no place for *damage* in my life. I'm good. You must be talking about someone else."

So, if your back is up just a little bit at the sight of that word, *damaged*, I really do understand. If you are an ASDP with at least one ACE score from your childhood, just being alive, healthy, and a high performer at work is a gigantic accomplishment right there. Many of us don't even make it to this point in life. So you have much to feel proud of.

(Hmmm. There's another word that packs an emotional punch: *Proud*. How does *that* word resonate with you? For many ASDPs, *proud* is as scary a word as *damaged*. If you were raised in a shame-based childhood, where parents exerted their emotional control over their children by intentionally or unintentionally making them feel unwelcome or unworthy of even the most basic human needs, ASDPs learned from their earliest days that feeling good about themselves—even for just a moment—will only get them in trouble. "Don't get too big for your britches." "Pride goeth before the fall." "Do you think you're better than the rest of us? Well, you're not." "Well, what did you expect, being all high and mighty like that?")

Okay ... now let's take a look at the other word: *Doomed*. You may never have used that word to describe your emotional experience of your life. But I bet you've wondered at least once if there was any hope for any chance of relief from the struggle or dread. As an ASDP, you were likely to have been born into a family whose damage story was already in full swing before you arrived. Generations of it, variations of it, starting with people—your ancestors—whose names are long forgotten. You know what they say: The fish is the last to know he's wet. Well, as an ASDP, you were born into a fish tank into water that needed to be cleaned ages ago. For you, your experience of life may have been on the continuum from good experiences to "yuck," from merely cloudy water to unspeakably gross water. And you've been swimming around in it, figuring that's just the way it has to be for you. Some people will even try to tell you that you chose that particular fish tank—and its unhealthy water—before you were even born. And now it's your karma to deal with it. How's that for feeling doomed?

So are you really doomed to feel damaged for the rest of your life? Going from one stressful moment at work to the next? Driving yourself to various degrees of anxiety because of misunderstandings and your own high expectations around performance and seeking approval? Are you doomed to never-ending and futile attempts to resolve childhood traumas through your adult relationships—especially at work? (Are you like I was and are actually unaware of how much our dysfunctional pasts are playing out in our current work life now?)

Well. No. Not unless you want to be. You are not doomed to living a damaged life, no matter how devastating your childhood might have been. The healing begins with your brain—and your mind.

Your Mind Can Heal Your Damaged Brain

In the last chapter, we talked about how adverse childhood experiences and early trauma actually physically change the developing brain. And, even today, those changes influence the way you experience day-to-day life at work. If you grew up in a childhood that suffered constant, unpredictable chaotic events, you might be carrying around a sustained feeling that any moment something horrible is about to happen. That's not you being all freaky and weird, indulging in attention-getting "the sky is falling!" fantasies that turn your workplace into a stress pool. That's your stress response system trying desperately to keep you safe, after having been exhausted to the point of malfunction because it started life constantly being flooded with cortisol.

Your ACE experiences also created a set of beliefs that influence the ways you react to other peoples' puzzling behavior and decisions you make in your work—beliefs about the way the world works, your worthiness to have a joyful place in that world, and the likelihood that you can actually achieve that joy. These are mostly unconscious beliefs. They're like the weather—influencing the way you experience day to day life, mostly in the background in a way that you barely notice them. But they're there. And like a hot, heavily humid day, they can drag you down and suck the energy right out of your spirit, limiting your career prospects and your chances for achieving a joyful outlook that carries you forward with momentum, optimism, exuberance, hope, in the company of colleagues who respect and appreciate you.

Here are some beliefs that ASDPs report having, once they're given the chance to stop and think about them. Do any of these beliefs sound familiar to you?

- It doesn't matter that my performance was excellent yesterday or for the past five years. I made a mistake today and now people may have lost some respect for me.
- If I ask for more than what I was offered, people will think I'm being selfish or demanding, with an inflated opinion of my value. And then they'll be mad at me.
- Promises and commitments were made to be broken.
- The business world is dog-eat-dog and no one can be trusted.
- I can't trust myself.
- If I slow down, I will be unsafe.
- Happiness is fleeting. A bad circumstance is forever.
- Self-care is selfish if there is someone who needs my help first.
- If I don't keep my head on a swivel at all times, catastrophe will sneak up behind me.
- Everything is equally urgent. Everything is equally important.

- If it's not perfect, it's potentially irredeemable and career-threateningly flawed.

- If there is one person who displeased with my imperfect performance, my career is on the line until I personally make sure it's fixed.

- The harsh, scolding voice in my head must be believed and obeyed. Beating myself up is the best way to keep myself motivated and performing at the highest possible level.

- When people are upset with me, our relationship is in danger of exploding irreparably. And whatever it is that they're mad about, it has to be my fault. The fact that I don't fully understand the problem is proof that I'm fundamentally wired weirdly.

- "No" is always more likely than "yes."

When you think about your life as an ASDP, it is possibly infused with stress, anxiety, and worry. You learned from your parents, probably from experiences that began before you can even remember, that life is full of unpredictable, chaotic, even, at times, violent moments. Other people's problems are more important than yours, so you can just hold your horses. Other people's needs are more pressing than yours, so don't be so self-centered. Don't be so full of yourself, or you'll get smacked upside the head.

Isn't that an exhausting way to be? It's a constant narration of how hazardous life is if you're not paying hyper-attention every single moment. Your inner narrator inside your mind is droning on and on about life, the world, and how it's all your fault that that last episode happened the way it did.

There has to be a way to start feeling better.

There is. It takes time, practice, and intention. You just have to be patient and gentle with yourself while you build up this new skillset.

Just a Little More Brain Science

(This part is going to be super brief. Neither you nor I are neuroscientists or psychologists. So we don't need to know all the scientific ins and outs. Just the good stuff.)

"People are who they are. They never change." I'm sure you've heard that before. (Probably from people who had some influence on your earliest beliefs about the world, and who didn't have a very high opinion of others—or themselves, most likely.) Maybe you've even said it, with every conviction that it's the truth. Well, it's not the truth at all. But we can't blame them for believing this. For centuries we thought of our brains as unchangeable after the Wonder Years of childhood. That belief is called the Doctrine of the Unchanging Brain. But then toward the end of the 20th Century, neuroscientists discovered that the brain itself was malleable, it showed significant physical changes in reaction to stimulus it was exposed to. Including experiences and new information.

The concept of the unchanging brain was replaced by the concept of *neuroplasticity*. And even better news: Researchers discovered something called *self-directed neuroplasticity*, meaning that we can change our own brains intentionally. It's not as easy as flipping on a switch, but the mechanism might be considered to be as simple: Replace negative beliefs with good thoughts. Do it with intention, attention, and a positive attitude, and eventually the switch flips itself. Not out of magical thinking or hocus pocus. But by making much better use of the 100 billion neurons in our brains looking for something more uplifting to do than ruminate over the daily news on cable.

Rick Hanson, PhD, senior fellow at the Greater Good Science Center at UC Berkeley, says, "You can use the mind to change your brain to change your mind for the better."

We are hard-wired for what researchers call *negativity bias*, which means we'll remember the bad events that happen to us, while quickly forgetting the good ones. It's a survival mechanism passed down to us through the ages as staying alert for dangerous animals—and making note of that plant that killed tribe members—ensured the survival of our species so that we could eventually invent cable news and this keyboard that I'm typing on. But first our ancestors needed to survive the lions, hundreds of territorial skirmishes, more than a handful of *coups d'etat*, revolutions, civil wars, car accidents, and frat party drinking games.

The outcome of all these adventures, misadventures, chance encounters, and marriage vows? Me. And you. And we inherited from all those great survivors a tendency toward stress, anxiety, and worry, which kept our ancestors alive before. And which we bring to work with us now. And sometimes we unintentionally (or, let's be honest, intentionally) cause other people stress, anxiety, and worry.

So how do we flip that switch toward a mindset that trends toward the positive? By making a point of noticing the good and worthy, and holding on to those noticings for dear life. Does it seem too simple to be respect-inspiring? Maybe. St. Paul and Marcus Aurelius talked about the importance of focusing on good things as a life priority from the time of Christ into the third century. And their words have endured to today. But maybe this mnemonic that Hanson devised will add more authority to the concept of the essential power of intentionally driving the good episodes of life into our brains and giving them the chance to stick:

H: Have a beneficial experience. That's self-explanatory.

E: Enrich the experience. Add more value to the experience by keeping it going; intensifying it in some way. Find ways to make the experience a multi-sensory one. Find ways this experience brings novelty into your life. Make a point of identifying the reasons why this event is relevant to your life.

A: Absorb the experience. Experience the sensation of intention-ally taking it into your awareness in such a way that your brain stores it for safekeeping—and for remembering again and again. Think about why this experience is rewarding, and notice how that re-warding feeling feels. You might, for instance, feel an uplifted mood or a sense of special appreciation. For instance, Martha gives the ex-ample of crossing the Lake Worth, FL, bridge over the Intracoastal Waterway for the first time in her convertible. She loves epic, cross-country road trips, so her memory banks are full of events that are wonderful and not so wonderful (like getting stuck on another bridge—this one the George Washington Bridge in New York, behind one of those huge trucks transporting a rack of at least 10 cars, the back row pitched precariously over her top-down car). Anyway, back to the Lake Worth bridge: She had just driven 1,999 miles to Florida from New Mexico. And now she was flying over beautiful blue water, bobbing sailboats, the sparkling ocean in the distance. And she says, "As I turned south on A1A, with the sound of rustling palm fronds overhead, all I could say was 'thank you God,' over and over again."

That was a beneficial experience that got absorbed. And a new neural pathway got created that day. Did it overwrite an old bad memory neural pathway? "Maybe," she says. "But I don't want to think about that part. I only want to cast myself back to that moment when all I could think of was 'thank you God.'"

L: **Link positive memories with negative inputs in such a way that the positive influence soothes the negative.** In his book, *Hardwiring Happiness*, Hanson writes, "You hold both positive and negative material in your awareness at the same time. You keep the positive material more prominent and intense, and sense it connecting with and gradually soothing, perhaps even replacing, the negative material. In this step, the flowers of positive experiences crowd out and gradually replace the weeds of negative thoughts, feelings, and desires."

In case you were wondering, Marcus Aurelius said, "Very little is needed to make a happy life; it is all within yourself, in your ways of thinking." And in his letter to the Philippians, St. Paul wrote: "Whatever is true, whatever is noble, whatever is right, whatever is pure, whatever is lovely, whatever is admirable—if anything is excellent or praiseworthy—think about such things."

Today neuroscientists tell us about how we can create lasting change through practices that support positive neuroplasticity. They have functional MRIs to discover and prove new knowledge about installing an outlook on life that supports a happy existence. But it all comes down to this: What St. Paul said.

Perfectionism Gets in Our Way

This morning, just before I sat down to start developing this chapter, a cartoon on Facebook caught my eye: The image is of a woman ironing her work outfit for the day, in a sweet, homey kitchen, complete with playing puppy and sleeping kitten, and front-loading washing machine. All the details project "cozy, normal." And "perfect." Except for one thing: The woman is your typical space alien with bulbous green head and slanted eyes. And the "outfit" she is ironing? A flattened suit of an entire, normal-looking person. Not just the clothes, but the whole body. Head, face, hands, everything.

The caption: "Me getting ready to act normal for work." The post has lots of laughing emojis in the comment thread.

The reason why it's so funny is because it's so universal. But then you connect its message with the way *you* feel inside, and suddenly a wave of sadness washes over you. You can relate. It's hard emotional work, this pressure to behave "normal" (or "competent," or "qualified," or "worthy") at work, when you feel anything but. As an ASDP, you probably already have at least a little bit of that "alien" feeling in your heart. And keeping up that mask of being normal is truly heavy lifting, even though for many of us, we are completely unconscious of how heavy it is. The inner critic in your head is constantly monitoring whether you're "doing it wrong" or "should have done it better." For ASDPs, the mask of normal requires a sheen of absolute *perfection*.

Perfectionism might be your "safe haven," that place that you're always aiming for, but can never quite reach. But you know what it looks like. Your behavior looks steady, calm, reasonable. Your performance is A++. You make judgment calls that reap impressive profits—or at least avoid expensive fines or losses. No one is asking, "Are you okay?" There is no crying in the restroom—at least not that anyone can see.

To exacerbate matters, we feel like we're being paid to be perfect at work. (HR and management might refer to their expectations as "solid performance" or "great performance," but those expressions translate into our reptilian brains as "better be perfect; one slip up and you're no longer *great*, or even *solid*.") Not only are we paid to be perfect, we are promoted and publicly recognized for our overachievements. We learn early in our careers to exceed expectations and we will go far. So we perfectionists go into overdrive to prove ourselves. But no matter how much we achieve, we never feel like it is enough. We beat ourselves up for both the big and small mistakes we make as if it is the end of the world. And we fix, work harder, and take on all of the responsibility for making things right to avoid our belief that we will get in trouble, make someone mad at us, lose someone's approval, get yelled at, or even possibly get fired. Those times when we're not perfect will show up in our performance reviews.

So we reach for coping mechanisms. Perfectionism is probably the most pernicious. It looks great on the outside—and is rewarded with approval, promotions and raises. But on the inside, perfectionism speaks to you in a hard voice of inner critic. It might have initially presented itself as a friendly voice there to protect you from yourself and keep you on the straight and narrow. But it has turned into the Incredible Hulk. It seems that there's just never any appeasing its constant, destructive badgering, as it starts to smash things up. Like your peace of mind, self-image, work-life balance, eventually, maybe, your reputation, and career.

For most of my life, I tried too hard to achieve a state that doesn't exist—flawlessness. "If I was perfect," I incorrectly believed, "then I would finally receive the acceptance from others that would make me feel complete, especially from my dad." Eventually, I included my bosses in this group of people who must be pleased. Psychologists would understandably observe that bosses—especially male bosses—would take the place of father figures in the ASDP life experience. So my drive to be perfect was never-ending. I was just now experiencing it at work, instead of at home.

I had been working at a large consumer packaged goods company for about a year when my manager asked me to complete a leadership assessment. I filled out a long survey and asked other people to give me feedback too. Once the survey results were in, I met with Ken Wright, the leadership consultant, who spent three hours with me to debrief my results.

I couldn't believe my ears. Ken, whom I had never met before, seemed to know everything about me from my survey data. He began by reassuring me that there were many plusses in my results, and that I had underestimated myself compared with how others saw me. He told me I had a general manager's profile—balanced and capable, top 15 percent of the leaders' profile. "Okay, this is good," I thought to myself, secure in the expectation that my overachieving self (in other words: perfectionism) would be noticed and praised.

But then he made four new observations:

1. Birth order. "You were probably the first born, right?" He told me that first-borns and only children grow up with adults, other siblings grow up with other children. Hence their performance standards are high. New parents tend to be focused on "getting it right," and that expectation is passed on to their first child. How did he know that? And why did I have that feeling of being on the verge of being busted?

2. Trauma in the family during childhood. "Was your dad angry?" he asked. "Was there alcohol, abuse, divorce, chronic illness, death, special needs siblings?" Ken went on to say that children don't differentiate a parent's problems from their own identity. If a parent is unpredictable, moody, angry and depressed, like my father was, children can unconsciously assume responsibility and believe that if they behaved differently, were "better," got better grades, etc., the parent's behavior would be better. Yes, my dad was a raging man, I told him. Unpredictable. Moody. Difficult. Angry. And nothing I did could "moderate" his behavior. No matter how I tried. No matter how I was still trying, even though my father himself was not very present in my life. Only now I was trying with everyone who worked with me.

3. Overly critical parents. "Did you often hear your father or mother say things that sounded like you weren't good enough?" Children who have overly critical parents learn to be pleasers or controllers. Yes, in fact, that was exactly what I had grown up with in my relationship with my dad. I often felt I wasn't good enough. In fact, that the voice I heard at the back of my head every day: "You are not good enough!" I once in a while still hear it, but in a much quieter distant voice. I grew up feeling on guard and judged. The feelings remained even though I was an adult on my own.

4. Being different. He asked me, "Were you different in some way?" Growing up hiding under my bed with my sister and dog in hopes of escaping our father's wrath probably made me "different." But when I was considering his question, I remembered feeling like an ugly duckling, growing up with big, thick glasses, long mousy brown hair, carrying extra weight, a band nerd who had very few dates in high school. On top of all that, I was an overachiever throughout my entire school career.

How did he know these things about me? From my survey answers and the responses from the people who worked with me. From what I said. How I approached work. And how I behaved. Then he gently said that I scored above the mean on *perfectionism*. "So that's good, right?" I asked, feeling pleased with my results and glad that others recognized this trait in me too. I sat up straight, ready to take on the praise that was just about to come my way. I got a wake-up call instead. I thought perfectionism was synonymous with outstanding results!

Ken said, "Perfectionism is the socially acceptable disease. It's fed by a fear of failure, rather than the desire for success. Healthy achievers rank *themselves* based on who they are. Perfectionists rank *themselves* based on how what they do is a reflection of who they are. They're never good enough." Those great results came with a high price on physical and mental well-being and long-term health.

The inner critical voice is relentless. The "never enough" experience drives many perfectionists to self-medicate. Which is why Chardonnay was one of my best friends for many years. In addition to alcoholism, perfectionists numb out through other destructive behaviors such as drug abuse, gambling, eating disorders, compulsive spending. Perfectionism, people pleasing, approval seeking are all interlocking pieces in the jigsaw puzzle of getting through the day—and life—with your inner turmoil undiscovered. Our work life feeds that drive in that we're expected to show confidence and can-do, not to mention super-duper results, no matter the challenge that's put before us. There used to be a deodorant commercial whose tagline was, "Never let 'em see you sweat." That's the workplace in a nutshell.

Many of us discover our adult perfectionism through our work experiences, which is why the workplace is such a great opportunity for healing from our past wounds. Here are some signs of perfectionism in action on the job. Do you relate to any of them?

We judge ourselves and others. We will be harder on ourselves than anyone will ever be on us. It looks like a form of idealism, and, in its best version, working on a high-performing team is very motivating.

But as a perfectionist, I made it very difficult for my team members to work with me. I used to cast a shadow of judgment (on myself and, by extension, others) that probably impacted the team dynamic in ways I was unconscious of.

We constantly feel that we're falling short of the mark. Aligned with "never good enough" you'll also find "never *enough* enough." Especially enough done at the end of the day, week, quarter. The To Do list is a constantly moving horizon, which can lead to stress-related illnesses, a work life balance that is consistently out of balance weighted in the direction of work, compromised self-care routines that disappear when work obligations elbow them out of your daily agenda, zero peace of mind.

We take things personally. We experience conflict, difficult conversations, set-backs as reflections on the way others see us as valued and respected members of their teams. We take simple feedback as indictment of our lack of worthiness. A straightforward conversation about how we can improve our performance may lead us straight into an internal vicious dialog, where our inner critic takes over, and sending us into stress, anxiety, and worry.

We take responsibility for everything. No matter what is going on around us, we believe it is happening because of something we did or didn't do or something about who we are. If a boss is angry, we assume we did something wrong. If someone is disappointed about the outcome of a project, we are sure we should have done more. If a strategy doesn't deliver the expected revenue and profits, we hang our head in shame, beating ourselves up for not anticipating what went wrong.

"I Would Be Perfect If It Wasn't For This Darned Perfectionism"

Growing up as ASDPs, many of us turned to our own inner guidance for the "parental" voice that we didn't get from the adults around us. You know how psychologists talk about the "inner child" we have in our hearts and minds throughout our life? As children, many of us developed the "inner adult," the voice that helped us get through the day. It was that voice that gave 8-year-old Martha the idea to bring a bobby pin to school with her. This way she would have it to pick the lock to get back into the house when her mother was already passed out by the time she got home from school. It was that voice that told her, "That's just the alcohol talking, it has nothing to do with you," whenever her mother would say despicable things to her that would still erode her self-image and confidence over time.

It was that voice that told me to run to my friend Debbie's house when my father's raging was beginning to build up steam. It was that voice that told me to just focus on my homework and grades so that my dad wouldn't judge me. I could be proud of the work that I was doing and bask in the positive and encouraging support I was receiving from teachers, who praised me and helped me feel valued. That voice became my advisor to seek a job at age 12 as a babysitter to earn my own income and have *those* parents come home pleased and appreciative that I had not only taken good care of their children, but had also cleaned their house. I know these early experiences set me on a course to a career that would be so good to me.

But somewhere along the line, for many of us, that inner voice morphs into the inner critic. Instead of wisely and kindly guiding you, you find that the voice in your head has become something of a scold. It talks to us about shame, blame, control, regret, hypervigilance, super-self-consciousness. The voice tells us, "Everyone else is responsible for determining your worth. Be perfect and please others, and then you will be worthy."

If you are an ASDP who grew up with hyper-critical, judging, and/or controlling parents (or caregivers), you may be surprised to read here that your perfectionism is normal. I bet you're even resisting that idea because you know first-hand how perfectionism can be ruthlessly tormenting. Or you may be where I first was, challenging the notion that perfectionism is not a good thing.

So hear me out on this one: Your perfectionism is a normal result of growing up with your head "on a swivel." The controlling, out-of-control adults in your childhood desperately needed you to be perfect. A "flawless" child meant that they were flawless parents, which, in turn, meant that they were flawless people. Which, in turn, fed the denial that is so common in dysfunctional households. So it was your job to constantly be on the lookout:

Was the kitchen sink perfectly clean? Were your table manners perfectly perfect? Were you perfectly respectful toward your elders (read: betters)? Was your weight so perfect that you're actually underweight? How were your grades? Perfect? How about your family's reputation in the community? Perfect? Did you shut the door perfectly? Or was it too loud? Did you overlook something? *Don't overlook anything!* If someone notices a tear, a bruise, a fleeting look of fear, unexplained absence from school or work, alcohol on anyone's breath, it's up to you to scramble and clean up the imperfection.

Did you stuff your anger so perfectly that it didn't ruin anyone else's day?

Your days of worrying about grade point averages are probably long over if you're reading this book. And you are likely to be well out of reach of a parent who might have randomly struck you, physically or verbally, with no reason or warning. But, if you're still struggling with perfectionism, like I did for years into my career, that skill you developed as a child has turned against you. And it's now threatening your health, peace of mind, and career.

Every time we let our inner critic have our mind's microphone, we're allowing it to cut an ever deeper groove into our brains, reinforcing the message of our unworthiness. But when we become conscious of and then quiet this relentlessly brutal self-talk long enough to really hear its destructive message, we realize that the real key to our peace of mind is to intentionally replace our inner critic with a loving, kind, supportive voice. Intentionally—and gently—reminding ourselves that we are the only ones responsible for determining that we are enough is the first place to start. That job belongs solely to us and no one else. And as we become more aware and conscious of how our adult professional reality and our childhood reality collide all of the time at work, we begin to rewire our brain. When we become awake to this new understanding, we can begin to give ourselves kind, supportive messages, overwriting those old grooves, creating new neuropathways that will lead us to more peace of mind, building a better career experience and a life that supports our joy and self-acceptance.

Our workplace is the lab where we can gently build the habit of taking back the job of deeply believing we own the right to tell ourselves that we are indeed good enough. When we actively practice self-supportive thoughts, intentionally grooving the new neural pathways we talked about above, we ultimately create the self-image of our choosing. We are surrounded by colleagues who can model for us a variety ways self-regard and self-acceptance look like when they're in action. While they might be holding secrets of self-doubt of their own, the ways people carry themselves inside a workplace culture provide all sorts of opportunities to pick the best behaviors, responses, attitudes, stress-management techniques.

The workplace has an even more powerful role in that it might be your first experience of actual *belonging*. Workplace cultures aren't perfect, of course. But your workplace is one of the few opportunities in your life to feel intentionally and specifically selected and invited to join a community. Remember, you are there because people wanted *you* above everyone else who applied for your job. They saw your value and your ability to fit in. And from this platform of belonging, you can start rebuilding your internal life that corresponds with the fabulous you that others can see from the outside. This is the beginning of truly authentic self-acceptance.

In her book, *The Gifts of Imperfection*, Brene Brown writes:

> Belonging is the innate human desire to be part of something bigger than us. Because this yearning is so primal, we often try to acquire it by fitting in and by seeking approval, which are not only hollow substitutes for belonging but also often barriers to it. Because true belonging only happens when we present authentic imperfect selves to the world, our sense of belonging can never be greater than our level of self-acceptance ... Practicing self-love means learning how to trust ourselves, to treat ourselves with respect, and to be kind and affectionate toward ourselves. This is a tall order given how hard most of us are on ourselves.

The Three Keys to Gently Dissolving Your Perfectionism

Have you noticed that I haven't used the expression *self-esteem* in this chapter? There's a reason for that. Self-esteem requires proof of concept in order to convince the critical inner voice that you're really okay, perfect or not. And that critical inner voice is going to say, "Prove it." And, since you're not perfect, you can't. You're eventually going to slip up on something. Everyone does; we're all human. So the critical inner voice wins. Every. Single. Time.

So, no, I'm not talking about self-esteem. I'm talking about *self-compassion* and *self-acceptance*. Your thoughts that are kind, encouraging, soft, considerate, supportive, forgiving. No matter how you're performing at work; no matter how you're pleasing people or disappointing them.

As you're reading these, are you imagining right now what horrible things might happen if you cut yourself just one tiny break? "But Susan," you might be thinking, "I know myself. If I let up for one moment, I'm going to slack off and screw up. I know this about myself; I've known it since I was a child. If I don't keep constant watch and out-perform everywhere, my life would be nothing but little dumpster fires all over the place. My only hope is constant pursuit of perfection. It's what high-achievers do. And I'm a high-achiever. Kind self-talk is just overindulgence and maybe even self-pity. That's the worst. Self-pitiers are insufferable."

Kristin Neff, associate professor in the University of Texas at Austin's department of educational psychology and author of the book, *Self-Compassion: The Proven Power of Being Kind to Yourself*, says that perfectionism is actually the culprit in poor performance. Not self-compassion. In addition to the toll that perfectionism takes on your health and personal habits that I listed above, perfectionism is also behind procrastination, strained workplace relationships where perfectionists are perceived to be untrustworthy and competitive with their colleagues. Want to improve your performance at work? Make a space for human failings, especially your own. Release your death-grip struggle with perfectionism, and you will one day find that perfectionism has released its death grip on you.

Your journey begins with self-compassion. In her research, Neff discovered three keys to building self-compassion—ultimately releasing your perfectionism:

Key 1. Self-kindness. Think about the constant voice in your head right now. If you heard someone talk to another person in that same manner, with the same judgments and messages, could you honestly say that the speaker actually liked the other person? Or would you cringe at the sound, feeling sorry and embarrassed for the target of so much vitriol? If you have the Incredible Hulk narrating your life for you, passing judgment on your performance and likelihood for success, your inner Incredible Hulk is actually desperate for a gentle, soothing, kind word. This takes awareness and practice and intentionality. When you hear the demoralizing, even hateful inner voice, notice its fear and replace its words with encouragement and forgiveness.

Key 2. Mindfulness (which we'll get to in greater depth later in this chapter). Monitoring and making room for your inner critic requires keeping a gentle ear tuned to what's going on in your thoughts. Without judgment. You might be compelled to ignore, exaggerate, even shout down the situation as it presents itself to you. Says Neff,

> Mindfulness entails observing what is going on in our field of awareness, just as it is—right here, right now … There is remarkable power in mindfulness—it gives us the breathing room needed to respond in a way that helps rather than harms us … One of the ways we harm ourselves most is through the reactive habit of self-criticism.

Key 3. Common humanity. What better place than the workplace to practice being aware of the fact that you're not alone in your internal struggles? As much as your inner critic and perfectionism might have made you feel driven to isolate yourself from the scrutiny and judgment of others, when you're at work, there is no escaping the community of belonging. It's in this intimate context that you learn every day how much you have in common with the rest of humanity, starting with your coworkers and their own internal struggles. Years ago, there was colleague who was upset because he felt like an outsider. He came to me for advice because he was thinking of leaving the company. He shared that he was sad because no one seemed to pay much attention to him. I suggested he start noticing what other people are doing. I shared with him that if he put his focus on others, he might notice that they were just as busy getting noticed as he was. He came back later and thanked me as he realized that when he put his focus on others, he began to feel less isolated. And he discovered that just about everyone else at work is working hard to be seen too.

Neff writes:

> We often become scared and angry when we focus on un-desired aspects of ourselves or our lives. We feel helpless and frustrated by our inability to control things—to get what we want, to be who we want to be. We rail against things as they are, and we cling to our narrow vision of how things should be. Every single human is in the same boat. The beauty of recognizing this basic fact of life—the silver lining, so to speak—is that it provides deep insight into the shared human condition.

Psychologist John Bowlby studied "attachment bonds" among adults who had attentive, loving parents, versus adults who grew up with cold, rejecting parents. The way parents responded to their children's needs installed in them an "internal working model" of their place in the world; how welcome they would feel throughout life, and what they could expect from others. Predictably, the children with cold, rejecting parents grew up "insecurely attached," feeling unworthy and unlovable. Close, stable relationships would be out of reach for them throughout their lives.

Unless … they had opportunities to build new experiences, new narratives, new "proof of concept" that they were indeed valuable, welcome, knowable, and lovable. The workplace becomes that lab for learning new truths about ourselves where we can safely drop our masks and discover that we're not aliens after all.

And then true self-acceptance can begin.

How Green Are My Peas? Changing My Mind About Mindfulness

When I think about this word, I'm always tempted to laugh. I honestly thought of it as something only masterful meditation experts ever achieved.

Not a regular gal like me. I had tried meditation many times and always felt like a failure with it. My mind would race on a million different distractions, never achieving what I thought was an elusive state of mindfulness. My mind felt more like 25 racehorses barreling down a track, thundering hooves kicking up track mud, splattering it all over my third eye. In the meantime, though my eyes would be closed, I just knew that my meditation mates had all achieved such a blissful state that they would be hovering six inches above their meditation cushions, their lotus poses, of course, being perfect.

I eventually gave up and concluded that mindfulness did not belong in my world. It was like golf for me. It was something I had tried, but then stopped doing because it was too hard. Another thing that was for others. But not for me.

But, one day I thought, "Maybe this mindfulness thing will work. Probably not, but why not give it another try?" I was at an exclusive, first class Southwestern resort that marketed itself as place for learning about and practicing *mindful living*. (Between you and me, though, I was there mainly for the horseback riding.)

They even had a program on mindful eating. So I signed up. After a day of riding in the desert, reading, lying by one of their pools, journaling, and then relaxing in the fabulous outdoor shower of my room, I headed to the restaurant for our special dinner. I felt great. I was suntanned, relaxed, wearing a cute summer dress and sandals I purchased at their gift shop.

About 10 of us showed up for the event, which was held in a private room at the resort's restaurant. Our guide was dressed how you would expect a woman in her 60s living in Southwest to dress—white blouse, jeans, silver white hair covering turquoise and silver earrings, necklace and bracelet. Her entire energy was warm and welcoming. Just looking at her made me relax.

Dinner began with the chime of finger cymbals. Ching! The sound seemed to reverberate around the room for five minutes.

As she talked, our guide reminded me of a kindergarten teacher telling us what to do in a very methodical quiet voice.

"Notice the colors on your plate. What do you see?"

"Notice the aroma of each item on your plate. How does the aroma make you feel?"

"Breathe."

"Are you feeling as hungry as before you sat down?"

"What feelings are you experiencing?"

"Does the smell remind you of anything?"

"Are you feeling happy, sad, relaxed, something else?"

"Are you remembering things from meals before tonight?"

I have to acknowledge that as I looked at my meal, I *was* struck by its beauty. The plates were a western design, and each item on my plate was colorful. The napkins, the stemware, the food together were like a rainbow. It reminded me of being in an art gallery and seeing artwork with splashes of bold color everywhere. I felt joyous. And relaxed. I liked this experience. The energy of the other guests was special too. I felt like I was in a far-away place dining with strangers who did not seem like strangers.

But then my stomach began to growl. I became mindful of this question: "When are we going to eat already?"

We finally were allowed to take small, slow bites of the delicious spa-prepared meal. Predictably, it was extremely healthy and completely delicious. My mind wandered to wishing someone would cook like this for me every night. Then my mind wandered to wondering if I had radicchio stuck between my teeth. Then, as our guide brought the meal to a close with a tasty desert-inspired dessert, a small scoop of delicious homemade vegan vanilla ice cream (no cows were harmed in the making of this ice cream) covered in a prickly pear sauce, my mind wandered to whether I could use the finger cymbals to call for seconds.

While the dinner that night was special, and I did thoroughly enjoy the mindfulness experience, I had no idea how to apply these principles to my daily life. The very next day, I went right back to eating super-fast, not noticing a single thing I was eating or experiencing as I didn't want to waste time mindfully eating when I was on to the next scheduled part of my day—a special class, spa treatment, or another horseback ride in the desert. Yes, exactly as I was living my life—never stopping. Always on the go, with a hovering sense of feeling unsafe if I slowed down at all.

Busyness, action, constant activities (what is referred to in the therapy world as having "process addiction," the addiction to being busy all of the time). With that as my underlying motivation, daily mindfulness continued to be elusive to me. I had bigger issues that clouded any semblance of mindfulness.

That was why the idea of mindfulness never felt relevant in my life. Mindfulness equaled slowing down. And slowing down made me feel unsafe. If people around me were "mindful," that meant they had slowed down long enough to judge me and consider the all the colors on my plate of flaws and shortcomings.

Plus those finger cymbals made me feel just plain silly.

And Then This Happened

"Yeah, I don't do mindfulness," I said dismissively to a colleague on the phone one day. I would have said, "I wouldn't be caught dead doing that phony, pretentious, uhm, stuff." But I was mindful of not wanting to sound too judgmental. And the possibility of making her feel shut down. Her response surprised me:

"Are you kidding me right now? You do mindfulness every day. You teach it. Didn't you know that?" Well, no. I wasn't aware.

Come to find out, you don't need finger cymbals, special candles, special recipes on special plates, mantras, zafus (those low meditation cushions that help people get down on the floor for their perfect lotus positions) to practice mindfulness. What you do have to do is pay attention to what's important, moment by moment, to respond to each moment with kind non-judgmentalism and curiosity. And to let your stomach growl, with no shame.

According to Daniel Siegel, clinical professor of psychiatry at the UCLA School of Medicine and executive director of the Mindsight Institute, mindfulness can be summed up as, "Being aware of what is happening as it happens without being swept up by preestablished mental activities like judgments or ideas, memories or emotions."

The practice of mindfulness is the finger that flips the switch of positive neuroplasticity. It changes the brain for the better, and then the brain returns the favor by bringing you a certain degree of happiness and peace of mind. More specifically, according to Shauna Shapiro, PhD, professor of psychology at Santa Clara University, here are the benefits of mindfulness practice:

- A strengthened immune system
- Decreased stress
- Lowered cortisol
- Better sleep
- Improved focus and attention
- Improved memory
- Enhanced creativity
- Enhanced innovation
- Encouraged ethical decision-making
- Reduced cultural bias
- Increased compassion

A glance at this list will tell you that mindfulness practice is good for your career.

Shapiro tells us that responding to each moment with a mental attitude of kindness and curiosity strengthens our capacity to learn and expands our brain's ability to support a happier life. In contrast, if we approach stress-filled circumstances of uncertainty and worry with shame, self-doubt, and judgment, we are actually flooding our brain's alarm center (the amygdala) with the stress hormones adrenaline and norepinephrine. And that, in turn, shuts down the brain's learning function. I expect you and I are alike in that we would rather learn in a state of open, receptive, kind curiosity.

Practicing mindfulness is also the key to neutralizing our emotional triggers, which we'll explore later in the book. In Part 2 when we go into Bumper Car Moments, I'll introduce you to the Rapid Power Reclaim method of bringing your conscious, aware self to stressful moments with your colleagues. The first step is all about bringing nonjudgmental curiosity to what might otherwise be a career "gun fight." Bringing the frame of mind that Shapiro calls "remembering what the most important thing is." **Slowing down** so that you're able to bring compassion and consciousness to the table—compassion both for yourself and for the other person and consciousness to our old triggers and self-limiting beliefs and being intentional about responding differently. **Introducing acceptance** into the encounter so that both of you can communicate in a safe emotional environment. And **committing to respond flexibly** so that you both can co-create an understanding of what the ideal outcome is for both of you.

I've slowed down long enough to accept the premise of the mindfulness concept. And my response flexibility over time has allowed me to bring it into my life. But no finger cymbals.

The One Question That Can Start to Dispel Your Distorted Thinking

You might have inherited these habits of debilitating beliefs. Or they might have been coping mechanisms you threw into gear to protect yourself as a child. But this unhappy legacy can stop with your adult self. *You* can be the one to put the stake in the ground and say, "Enough!" You can be the one to choose a more joyful, confident way to experience life—and then model new skills, behaviors, and beliefs about the world for future generations. You start by changing what you say to yourself and your outdated beliefs about people and the way the world works. Psychologists call this your *explanatory style.*

Recovery from these distorted ways of thinking starts with mindfully, consciously, identifying the thought. And then intentionally challenging its legitimacy. Get into the habit of asking yourself (and whatever family members are willing to join you on this adventure) this single powerful question:

Am I sure?

Here's what this looks like as a moment-by-moment practice:

"I have to be perfect all the time. Falling short of perfection will be held against me forever."

Am I sure?

"It's my job to please others."

Am I sure?

"People can't be trusted."

Am I sure?

"My boss is in a bad mood. That must mean I did something wrong."

Am I sure?

"I just got frowned at by a stranger. I've just been harshly judged."

Am I sure?

"I will never be happy."

Am I sure?

"My past defines who I am today."

Am I sure?

"If I'm not explicitly invited, I am specifically unwelcome."

Am I sure?

"People can't change once they're adults, which includes me."

Am I sure?

"I don't deserve to be happy if someone else is unhappy."

Am I sure?

"If I have what someone else needs, I must give it to them, even if the sacrifice hurts me in some way."

Am I sure?

"I can't say no if that would disappoint others."

Am I sure?

"The odds are stacked against me forever."

Am I sure?

"Uncertainty means certain disaster or disappointment."

Am I sure?

"Everyone else is perfect, happy, healthy. When they find out the truth about me, they'll lose respect for me and I'll be rejected."

Am I sure?

"Everyone else is stupid and screwed up. I'm the only one who sees the world correctly."

Am I sure?

"Everyone else has it figured out except me."

Am I sure?

These statements come from ASDPs I know. Do you recognize them as thoughts of your own? Or maybe you can think of others not listed here.

Why "Am I Sure?" Can Change Your Life

When you consider the above list of sample beliefs, you might recognize some. Or their example might bring to mind others that have become so ingrained in the way you experience life that they're practically unconscious at this point. Either way, they are beliefs that might have kept you safe at one point. But now they serve to keep you playing small as you become a working adult. Aren't you ready to play *big* in your professional life?

So three simple words. Am. I. Sure. Can they really change your life? Yes. Here's why: They make you stop that headlong run into a self-destructive thought pattern. Undo those messages, one by one, every time they come up as undeniable beliefs. "Are you sure?" Mindfully look at each one as it comes up and you'll very likely come to believe that, huh, maybe there's a more helpful way to experience each moment as you learn healthier ways of taking on challenges at work.

Don't blame yourself for carrying those beliefs into your adulthood. But it can all stop with you. There is almost always a more empowering, compassionate way to interpret other people's actions and create a more empowering view of the world for yourself.

Now you have the single most important question to ask yourself every time a debilitating belief comes up for you. And as you reprogram your mind to take a moment and ask that one simple question, you are reaching into the future and influencing new generations to choose a more positive way to look at a happier life.

Yes, I'm sure about that.

Chapter 5
Why the Workplace is a Lab for Emotional Healing

FOR ME, BEFORE my corporate jet encounter with the Pirate, showing up every day as the sweet little puppy dog was not working for me professionally. The stress of this constant and futile approval-seeking that I was subjecting myself to was threatening my physical and emotional health. I can only guess what unconscious buttons in these guys that my ridiculous behavior was pushing.

I wish I could say that the corporate jet moment of truth put a permanent stop to my people-pleasing behaviors and drive of approval-seeking forever. To be sure, it had a significant impact on my self-awareness and my understanding how my behaviors invited certain kinds of unhealthy interactions with others. And I'll always be grateful to my coach for helping me see what kind of dynamic I was creating that resulted in the exact opposite of what I really wanted. I wanted approval, respect, and a sense of validation and belonging. But the ways I went about going after those feelings were creating a dynamic that resulted in exclusion and disrespect.

It wasn't until years later that I only just began the process of connecting the dots between my drive to please others—often at my own expense in some way—and what beliefs about myself that I had brought into my adult life from my childhood. Growing up I was driven to do anything I could to prevent another raging episode by my father. And I concluded that being the best girl ever—good grades and perfect, un-provoking behavior—would keep me safe from his rage one more day. And then another one more day. And then the next.

What beliefs and behaviors did you learn as a child that you have un-consciously brought with you into your career? How have those beliefs and behaviors held you back from achieving the full potential that you know you are capable of? For me, it was the behavior of unconsciously seeking approval, more often than I care to admit, which resulted in some col-leagues disrespecting me while I poured my life into my work—at the expense of anything that even resembled anything like work/life balance. For Martha, it was the belief that people can't be trusted, which resulted in her choosing a solitary career path of being a writer. For someone else I know, it was the belief that the only way to be heard and respected was to behave outlandishly at work, yelling and shouting in meetings, and having over-the-top reactions to perceived slights. Someone else I know took on an unrelenting workload, without complaint, believing that if other people thought it was reasonable to heap the work on her, treating her like a pack mule, their demands and expectations must be appropriate. And her struggle was her own problem to cope with quietly. Someone else I know sees himself as a perpetual and helpless victim, always on the receiving end of other people's maliciousness.

Those are only just a few examples of dysfunctional beliefs that are natural conclusions about the world that an ASDP might have learned as a child. And those beliefs are getting in our way. They are seriously negatively affecting us in ways that we may be completely unaware of. As many ASDPs have told me, "The formula of being driven, overachieving and constantly driving ourselves works for many years, until it doesn't anymore [failed marriages, not taking care of our health, eating/drinking/spending too much, depression, moving away from our faith, etc.]. And then one day it all comes crashing down."

So as much as we'd like to think that we left our painful childhood pasts behind us as we grew up, the workplace (and all those experiences we have working with colleagues who may represent to our subconscious vari-ous people from our young pasts) gives us fresh opportunities to discover what areas still need healing. And what opportunities we have to design and build full, healthy lives of self-acceptance and joy—in all aspects of our lives, not just work.

Does this principle of using the workplace as a venue for emotional healing surprise you? As a culture, we have been taught to regard the typical workplace as a place of *further wounding*, not healing. Society will tell us that the workplace is an unhealthy environment where people mistreat each other, where we suffer stress-related physical ailments like high blood pressure, diabetes, addictions, and even cancers. But I'd like use this chapter to invite you to look at the workplace through a different lens—the workplace offers many opportunities for healing, for finding your place in the world where you are welcomed by people who are glad to see you, and where you can fill your life's days up using your potential and gifts to enjoy positive experiences and celebrate accomplishments. It's a place where not only are you financially rewarded so you can take care of your fundamental material needs, but where you can also find meaning through fulfilling work and that sense of belonging that may have been missing up until now.

Exactly How Does This Healing-At-Work Thing Work?

When our friends think we're overidentified with the work we do, they'll remind us, "You're not your job." And they're right. And when our friends think we're overidentified with our wounded past to the point where we let the pain get in the way of our happiness, they'll tell us, "You're not your past." And they're sort of right about that. We learned about life and the world through our childhood experiences. And we bring those beliefs with us into our adulthood.

You've probably heard the expression, "Our past gives us lessons, but it's not a life sentence." When our wounded past consciously or unconsciously collides with our day-to-day career experiences, we're presented with a choice: We can allow these impacts from the past—they occur in ordinary, everyday episodes that I call Bumper Car Moments—to wreck our reputations and threaten essential career-building relationships. Or we can be conscious of how these Bumper Car Moments can help us understand ourselves better and heal old wounds and correct limiting beliefs that we have dragged with us into our adult lives. We can use Bumper Car

Moments as opportunities to practice different responses and gradually quiet the limiting belief voices that cling to us like burrs. And where better to experience a whole array of Bumper Car Moments than in the workplace?

We can do all that by intentionally rewiring our brain—taking advantage of that neuroplasticity we talked about earlier in this book—using positive (and sometimes even negative) experiences that we have at work to build new neuropathways that will eventually give us a brain that supports a calmer, happier, more focused, more productive, more optimistic sense of what we are capable in life overall.

In his book, *The Power of Neuroplasticity*, author Shad Helmstetter writes:

> What goes on in your mind and in your life changes your brain physically. When you think or do something repeatedly, your brain actually changes its physical structure. Your environment, your experiences, your emotions, your attitudes, your self-talk, all of your perceptions—your brain is imprinting itself with every message it gets. And this discovery means that because your brain is constantly rewiring and changing itself, you are creating it at this moment, the person you're going to become tomorrow, and you are physically wiring that person into your brain.

Martha and I are fond of reminding our readers, "The rest of your life is yours." Neuroplasticity is the foundation of this statement. As much as we are truly affected by our past experiences and influences from others and their limiting beliefs—especially when we were children—we can start creating the rest of our lives starting now. Not by wishful thinking. Or artificially forced "positive thinking." But by understanding the power of neuroplasticity and its therapeutic sibling, positive psychology, which is far more substantive than I initially understood it to be. And recognizing that we have all around us the tools and experiential opportunities to create the people we want to be. Not the people we were told we were by powerful, tormented early influencers who were struggling mightily with their own lives and taught us to see the world (and ourselves) through their own eyes. Those are lessons and beliefs we can start to undo any time.

So "healing in the workplace." Is this a promise with an endpoint, after which everything will be rosy, happy, all the scars will disappear, your career will skyrocket, and all holiday family gatherings will be conflict-free? Well, that would be nice. And unlikely. (In fact, the healthier you become through healing at work, it's possible you will see pushback from your family of origin because you might be demonstrating new ways of relating to them, to the world and to yourself that will feel like an affrontery, a rejection of established family cultural patterns. And someone might take it personally. And then make it their business to tell you all about how they don't like the way you've changed. Change the rules of engagement unilaterally, and someone will likely tell you that they object. Just fair warning.)

Your family relationships will still be there. Your memories from the past won't magically disappear. So, no, there is no endpoint with emotional healing, and there will be lingering scars. But with the healing that you take on in the workplace, using the equanimity- and awareness-building tools that you will be acquiring through the practices of positive psychology, neuroplasticity, and leveraging Bumper Car Moments at work, the power that the old wounding beliefs have held over you for so many decades will gradually give way to a healthier practice of separating yourself from other people's issues, optimism, a grounded sense of compassion with boundaries, and a positive outlook. And those, in turn, will support and empower you as you discover new levels of self-acceptance and joy.

But what about those scars? Imagine having an accident with a kitchen knife. It's severe enough that you have to go to the emergency room, which then sends you straight into surgery. It's bad. And it needs expert attention. (This is just a metaphor, so don't get too caught up in the grossness, especially if you don't like the sight of blood.) Will there be a scar? You bet. But there will be one anyway. Would you rather have the scar from the damage? Or the healed, smoothed over evidence that you cared for yourself so much that you took action to stop the pain and the bleeding?

Your past will leave a mark. Depending on how horrible your past was, the mark could be intense too. But wouldn't it be better if that mark told the story of how you prevailed? And healed? And found new opportunities to contribute your gifts to the world in healthy, meaningful ways?

That's what the workplace can do for you. And all those relationships around you.

Exactly how does this work? Not by single-mindedly focusing on banishing the bad. But by replacing it—or, even better, *displacing* it—with an ever-growing accumulation of the good. When you pour more water into an already full glass, the water that was already there sloshes out. When you focus on pouring healing experiences, beliefs, and attitudes into your life, the new neuropathways will eventually render the old harmful beliefs, experiences, and attitudes obsolete. And your brain will start pruning and discarding those old, unwanted connections.

To be clear, the principles behind this message of healing in the workplace aren't intended to replace whatever therapy program might be underway for you, either now or in the future. This framework is to *support* your growth and healing by using the elements already existing in your life as a working adult. Even if you're working at home, which is very much the situation all over the world as we're writing this book in 2020. It's based on the philosophy and observations initially introduced by Martin Seligman, professor of psychology at the University of Pennsylvania, and author of multiple books on the practical application of positive psychology. He has written over the years that he first discovered the need and role for positive psychology when he observed that his patients who were healed of their psychological pain weren't necessarily happier people. They were healed "empty" people.

The removal of the pain didn't automatically mean they had the skills and abilities to live lives that he would later describe as *flourishing*. To take the healing that extra step requires intentional noticing and onboarding of positive experiences. "Taking in the good," as his colleagues would eventually phrase it. This can all be done by leveraging workplace conflict as your own laboratory for healing.

He writes: "Positive psychology holds that one of the best ways to help suffering people is to focus on positive things ... Experiences that induce positive emotion cause negative emotion to dissipate rapidly."

And then the idea is to keep repeating these experiences to further support the neuropathway connections that you want. In his book, *Resilient: How to Grow an Unshakable Core of Calm, Strength, and Happiness*, Rick Hanson wrote, "In essence, you develop psychological resources by having sustained and repeated experiences of them that are turned into durable changes in your brain. You become more grateful, confident, or determined by repeatedly installing experiences of gratitude, confidence, or determination. Similarly, you center yourself increasingly … with an underlying sense of peace, contentment, and love—by having and internalizing many experiences of safety, satisfaction, and connection."

(Notice those last three words: *safety*, *satisfaction*, and *connection*. If you know the famous triangle that makes up Maslow's Hierarchy of Needs, you'll recognize those as the first three must-haves that everyone needs in order to build the foundation of a satisfying life. And, assuming that you work for a company that cares about such things, isn't it reasonable to be able to look for safety, satisfaction and connection at work?)

Over the years, Seligman has been joined by hundreds of students, researchers, and scientists to further learn how positive psychology lays the foundation for a more rewarding life experience. And Seligman himself continues to refine his thinking on the subject. In one of his more recent books, he intentionally moves away from such words as *happiness* toward *flourishing*, which supports a fulfilling overall experience of well-being, without necessitating an ongoing positive feeling of happiness. You can flourish in the workplace, but, really, can you realistically expect to be happy 100 percent of the time?

Seligman writes that well-being theory features five elements that make up the actual experience of well-being (or flourishing). And, delightfully, you can identify and experience these elements at work:

Positive emotion. Seligman illustrates *positive emotion* as the *pleasant life*. In the workplace, you experience positive emotion on a day-to-day basis where the culture is congenial, trusting, you can focus on your work, setting aside the habit of hypervigilance long enough to get the work done, and the meeting concluded. Positive emotion comes when you generally like the work you do. It's challenging but not so challenging that you experience toxic stress. You feel generally welcome, accepted and appreciated for who you are and your contributions to your community of coworkers. You may not realize the pleasantness of your life until one day you realize, "I'm not white-knuckling it here." Maybe for the first time in your life.

That's positive emotion.

Engagement. Your company probably already has some kind of employee engagement or experience survey, which measures a wide variety of ways your company's culture and values play out on a day-to-day basis. Many companies start out their engagement journey by using off-the-shelf products like the famous Gallup Q12 Employee Engagement Survey. But as they gain more sophistication and experience in identifying what exactly they want to offer employees as an engagement experience, they customize their engagement descriptors. You'll see some variations of these kinds of statements: "I trust that my supervisor cares about my professional development." "I have the time, resources, skills, and materials that I need to do my job well." "I am proud to tell my friends that I work for this company." "I fully understand what is expected of me on a day-to-day basis." To the non-ASDPs, these kinds of statements feel ordinary and the very least that can be expected of their daily working experience. But to ASDPs, who grew up in some level of chaos, where their needs might have been routinely put last on the list of family priorities, and where communication was unheard of, these kinds of descriptors are exotic indeed. To be able to go to work in a culture where these experiences of safety are expected is quite the exotic experience for hundreds of thousands of people who can't shake the feeling that "the other shoe is about to drop."

Positive relationships. No workplace is perfect. And I don't know a soul who can't tell you many, many stories about being on the receiving end of toxic internal politics, leaders, and colleagues at work. So I wouldn't dream of trying to convince you that all workplace relationships are positive and without conflict. I also deeply believe that some of the most difficult negative relationships at work can teach us meaningful ways to develop more positive relationships with ourselves.

The workplace gives you wide opportunities to develop relationships with people you would never meet otherwise—people who depend on you (and you depend on them) to work as teams to achieve mutually critical goals. Workplaces where the leadership places a high priority on safe places to learn, innovate and even fail provide an environment where your well-being is fostered in the company of people of many different backgrounds, with many different expectations other than to work together in harmony toward objectives you all share.

Even just having the experience of being in the company of people who are just kind to each other can be eye-opening. Martha recalls a time when she was visiting some family friends on Cape Cod the day after the patriarch had died unexpectedly. "I was the outsider in a living room full of people coming to Chatham from all over, all in various stages of grief. I discovered that I was unconsciously braced for a snarky comment or someone zinging an insult to another family member. But that wasn't happening. I'll never forget the a-ha moment when I thought, 'Oh my gosh, this is how families act when they're nice to each other.' It was such a moment of revelation that I remember it to this day, over 20 years later."

Meaning. You don't have to feel that you're saving the world in the work you do. And sometimes, even when you *are* saving the world, some days are so bogged down in administrivia that it's hard to find the meaning on any average day. One of our friends works with Doctors Without Borders, which is one of the most meaningful jobs in the world. And even she will tell you that she knows that it's time to come home for a rest leave when she finds the sound of gunfire going on outside the walls of her compound to be more irritating and disruptive than frightening. "I needed to get these emails written and the noise was distracting," she'll say with the same kind of roll of her eyes that is more expected from someone who is irritated by the line at the post office being too long.

So *meaning* isn't about what you do and who you're doing it for. It's about the relevance of the work to *you*. In Martha's research into the ordinary people love their jobs, she discovered that *meaning* breaks down into three categories. Each individual must be able to see how their work does one or more of these three things:

Relieves pain
Restores hope
Brings beauty into the world

No one else has to agree with you, or approve of the connection you make between meaning and the work you do. You must be able to see it for yourself. And when you do, you can see how your very existence benefits the world and humanity. No matter what your job is—unless you happen to be a drug dealer or a hit man—your job (and therefore your work) benefits mankind. Find that connection and you'll get some of that positive emotion right off the bat.

Finally, Seligman identifies **Achievement** as the fifth component of well-being. We all want to know we're competent, capable—especially if each accomplishment is successively more complex or challenging than the previous one. That is achievement. It's a closed loop experience where we open the loop by setting an objective (or agreeing to take on an objective that our managers set for us). Then we pursue that objective until we accomplish it. And that's when the loop closes so satisfyingly.

You make plan for the month. Or the annual budget you've just rewritten is a doable savings of many millions. Or you ran that sensitive negotiation in such a way that everyone believes it was a win/win, the pleasure of these achievements resonates in your neural pathways long after the project is completed and the entire team is on to the next one. If you're an ASDP, this could be the first time in your life that you had the chance to see a project from beginning to end. It could be the first time in your life when everyone around you did what they said they would do. And together you carried your shared goal to the finish line.

These five elements combine to make the acronym PERMA. And Seligman points to them all as a group of essential ingredients for the creating and sustaining of well-being (or *flourishing*) for anyone, anywhere in their life experiences. But we're especially interested in the workplace situation, and how you can use its opportunities for supportive experiences to build new neuropathways in your brain and use those positive experiences to displace the old beliefs and memories about who you are in the world.

So here are other opportunities that your workplace and professional life can help you build another you over time:

1. The workplace helps you create a new identity—one that's real and more authentic to who you really are than the one you adapted from your family of origin. When you were hired, you were hired because they actively wanted *you* ... you above everyone else who applied for the job. They don't know you're an ASDP, and if you don't tell them, they never will know. Your colleagues take you at face value; they see you for who you are today. They don't see you through the eyes of your controlling, negative parents, caretakers, or abusers. You're coming in good.

2. The workplace gives you the opportunity to experience psychological turning points/new rites of passage that are independent of your wounded family of origin. We all know about the rites of passage in life that have been common for thousands of years: birth, marriage, aging, children and then grandchildren, even, I suppose, in some cases, divorce, are all rites of passage. They take us from one phase of life to the next natural stage. Along those same lines there are also psychological turning points that give us wisdom, insight, and experiences that can change us forever. These psychological turning points at work include moments of inflection when you discover your true nature in significant episodes. Like the time you stood up for yourself. Or the time you stood up for someone else. Or the time you successfully negotiated a pay raise. The time you waited to see if you would be one of those chosen to be laid off. And how you handled the news when you finally got it. Psychological turning points don't have to have happy endings. Nor do you have to like what you're learning about yourself. But even unpleasant or unwelcome outcomes can be used as a source for good and important personal growth.

3. The workplace is a lab that offers us the chance to acquire learnable skills that play a role in healing our secret wounded parts. Healthy, healing workplaces offer personal and career development opportunities just as a matter of course. But the courses—like, say, handling sensitive conversations, time management in chaotic conditions, or overriding your anxiety to trust someone at a crucial time—can be applied at home and in other parts of your life.

4. The workplace gives us the opportunities to build new professional families of sincere love and connection. We're often warned by career experts not to get too emotionally attached to our coworkers; that the workplace isn't family; it's just a bunch of people working together until they're no longer working together. No muss. No fuss. People come, people go. Org charts aren't family trees. We learn soon enough, though, that inside the "family" of the workplace community, we build a connection with people that is as deeply rewarding—if not more so—as with our real family members. We go to their weddings. We go to their funerals. We celebrate milestone moments in their lives in between. (A female colleague was actually my birth coach when I went into labor unexpectedly with Joe, my first born, while I was on a business trip without my husband.)

5. The workplace—and our careers—give us the opportunity to take the best of what our families taught us and honor them by living out the values they handed down to us. The values we want to keep. The values that will see future generations toward even greater healing. Maybe starting with forgiveness.

We never finish learning about ourselves and life. Even if by the time we enter our professional years we think we finally have it all together—especially once we have started building lives of our own—we discover through workplace experiences where our unhealed bits are.

And at last, we have the tools and knowledge we need to mend and build ourselves to be the people we truly want to be.

Chapter 6
Self-Acceptance:
The First Person You Hire Is Yourself

NOT ALL ASDPS are alike, of course. But we are often marked with two common characteristics: To some degree, we are mystified by what "normal" behavior is all about. And we crave connection with someone who is kind and gentle, who can show us how to be effective, wise, and emotionally intelligent adults. It's likely that we didn't get a whole heck of a lot of either of these in our childhood home. Even if one parent was reliably loving, supportive, and sober (like my wonderful mother was), if the other parent role-modeled terrible, raging behavior (like my father did) as a coping response for frustration, shame, and out-of-control feelings, we're going to learn those crazy behaviors just by watching him. Even if we consciously resolve to not copy those behaviors as adults ourselves, we're still left with big holes in our self-definition. Who am I? How do I behave? How do I cope with stress? How do I express my anger at someone, when I just don't know how to do that so that the relationship isn't wrecked?

We also believe deeply and often unconsciously that it is another person's job, not ours, to tell us we are worthy. We crave validation from others. We grow up thinking it's our job to get others' approval and praise. But the only approval that really counts (and is sustainable) is the approval we give ourselves. And until we resolve our issues with self-acceptance, that craving will never subside.

It's hard to feel self-acceptance when we know our toolbox of adult behaviors and interpersonal skills is only partially complete. And so we turn to trusted friends. We even hire coaches and consultants to help us fill in those knowledge gaps. In Martha's case, she escaped to books, losing herself in solitary stories as soon as the doors began to slam in the house. Reading, says memoirist Mary Karr, is our only socially acceptable form of dissociation.

As for me, I escaped into the challenge of pursuing stratospheric grades, winning the approval of teachers, excelling in competitions that required intense discipline, overworking and achieving in my career. My drive for approval was insatiable. And so along the way, I kept unconsciously attracting different variations of my father in the form of teachers and other influencers.

In my constant yearning to learn and grow, I found myself once again in futile relationships with power-tripping people who I entrusted with my well-being and what I hoped would be, finally, peace of mind. I permanently damaged my back, for instance, trying to please a distant but demanding and controlling riding instructor, whose carelessness actually placed me in physical harm's way when I was young. In my eagerness to respond to her demands and expectations and neglect, I put myself in the dangerous situation she had set up for me. I predictably fell off a young horse and lay there in the dust by myself in the practice ring at a horse show, waiting for an ambulance, with her nowhere to be found. I was 20 then. And I suffer chronic back pain to this day.

In my professional life, I have known people who could also be described as power-tripping. Recall my golden retriever puppy dog story and the men I worked with then? For an entire year, I was that puppy dog looking for those guys to pat me on the head and tell me what a good girl I was. Seeking others' approval is a sure sign that we are void of self-approval, which is an internal job. Either I get others' approval and still feel perpetually empty or I find ways to improve my own self approval and feel full. We have a choice of going after one or the other which will either support or deplete self-worth, self-approval.

This was long before I understood the concept of the two career paths. I was skilled at beating myself up when another's approval did not come. I judged myself. The concept of self-acceptance wasn't even on my radar.

I seemed to attract people who knew just how to push my buttons, setting off my triggered responses. This is a characteristic of the Unconscious Wounded Career Path experience. I once had a boss who used anger to control others. Anger is a huge trigger for me. I was constantly on guard with this manager. Some days there was kindness. Other days a raging maniac. It never occurred to me that my responses in this situation were dramatically amplified by my relationship with my angry father. All I could think back then was run and hide under the bed—even though, let's face it, there's no bed in the workplace. Still, I felt exactly how I felt when I was little.

Looking back now, I can admit that I unknowingly assigned the duty of approving me as a human being, not just an employee, to authority figures at work. Especially men. A very long time ago, I worked with one older colleague who was incredibly talented and smart. He had an important title and I looked up to him. I admired him. He seemed to know all the answers and how to handle any situation, with complete confidence. He knew how to work the corporate halls because of his extensive network. He offered me career coaching and paid attention to me. He noticed me. I felt seen. I felt approved of.

Over time, the professional boundaries began to blur. Before too long, we were not only going for after-work drinks to discuss work and my career, we were going to dinner too, and then back to my apartment. Yes, we began a personal relationship. And although I did not work for him, he could have influenced my career. So we kept our relationship a secret. I had no idea at this young stage of my career that this was completely inappropriate.

My colleague assured me he knew best. I agreed with him. He set the terms of the relationship. I never argued. He was the voice in the relationship. I never spoke up. I learned that if I did, I would be ignored. Not looked at in meetings. Not called after work. Not invited out after work for a drink. I saw him as smarter than me. Wiser. More insightful. More mature. More worldly. He was in control. I was the follower. I was a small-town girl from a small-town world. He was from a big city. I was always on my best behavior, hoping to get his attention and approval. He was superior. I was inferior. My energy was like a circus dog jumping through hoops to get the treat. And in my neediness to delight and be validated by somebody else, I basically replicated the relationship I had with my dad, with this man. And here is the thing, I was completely unaware that I had created a clone of my relationship with my Dad, playing out a familiar script and scene from my damaged past right smack in the middle of my new career.

Anyone who has been in this kind of emotionally abusive relationship will agree with me when I say that some positive value does come along with the punishing experience. With my dad, I learned how to interact and connect with others. I gained a global view on life. He encouraged me to do whatever I wanted to do. Likewise, I benefitted from the relationship with this man at work. He helped me navigate the company politics. He was generous with his advice about how I should do things and gently corrected me when my performance could be improved. I believed he was helping me to become a corporate talent. However, just like with my dad, there was always a cost to pay. With my dad, there was always the prospect of the un-predictable exploding volcano of rage. With my work colleague, I was often left feeling rejected. Abandoned. Not good enough.

While the following statements were never directly said, they were very clearly the rules of the road in this relationship: "Don't argue with me be-cause I will win." "I'm stronger than you." "Don't challenge me." "You're not entitled to your opinion." "My opinion's right." "Yours is wrong."

This is exactly how I stayed small in my relationship with my dad and in my relationship with this man. I continued to give my power away, "waiting for the axe to fall," and essentially retraumatizing myself for a year at work. The guilt and shame that I experienced was overwhelming. I hated secrets. I knew I should not be in this relationship, but I stayed because his attention made me feel important. I had unconsciously allowed my child-hood to translate into my working career and was completely unaware it.

We may think we can escape our past. We can literally try and escape the misery of our life, the parts of our childhood trauma. We can try to hide away from the past and just go to work and make work be our entire life. But here's where the joke is on us. Our past trauma will follow us there, too. We are facing a big problem right now in our workplaces. Too many of us are escaping our pasts at work. We think our careers will give us relief from our difficult childhoods, but we will encounter them when we least expect it. It's the same monster wearing a different mask. This is the Unconscious Wounded Career Path. And self-acceptance is completely invisible in the fog of our ASDP backgrounds.

Some of us are seeking validation from a colleague or boss. Some of us are overachievers and are working 70+ hours a week. This is a trauma response. Let's work ourselves to the bone to prove ourselves to our bosses so that maybe, just maybe we will feel a moment of satisfaction that we are "good enough." Until the next day when we start all over again. Work becomes a perceived escape, but we start to realize our past patterns are playing out every day in our workplaces—withdrawal, performance anxiety, adrenaline, overachiever, Type A, over analytical, bully, and action compelled by perfectionism.

I eventually ended that relationship, but it would still be a long time until I would come to understand how unaware I was of how my past affected my behavior at work. Back in those days, I could never imagine I would find a place of greater self-acceptance. And I most certainly would not have been able to give self-acceptance advice to Martha, had I known her 15 years ago when she was caught up in her own *danse macabre* with a control freak she had come to depend on and trust—to the point of betraying herself.

"He was a colleague turned writing partner," she recalls. "We never wrote a book together, but we supported each other while writing our own books. We trusted each other with our ideas, our creative insecurities and eventually the complexities of our private relationships. He made me feel safe, known, understood, respected, appreciated, and accepted. All feelings I had never experienced at home while growing up. As it turns out, I should have given those feelings to myself before looking to anyone else for that kind of emotional support."

She continues: "Looking back, I can pinpoint the exact moment our relationship was over. It seemed like such a small thing at the time (isn't that the way with all those turning-point episodes in life?). But, from a distance, I can now see how positively monstrous that moment was. It was the night before my father's funeral. And my friend had cleared his calendar for three days (he is a mental health professional and is paid by the hour, so this sacrifice was significant), flew out from the West Coast to Washington, DC, to support me during this tumultuous time. We were sitting outside at an Annapolis waterfront restaurant, and I was taking my first breather in over a month of all the emotional trials of dealing with family dynamics, memories, and clearing out my father's apartment—which he had left fully expecting to return. So, as you can imagine, I was still in shock.

"But for that one soft night at our waterside table, I was safe. I was with my trusted friend. I was taking in the wonderfully humid Chesapeake night air, relaxing to one of my favorite sounds: Sailboat cables clanking in the breeze against aluminum masts. Everything, for the moment, was safe and okay. No drama. The only thing on my mind was the drink and crab cakes I had ordered. And they were on their way. Everything was good. Breathe.

"Then out of the blue, he said, 'So tell me, who are you going to vote for president in November?' Wait a minute, what? In those days I was completely apolitical, we had never talked about politics in all the years we were friends. And he chose this time to bring up such a question? Confused more than anything, I tried to back out of the topic. But he persisted, pressing a political argument that I really didn't care about one way or the other. Finally, he smugly laid down the gauntlet of all-or-nothing challenge, 'You're either with us or against us.' I was speechless.

"To my amazement, we were having our first fight. About something he had started and that I didn't even care about. The night before my father's funeral, at a time when I was my most emotionally vulnerable and physically exhausted. I was assuming I could, for just a few hours, lay down the armor of my hypervigilance. But, instead, at that moment, our friendship was over. I just didn't know it yet. If I had to live that moment over again (and believe me, I have in my mind multiple times), I would have stood up from the table and walked away.

"The friendship was over, but the troubles had just begun. From that night onward, it was like his warm, nurturing, accepting personality was eerily taken over by the cold, harsh, judging, withholding aspects of my dead father's personality. I was watching myself bend over backwards to regain the sense of safety and acceptance that I had been craving my entire life—and that I had once known with him. But instead, the following months were marked with tears (mine), begging (me), a battle of wills over a Steinway baby grand piano (mine), and a bizarre threat from out of nowhere (his) to have me arrested for breaking and entering should I ever use my copy of his house key to retrieve my piano. And hundreds of dollars I compulsively spent in gifts trying to win back his approval. All he had to do was casually mention his admiration for something—like an entire set of Le Creuset pots and pans—and presto! It belonged to him. I was standing outside myself, watching my own bizarre behavior, I knew what I was doing, and I still couldn't stop. Intellectually, I saw the compulsion for what it was—my own form of manipulation, I suppose—but a powerful momentum was already in play. And I couldn't stop myself.

"Whatever I desperately tried, my friend was gone and in his place was my father's shadow ghost. It was like a *Twilight Zone* episode. I was losing twice. I realize now that I was subconsciously trying to get both of them back.

"It took me almost 10 years to be able to even think this guy's name without my blood pressure skyrocketing with rage. I can work myself up into a lather even now, if I give myself half a chance. But I don't because there's no point. It's bad for my brain. Life goes on. And I have better things to do with my neuropathways.

"The enduring value of this experience in my life isn't the hurts-so-good experience in telling the story about how someone was mean to me. Who doesn't experience episodes when others are cruel to them? The enduring value comes from being able to stand outside the drama and help others see what can happen when someone suffers from lack of self-acceptance. Boundaries disappear. Tears are shed. Thousands of dollars are wasted. Years drain away in the futile struggle for some kind of resolution or peace of mind. It's an exhausting way to live. And everyone deserves better. Including my former friend, by the way, who never volunteered for the assignment of being my validation mirror. And clearly, my need triggered his own anger issues that were more powerful than his better nature. So he was suffering too."

Here are two examples of the desperate need of two ASDPs to be accepted and supported by someone we respect and admire. To finally see ourselves positively through the eyes of someone we trusted—as opposed to unconsciously allowing ourselves to be defined and manipulated by people who were dealing with their own issues. We stayed small. We allowed the other person to be the dominant one. We stayed quiet and did not speak up. We twisted ourselves into being someone we were not, because if we had spoken up or stood up to them, all hell might break loose. We thought we had found a safe place in the presence of someone else. But instead we paid the price with additional chiseling away of chunks of our own sense of self.

These are stories (and there are plenty more all over the world) of what happens when children start out life not getting the emotional basics they need—and deserve—to grow up with a healthy sense of self and who they are. They struggle to give themselves unconditional, positive regard because they didn't see it reflected in the eyes of some of the people who were supposed to take care of them when they were children. As we will learn in the next section, when we ASDPs didn't get the emotional basics that we deserved in childhood, just for being alive in this world, we unconsciously find ways to rationalize why we don't deserve to have that emotional foundation from our caretakers. And then many of us spend our lives desperately trying to build that foundation ourselves, using people-pleasing, perfectionism, appeasing behaviors to pull it out from others.

If we believe there is a chance that there is someone in this world who might love and accept us for who we are, and make us feel safe in our own skin, we willingly hand over the keys to our emotional castle—willfully turning a blind eye to all the indications that this person is deep down not our champion after all. Where others, standing at a distance, can see what's really going on and where our boundaries are being violated, we're too close to see that the champion we're desperately trying to appease is in fact ... a dragon with his or her own issues and needs that they might be futilely trying to get us to meet. And worse: Even when we have finally identified that dragon, we are too locked into the relationship to be able to back out of it, without tearing our own flesh in the process. Do we stay or do we go in the destructive relationship? Either way, it's horrible, and we punish ourselves even more for the failure. Because we think we don't deserve anything better; because there was something we did—or didn't do—to bring the crazy into the relationship. Or so we tell ourselves. Because, after all, we grew up being told that just about everything that was going wrong was somehow our fault—or that we somehow made it worse.

This is what lack of self-acceptance looks like.

Author and psychologist Tara Brach calls it *self-aversion*. The only way we can make sense of our negative experiences interacting with the world is to believe that we must be fundamentally flawed or bad somehow. We believe we get what we deserve. And we deserve mistreatment because we're foundationally just plain wrong. Of course, none of that is true. But we struggle to integrate that fact into our psyches. It's a Catch-22: We have this deep-seated, mostly unconscious, belief that we're too flawed to deserve better feelings about ourselves to take the necessary steps to walk ourselves toward our own unconditional, positive, self-regard.

Brach says in her audiobook, *Radical Acceptance*:

… [There's] a feeling of deficiency that's right at the center of the most painful and paralyzing of experiences … 'I'm deficient, I'll be rejected.' It affects our ability to be intimate; our capacity to be creative. It drives our addictive behaviors. I've noticed that the most uncomfortable language describing deficiency is feeling shame. We're even ashamed of the word *shame*. But it's an important word; it points to the deep pain of self-aversion … When we feel deficient … we feel shame. And that shame ties us up in knots. It gives rise to the most profound sense of self-aversion and feelings of unworthiness.

Brach continues:

It's alarming to me just how habituated we are to the perception that 'something is wrong with me,' to feeling fundamentally not okay. It's like an invisible but toxic gas. We're always breathing it so we're not aware that down deep we've just assumed that something's wrong with us. Belatedly we start realizing that we've been living out our days compensating for this feeling. Our lives have been wrapped around trying to avoid feeling bad about ourselves, to make up for not being okay.

That sets the stage for my negative experiences with my former colleague. I fueled the unhealthy dynamic with him in my need for his validation, which he often gave. And, I just accepted the moments of subtle mistreatment as an attack for me to absorb so we could return our relationship to what I had perceived as "normal." And Martha didn't have the presence of mind to realize how appallingly manipulative it was for her friend to intentionally pick a fight with her on the one evening when she specifically needed emotional safety and serenity. Being treated wrongly for an ASDP is normal because wrong is a state of being we're used to. We believe that if it's not right and comfortable for the other person, it has to be our fault in some way. It's our job to fix it, whatever the cost to our own well-being. And nothing will be right until we do.

We spend our early years seeking out that sense of safety in external relationships, not fully grasping the realization that the foundational safety must come from ourselves. And then many of us grow up to spend much of our careers seeking the external validation from professional relationships, especially from people we perceive to be in authority. The balance to strike, of course, is to know how to move through life as our own champions without being so defended that we never let anyone into our inner circles of intimacy and trust. And learn to welcome praise, kind words, and external validation from our bosses and colleagues when they come, while knowing deep inside that we already knew we did a good job.

That balance comes from self-acceptance. The workplace is a wonderful lab of experimentation, experiences, and relationships that will help us build true, healthy, self-acceptance. Even when those opportunities come in the form of conflicts.

How Self-Aversion Shows Up At Work

In a harrowing kind of way, though, this very workplace lab that will help us build a path to self-acceptance is, for many of us, our earliest adult indicator that we haven't left our damaged past behind. Even though we're all grown up and making our way in the career world. In fact, our work lives, and our work relationships, often serve to magnify where healing is desperately needed. For Martha, growing up in an emotionally harsh family life that was rejecting and judging, the exposed vulnerability she felt in her earliest workplace relationships sent her running to an isolated work style where she can thrive working from home. For me, the constant need to anticipate and prevent unpredictable rages from my father made me exquisitely attuned to other peoples' expectations, moods, and opinions. Especially when it came to my professional colleagues' opinions of me. And I almost ruined my health coping with the pressure of the never-ending pursuit of perfection.

As Martha and I continue to speak with ASDPs around the world, we hear stories of professionally successful adults who are haunted by emotional triggers from their damaged pasts of sexual or emotional abuse; any number of those adverse childhood events we described in Chapter 3, a feeling that at any moment "the other shoe will drop," or "there's an axe above my head hanging by a fraying rope." One very successful consultant I know, who once held a highly sensitive—and dangerous—international career that served critical national security interests, told me that his entire adult life was haunted by the childhood memory of his father telling him, "You're doing it wrong."

We are commonly drawn to professions that prove our early negative messages wrong—or right. For my friend, "doing it wrong" literally could have gotten someone killed. His country counted on him to do it right, every single time. His family needed him to do "it" right so that he would come home safe. He spent his first career proving his father's ghostly message wrong. Again and again. Until his health and reprioritized values prompted him to switch careers altogether and lead a life that offered him some peace of mind.

The impact on our little kid brains is real and intense. "When parents are the most out of control, they are the most threatening to the child's survival," as John Bradshaw writes in *Healing the Shame that Binds You*. When this happens, cold, hard, bone-chilling fear is encoded in our central nervous system, which triggers the fight, flight or freeze response designed to keep us safe from dying. Even as adults, when we experience a situation that reminds us (in most cases completely unconsciously) of what happened to us when we were little, our body reacts instantly. When something or someone at work triggers that deep dark fear threatening our sense of safety, we have an immediate physiological response in our body that feels like a strike of lightning.

For me, after a traumatic childhood of chaos, rage and fear, I know I stayed alienated from myself even after my dad died. For me, my central nervous system is programmed to react immediately and intensely when I feel judged, scolded, bullied, made to feel small, stupid, or played for a fool. My physiological reaction is to feel instant fear. Then I want to cry. I feel a pit in my stomach; I feel my body tense up and get tighter than a drum. I experience rapid breathing, and I want to run away. My entire body goes on high alert, and I sense danger.

I compensated for those feelings by working all the time, trying hard to prove myself, always. I worried during the day if I was doing enough, should be doing or not doing something differently. At night I obsessed about work. If someone seemed unhappy with me, I obsessed about that. If someone was angry, then I just knew that it was I who had done something wrong. Given that I was a pleaser, plus a perfectionist, my work quality was always very high and thus my performance ratings were very good. Outsiders saw my career trajectory as something to admire. But, in fact, I was constantly under the gun. From the fear of being judged. The fear of being wrong. Fear of being punished.

Our ability to achieve greater self-acceptance will help to reduce the intensity of our fight or flight encoded memories when they get triggered at work. At work, we are rarely, if ever, truly in a life-threatening situation. But when we are consumed with what others think of us, when someone does something that feels like they are rejecting us, our central nervous system kicks in, catapulting us straight into reaction. Rarely are we at our best selves in these circumstances. And we tend to overreact emotionally, even if invisible to the people we are interacting with.

Greater self-acceptance allows us to take the time and space between the event and our reaction to consciously choose the response that serves us best, protecting our boundaries, while preserving the relationship—and our self-respect in the process. And remembering that we are not the small children of our pasts. We are professionals in our careers. And we can consciously choose a different reaction to a moment when our central nervous system gets triggered by something that happened to us at work.

To see the three of us—me, Martha, and our consultant friend—standing together at a convention hall, you could think: "Now there are three professionals who have it all together." Shoes polished. Hair brushed. Impeccable posture. Saying smart things to one another. Maybe laughing at a clever, professional joke. We have it all together. Even though we carry raging memories around in our brains. You'd never know it to look at us.

What would people never know to look at you? If you are an ASDP, you are likely to be struggling with some kind of historic belief in your mind—unintentionally implanted by your early caretakers—that the shame of who you are makes you unworthy. John Bradshaw defines shame in the following ways:

- We are divided within ourselves.
- Shame leads to false cover up.
- It is a rupture of the self with the self.
- Self becomes an object of its own contempt, which creates the experience of ongoing inner torment.
- A sense of being a failure.

How do these feelings actually show themselves at work? Maybe some of these experiences will feel familiar to you:

- You constantly feel like you have to prove yourself, despite strong performance and enviable accomplishments.
- You approach your work with a sense of pessimism or dread.
- You feel a sense of self-consciousness that's so intense it makes the simplest task overwhelming.
- You freeze when you should be standing up for yourself.
- You over-react in minor conflicts.
- You take things personally when no offense was intended.
- You beat yourself up for imperfect work, minor conflicts and misunderstandings.

- You self-sabotage, procrastinate, struggle to focus on your work.

- You mysteriously find yourself to be the target of other people's blame or ridicule.

- You find that your worst enemy is the voice in your head—the Harsh Inner Critic—that demoralizes you before you even begin the project in front of you. You're exhausted by the efforts required to override the negativity already playing in your mind.

When Every Day is Take-Your-Dysfunctional-Family-to-Work Day

As we've already discussed, so many of us ASDPs grow up counting the years, months, weeks, days before we can leave our dysfunctional childhood life and enter adulthood—with our own apartment, car, job, and everything. And then we discover that leaving the wounds of the past behind isn't just a matter of changing addresses and day-to-day relationships. We find ourselves repeating the old patterns in our adult interactions. And that's when we're brought up face-to-face with the fact that we have just brought so many of our old roles and behaviors to work with us. And we find ourselves thinking, "Oh my gosh! *This again*? Why am I experiencing these awful relationships at work *now*, when I thought I left that behind me?"

This is when many of us discover that our first workplace—our first "job"—happened well before the one that came with our first paycheck. Our first workplace was our family home. Our first resume is the one handed to us by our caretakers. However they approve or disapprove of us (including our track record of behaviors and "that time when …") is how we're taught to approve or disapprove of ourselves.

This is where we learned how to perform roles, behave and function in a way that earned us praise, or at least didn't exacerbate the chaos. This is where we learned how hierarchy works. How to cajole, appease, please, and negotiate. And how objectives are met. Or not met. How we cooperate with each other as a team. Or betray each other in a swirl of interpersonal self-serving politics. This is how we learned how to keep "company" secrets safely behind closed doors.

Some parents tell their children, "Your job is to get good grades." In the case of ASDPs, we had jobs too. One job, for many of us, was to help keep the lid on the family powder keg.

So here we are, all grown up, showing up for our first paying job. Our second job. Our seventh job. And we are surrounded by coworkers who bring their own emotional baggage to work. And we're all playing out roles and behaviors that we had thought would be safely buried in the past. But what we're really doing is bringing our unconscious beliefs about ourselves, life and ways to interact with others into a workplace where others are doing the same.

Cassandra recalls this story from her childhood and early career:

"As I was growing up, my family decided that I would be the one to be put down, criticized, and ridiculed. That was my role, my assignment, my job description. But I knew I was born for a better life than my family members believed I deserved. So I just kept my head down, my bedroom door closed, my nose in books. Now and then, some family member would come find me, bust the door open, and violently remind me that I was being too, well, whatever. Too proud. Too vain. Too full of myself. 'You need to be knocked down a peg, come over here.' These humiliations made me a weird, jittery kid, who attracted teasing at school. 'They don't have the advantages you have,' my mother would advise me when I would come home from school. If she was still sober, I could tell her what had happened during the day. 'Just laugh it off.' So I learned to laugh awkwardly when people teased me. Which was probably also weird.

"Fast forward to my third professional job. My new boss said he hired me because he 'saw something' in me. At first I thought he was saying that he saw *hidden potential.* But it wasn't long before I realized that he saw *himself.* He was also an ASDP, raised by a single, alcoholic mother who died horribly in a fire started by her lit cigarette when she was passed out in her easy chair.

"So there we were, two damaged people, bringing our traumatized family roles to work every day. He developed a strange kind of crush on me—it was more like a fascination because he thought he could rescue me from the tapes of self-loathing that were obviously playing in my head all the time. He actually said as much. He over-compensated for his feelings and giddy energy by constantly teasing me and putting me down with insults wrapped in jokes. Always in front of others, of course. 'Just kidding,' he'd say. And, following my mother's advice, I'd 'laugh it off.' I lasted one year there.

"Years later we saw each other again at an industry reception at a penthouse hotel suite overlooking the San Francisco night lights. We were 10 years away from our time working together. And 3,000 miles away from that office. But otherwise nothing changed. I stood there, with a stony smile on my face, laughing nervously as he hurled 'just kidding' insults at me, one right after the other. In front of industry colleagues and even a client of mine whom I had brought as a guest.

"As my client and I finally walked away, I kept saying what a great guy he is. Maybe a little uncouth but mostly a great guy. A really nice guy, really. Really.

"She just looked at me, wordlessly. And then she said the thing I will never forget: 'Great guys don't humiliate their friends in front of others. Never mind clients.' I was so used to that kind of humiliating teasing, I had no clue how abusive it really was. I had to see it through her eyes.

"We were playing out our family roles and having ourselves a big old Bumper Car Moment right there in that San Francisco penthouse suite, decades away from our own damaged childhoods. In front of everyone. It's been another 20 years since that night. Haven't seen him since. And I don't especially want to. Even though I still catch him checking out my LinkedIn profile now and then.

"I look back on that early time, and wonder, 'What was I thinking to put up with that kind of behavior?' I know what I was thinking. It was still my job to absorb attacks from people who felt compelled to 'knock her down a peg or two.' It was *my* job not to humiliate *him* in this reception in front of our professional peers. I don't know what was going on with him. But it was a comfortingly familiar dynamic for both of us. But now just the memory of it makes my stomach turn."

Cassandra was just playing out the role she had been raised in—the scapegoat role, probably, which I'll describe below. Her former boss isn't here to tell his side of the story, so we can't be sure what role he was acting out. But my guess is that at least a part of it was "rescuer." He saw the wounded child in Cassandra when she was a job candidate. And it made him feel great about himself to be the one who might be able to lift her from her damaged past. Until his own feelings ran away with him.

If you have studied what it means to have grown up in a dysfunctional household, you probably have already learned about common roles family members take on to support the damaging home culture. And you probably have asked yourself which role(s) you were assigned and how they have influenced the way you experience your adult life today.

That dysfunctional family role might have helped you somehow survive a rough and rocky childhood, because it helped you function inside the organization that was your nuclear family. But you might be unconsciously playing that role out even today as an adult at work. I'll share these roles in a minute.

When you watch your coworkers' mystifying behavior, have you ever wondered if they're playing out the roles they learned in their own dysfunctional childhoods? Do you find yourself reacting irrationally or out of proportion to someone else's inexplicable behavior? What you might have going on is the collision of dysfunctional family roles—the collision of your two realities at work. The collision of two different sets of limiting beliefs colliding into each other. These two realities are your adult professional reality and your childhood reality. Sometimes our childhood reality steps into the lead role at work, and we are completely unaware there has been a change of actors on the corporate stage. And the other person is probably also wondering why *you* act the way you do.

A Recipe for Bumper Car Moments All Over the Place

Let's look at some of the roles that psychologists have identified as common in dysfunctional families. In most cases, there is a central individual around whom everyone else spins in an orbit, adjusting their speed, path, behaviors, energies in response to what that individual is doing, what crisis has reared its ugly head. That person is most likely an adult, normally in the role of an essential caretaker. But instead is an alcoholic, rage-o-holic, overbearing, narcissist, overly critical, judgmental, addict, criminal, etc. Whatever the person's behavior is, it requires an "all hands on deck" approach by the rest of the family, to keep the secret, to keep the damage contained, to stay safe, to stay employed, to try and manage the energy so it doesn't go from a spark to forest fire in seconds. Roles are unconsciously assigned. But they stick deep into each family member's future, following everyone into future relationships—even the ones at work.

The roles we learn as children are the behaviors, we grow up believing will help us get along in life. Do you see yourself in one or more of these roles?

The Hero. The Hero is also known as the Golden Child. This is the good kid. The one who never causes anyone any problems. Heroes carry the weight of the entire family on their shoulders. It's up to them to keep up the mask, the fiction, that the family is perfect. The Hero is the one "most likely to succeed," working hard to achieve outside the family. Parents count on the Hero to serve as proof to the outside world that they're good parents, raising a family destined to be successful.

At work, Heroes are the ones who feel the urgency of the work that must be done. Heroes might be leaders, overachievers, perfectionists, but this drive sets them up for burn-out and stress-related illness. If you're a Hero, you might be causing resentment at work because you could be taking away your coworkers' chance to shine, or they may perceive you as being too hard on yourself, setting unrealistic expectations of yourself and others and working all of the time to make sure you are always proving your worth. In the end, the Hero feels tremendous responsibility and duty to be seen as a leader, one always in charge, yet underneath they struggle to escape their self-limiting beliefs that drive them to perform.

The Enabler. The Enabler is the caretaker of the group, supporting weaker members; doing their work for them; covering up for someone who is saying, "Come on, it's just a little white lie." They are also known as Rescuers. Enablers draw their self-value from the belief that only they can keep the team intact, protecting everyone else from suffering the consequences of their irresponsible actions. In their hearts, though, Enablers resent their family members, and then later coworkers. They are the self-appointed martyr of the group, and they keep track of all the prices they have to pay to support the troubled situation.

At work, they are the parent of the group, including the boss. Enablers are the ones everyone can count on to get them out of a jam. Before long, the rate of incoming jams picks up because everyone knows the Enablers will deal with it. Until the Enabler stops (by quitting, for instance). And then the organization discovers that the Enabler may have, in fact, built a house of cards.

The Scapegoat. In the family setting, the Scapegoat is the one who constantly gets in trouble to take the family's attention away from the main trouble. The Scapegoat in this way acts as something of a pressure valve, releasing stress in small, manageable increments while the big problem continues to go unaddressed. The Scapegoat, for instance, will get arrested for speeding, while an addicted parent is about to lose the family's only source of income.

Scapegoats also have a way of telling it like it is. At home, they are defined as hostile, defiant, angry, oppositional. At work they might be experienced by their bosses and coworkers as resistant, argumentative, mavericks, insubordinate. They are the most likely to threaten cohesive corporate cultures where "getting along" is a cherished value. Other ASDPs in the organization might treat the Scapegoat as the target and victim of office politics.

Scapegoats do bring a gift to their organization—their willingness to see the potential downside of scenarios. Heroes and Enablers are more likely to consistently see the positives of proposed initiatives and risks. The Scapegoat will see where the hazards are hidden and isn't afraid to speak up about them. It will be the Scapegoat who launches the conversation around prevention, mitigation, risk assessment.

The Lost Child. Like the Hero, the Lost Child is rarely in trouble. Lost Children make it their business to stay invisible, out of the way, small and quiet, easily overlooked and underestimated. They're loners and shy, likely to have awkward social skills. Very much like Cassandra, they grow up dealing with reality by separating themselves from it altogether, living in a world of their own.

When they start their working years, they likely remain a wall-flower. They're likely to be living with overpowering secrets or beliefs about themselves. And they have concluded that keeping to them-selves is the best self-protection mechanism. But when they are given the support they need to come to grips with whatever their secret might be, it's not unusual for them to blossom. The workplace, with a caring, observant leader, can be their opportunity to emerge from their shells and become the people they were born to be all along. Unfortunately, they make such great, solid, B and C players that super-visors might not be incentivized to develop them.

The Mascot. They are similar to Scapegoats in that they use antics and distracting behavior to take attention away from larger, more ur-gent and critical issues. They're the class clown at school, the jokester at work. Cassandra's boss might very well have had a little bit of Mascot in him in the way he used humor to release his own tension around her.

At work, they can be charming, at first. But they quickly become annoying because they waste too much time cracking jokes and mak-ing a spectacle of themselves. Naturally not all entertaining, light-hearted colleagues are harboring a dark, ASDP secret. But it's a fair bet that they are carrying around a heavy heart load if their humor is too much, inappropriate, or wastes time in serious meetings where there's work to be done.

If you're an ASDP, or you know one, you probably recognize some of these personalities. In families, it's unlikely that there would be multiples of any one personality. But imagine how they might all convene inside a work environment, each bringing their own reality, beliefs about themselves and others and interpretations of life's events to work with them.

That's when you'll see Bumper Car Moments, with everyone involved—including innocent bystanders—wondering what the heck just happened?

You have at least two realities that come along with you every time you step into your workplace environment. You have your current adult self, competent and professional. You also have your past, wounded, largely unconscious self, trying to protect you based on childhood fears and limiting beliefs. As if that wasn't complicated enough, all your coworkers are carrying two realities with them, as well. You can be very sure there are multiple points of view, multiple interpretations and multiple meanings in any encounter where there are two or more people experiencing a situation differently.

You might be the only person who sees the many opportunities to heal from each Bumper Car Moment. Are you personally responsible for making everyone feel better after the Bumper Car Moment, now that you understand how all the personalities convene and clash?

What do you think? The best you can hope for, starting out, is a sense of peace and equanimity that come from holding the hope and expectation that in a time of confusion and conflict, everyone is doing the very best they know how. That's the start of self-acceptance.

Greater Self-Acceptance is Our Key to Healing at Work

Self-acceptance is **being grateful for and valuing all that you are**. This is not about being self-centered or selfish. This is about appreciating and valuing all parts of who you are (even the ugly and dark shameful parts) in healthy ways; loving yourself actively; being compassionate and kind to yourself. And giving yourself credit for all that you have gone through and accomplished to get yourself to this point in your life.

Self-acceptance is about taking control and ownership of the shape of who you are, your story, your self-definition, your sense of the role you play in this world. What you have to offer. And what you're just not going to give away anymore or delegate to other people.

You might be thinking, "Yeah, that all sounds good but there is no way I can be grateful for and value all that is inside me. If you knew what was inside of me, you would judge and reject me. You might run away as fast as you can. Maybe even vomit." I know. That was exactly what was in my head along my own journey. I get it. And you may not believe this yet, but you are on this earth because you are special. You matter. You are worthy.

There is no one else like you and you have important things to do during your life. All that has happened to you, both good and bad things. All that you have done, both good and bad things. All that you know, and all that you don't know yet. Every part of who you are matters. Without all these things that make up who you are, you would not be you. And you would not be ready to do what you are meant to do throughout the rest of your life.

The journey toward greater self-acceptance includes learning how to find the value of every negative thing that was either done to us or that we did to others. As odd as this may sound, the further along my own journey of seeking greater self-acceptance, the more I realized that my dad, who was so very difficult, may have been my greatest gift giver in teaching me that no one is in charge of determining my self-value, self-worth, or degree of self-acceptance, except me. Through my perceived view of never being able to please him and feeling responsible for his rage, he was in fact teaching me not to spend my time looking to others to approve of me.

I've also realized along my journey that the most painful, hard, hurtful, challenging, difficult relationships and moments in my life, were in fact, the greatest teachers of learning to accept myself. I know this may not make sense right now, but it will. Every negative thing that happens to us or by us creates opportunities for deep learning about who we are and how we want to define ourselves. When we realize that it is no one else's job to decide if we are worthy, valuable or good enough, we are on the road to discovering greater self-acceptance. We may not like everything we see, but this is the road that will lead us to more joy not only at work, but in life too.

Following are other definitions of self-acceptance. Hopefully one or more of these examples resonates for you. I love all of them. Perhaps you have a definition too?

Melody Beattie, author of 18 books including *Co-Dependent No More*, writes that self-acceptance means that "for the present moment, we acknowledge and accept our circumstances, including ourselves and the people in our lives, as we and they are." She goes on to write, "Not only are we comfortable with our circumstances and the changes we have endured, but we believe we have in some way benefitted from our loss or change even if we cannot fully understand how or why."

In his book *The Pursuit of Perfect*, Tal Ben-Shahar connects the lack of self-acceptance with perfectionism. In contrast, he says, self-acceptance makes room for "optimalism." Perfectionists and optimalists have different relationships to failure: Perfectionists are driven by the fear of failure and their "primary concern is to avoid falling down, deviating, stumbling, erring." They try "in vain to force reality to fit into straight line vision of life where no failure is acceptable." In contrast, optimalists understand that "going off course is not always a negative thing, and it can present choices and lessons that may not otherwise have been recognized."

In his book, *Honoring the Self: Personal Integrity and the Heroic Potentials of Human Nature*, Nathaniel Branden wrote: "If I can accept that I am who I am, that I feel what I feel, that I have done what I have done—if I can accept it whether I like all of it or not—then I can accept myself. I can accept my shortcomings, my self-doubts, my poor self-esteem. And when I can accept all that, I have put myself on the side of reality rather than attempting to fight reality. I am no longer twisting my consciousness in knots to maintain delusions about my present condition."

Martha, who has spent much of her career writing about personal mission through work, says: "Part of self-acceptance is the knowledge that one's mission and purpose in life is more important than any potential for embarrassment, objection, rejection, etc., any discomfort at all that is around the question *who are you to* ... Once you start coming to terms with self-acceptance, the question very naturally becomes, *who are you not to*? And soon you run out of excuses, and you start seeing doors opening up everywhere."

Kristin Neff writes, "Self-compassion [which I equate with acceptance in many ways] honors the fact that all human beings have both strengths and weaknesses. Rather than getting lost in thoughts of being good or bad, we become mindful of our present moment experience, realizing that it is ever changing and impermanent. Our successes and failures come and go— they neither define us nor do they determine our worthiness."

Hopefully by now, you are coming to understand that self-acceptance is about having a healthy relationship with yourself where you are kinder to you, you pay attention to what you are feeling and what you need and then speak up to create that in your life. Achieving self-acceptance is about re-connecting back with yourself. It's about standing up for yourself—not ashamed of even being in the position of having to stand up for yourself. It's about healthy boundaries. It's about giving ourselves what we need—meaningful work, restorative rest, healthy boundaries with respectful friends and colleagues—to thrive and achieve our full potential.

Steps to Greater Self-acceptance

In addition to practicing leveraging workplace Bumper Car Moments and the Rapid Power Reclaim to heal your past (we'll dive deeper into this area in Part 2 of this book), here are practical actions you can take toward becoming more self-accepting.

Have fun with this list. These steps come from my own experiences plus the advice of many wise authors. Think about how you might adapt these to your workplace.

And remember to give yourself credit for your wins, even if you're in the habit of dismissing your achievements because of old "you're not good enough" coding. William James said, "The deepest principle in human nature is the craving to be appreciated."

1. Get clear on the underlying fears that are keeping you from achieving greater self-acceptance. I had never connected my being a pleaser and a perfectionist to any underlying fears. I had also not connected my desire to drink to a way of avoiding feeling all these fears. The fear of not being good enough, being abandoned, getting in so much trouble, I might die from the punishment, and the fear of anger.

But Sue Paige, of Pathways to Successful Living, opened my eyes one day. As I was going through my list of fears, she helped me see that this lengthy list is what drives my need to be liked and my desire to do things perfectly.

"When are you going to stop letting your fears control you?" she asked.

She changed my life with that one simple question!

I had never thought of my need to please others and perform as being the result of my fears controlling me. If I am afraid of being rejected, yelled at, judged or abandoned, I will do whatever I can to avoid upsetting someone, doing anything that could be viewed as displeasing or offensive. This insight has caused me to look at what I need to do to stop letting my fears control me.

Sue's loving advice was to look for places where I might not speak up and set clear boundaries with others for fear that they may not approve of me. For instance, letting people know what is really going on with me if I am uncomfortable, I don't like something, or I need to let someone know how I am responding to them. Respectfully disagreeing with others, especially men in authority, when I don't support their direction or decision.

Now that fears have a spotlight shown on them, it was eye opening to see how much they were influencing my behaviors. We all have fears. It's normal. It's a condition of being human. Some deny it. And we all have issues. Real and perceived fears evoke feelings and emotions that can directly affect the degree we can achieve greater self-acceptance. Our opportunity lies in understanding what our fears are and taking back control of our lives and not letting the fears dominate us. Fear comes from the past—what has happened that we don't want to repeat. And our worries about the future—anxiety about what might happen. In this preoccupation with our past and or future, we can lose the only priceless possession we own—the present.

Here is a list of fears that I have unearthed in my own life as I've gone through the work of exploring exactly that has kept holding me back:

- Fear of judgment
- Fear of rejection
- Fear of being alone
- Fear of being excluded
- Fear of anger
- Fear of being laughed at
- Fear of disease
- Fear of hell
- Fear of the devil

- Fear of looking stupid
- Fear of being unlovable
- Fear of failure
- Fear of being manipulated
- Fear of not being able to love
- Fear of being fat
- Fear of getting old
- Fear of letting people down
- Fear of a sexually transmitted disease
- Fear of dementia
- Fear of later life suffering
- Fear of not being good enough

2. Review what people-pleasing behaviors might be damaging your career. What do you do at work to get others to like you, even if it comes at the expense of your self-acceptance and career? Write out the consequences of people pleasing at work and the impact of not being honest with others about who you really are. Remember that people pleasing keeps you separate from others. People pleasers in the workplace may be viewed as:

- Political and inconsistent
- Brown-nosers
- Self-serving, potentially at the expense of the team
- Disingenuous and manipulative, therefore untrustworthy
- Easily manipulated
- Looking needy
- Competitive
- Working ridiculous hours so perhaps they aren't smart in how they work
- Uncertain, ill-equipped to provide and commit to essential professional perspectives
- Uncomfortable "in their own skin," causing others to feel uncomfortable too

Write out new ways you will show up at work instead of being a people pleaser. This doesn't mean you won't still do great work or have people praising you for what you have done. This is about showing up as you and rather than constantly being driven to accomplish to have others tell you how wonderful you are, focus on the feelings of satisfaction you experience when you do a great job. This isn't about becoming argumentative for the sake of being argumentative. It's about allowing yourself to be in touch with you throughout the day rather than being consumed with what others are thinking about you. Decide on new ways you will handle the times where you go into automatic people pleasing and come up with some counter behaviors that are centered on feeling good because you know you have done a good job.

3. Factor your own self-interests in your career decisions. I'm not suggesting that you engage in unethical self-dealing, get in trouble with your boss, or plot against a colleague. But ASDPs commonly put their interests last in business situations. They take on more work than they can reasonably do well, at the expense of their personal lives or health. They will accept a lower salary offer because they don't want the hiring manager to think they're not team players. They'll let a colleague take a plum assignment that by all rights should have gone to them—saying to themselves, "I'll make it up later." They'll let others take the credit that's rightfully their own. There are no boundaries. Even if ASDPs try to set them, it's often half-heartedly, and colleagues know that they're permeable. Even the question, "Is this decision good for me?" feels like a crime against humanity, or at least society.

It's not wrong to put yourself first, at least in early phases of a decision-making process, before you take your thinking public. You may end up putting other people's priorities before yours (like, for instance, your boss's). But no one will consider your perspective until you do.

4. Welcome interpersonal challenges as opportunities to practice new skills in self-acceptance. You may have grown up believing that your job in life was to prevent—or at least mitigate—overwhelmingly frightening drama in your family of origin. Now that you're an adult, and you can see the situation from a distance, would you ever put those feelings of responsibility on to a young child? Of course not.

And yet, it's possible that you take them with you into the workplace. You'll do anything and everything to avoid interpersonal challenges, whether it's possible someone is mad at you, or you are a third-party wondering if there is something you can do to step into someone else's conflict that you have nothing to do with. In these moments, we personalize the other person's anger. When in reality, their anger belongs to them. Their anger is their *property,* to use an expression by Melody Beattie that I found in her life-changing book *The Language of Letting Go.* In her May 13 installment, she writes:

> What other people choose to say and do is their business ...
> Our property includes our behaviors, problems, feelings, happiness, misery, choices, and messages; our ability to love, care, and nurture; our thoughts, our denial, our hopes and dreams for ourselves. Whether we allow ourselves to be controlled, manipulated, deceived, or mistreated is our business ... If something isn't ours, we don't take it. If we take it, we learn to give it back. Let other people have their property.

These moments give us a chance to practice separation from the other person's behavior.

Interpersonal upsets at work—whether you are personally involved, or you're watching from the sidelines—aren't automatically your fault. Sit back, watch, observe, and know what your responsibility in the conflict really is. And then consciously, step by step, address the situation without defensiveness, emotional reactions, getting caught up in the battle. You won't do it perfectly every time. And it may happen that others will be angry with you. And you know what? It's okay. Look at your part in the play and take accountability for what you may have done or not done in this scenario. Own it and move on. The other person's anger belongs to them. It's very possible they themselves are unconsciously behaving this way because their own childhood reality has come crashing into the moment. If they appear to be over-reacting, this is often a signal that an entirely different script is playing out in their own mind.

If you do your best, that's the best you can do.

5. Reduce perfectionistic behaviors that separate you from self-acceptance. Neff suggests there are some steps you can take to reduce the negative effects of perfectionism. We took her concepts and overlaid the workplace context.

Do you have an underlying drive to prove yourself? Do you engage in ruminating thoughts that play in your head second-guessing how you handled a work situation—either feeling you should have done more or less or whatever?

Take a minute and assess the consequences of perfectionism and impact on your career. Here are some starters that I know many professionals and executives experience:

- Effects of always feeling you need to prove yourself
- Disappointment, depression, sadness when you fail
- Underlying sense that you may get fired
- The effort and energy it takes to manage your image day in and day out
- Impact of perceived failure on sense of self
- Impact of dread experienced if image is threatened

6. Practice gratitude daily. When we begin to appreciate all that we have, we are less likely to focus on ways we are inadequate. Melody Beattie wrote, "Gratitude unlocks the fullness of life. It turns what we have into enough, and more. It turns denial into acceptance, chaos to order, confusion to clarity. It can turn a meal into a feast, a house into a home, a stranger into a friend. Gratitude makes sense of our past, brings peace for today and creates a vision for tomorrow."

In 1999 I started a practice that literally transformed my life. I had picked up the book by Sarah Ban Breathnach called *Simple Abundance*, in which she suggests keeping a gratitude journal as a way of tracking all the gifts and miracles that are right in front of us every day. But we tend to overlook them when we're caught up in the flurry of life. I bought my first journal in 1999 and began to capture five things per day that I was grateful for. It didn't matter how big or how small it was. If I was grateful for it, I wrote it in the journal. I would reflect on my day thinking about special moments that stood out:

- My sons' smiles and laughter
- A kind word from a boss
- Time off work with pay for my maternity leave
- How the rain made the trees sparkle like diamonds
- Working with smart people
- A quiet morning offering time for renewal
- A call from a friend
- A hot cup of coffee with extra cream first thing in the morning

Most days, it was easy to come up with five things I was grateful for. Occasionally, I would struggle to come up with something. Then I would be reminded by another's story how blessed I was to have a healthy body, or the ability to see and hear, the ability to do all the things I love to do that require physical and mental capabilities.

I just started my 22nd consecutive year of my gratitude journal. As I was taking my most recent journal to my closet to stack on top of the other 21, I couldn't help but be amazed by how many riches were stored in those journals! Twenty years of taking time each day to give thanks for all the big and small blessings in my life. Living a life of gratitude for all that is already in my life, created wealth beyond the imagination. Gratitude brings abundance. The more gratitude, the more abundance. The more gratitude I feel, the better I feel about my life. About myself.

I know how easy it is to wish I had more. It is an easy place to go some days. However, the daily ritual of writing out the five things I am grateful for today, transformed my life. Have you considered your own gratitude practice? It literally takes less than a minute a day.

7. Master your emotional triggers. Triggers are awful. They're scary. And they are very real. I would never in a million years just flippantly say to you, "Just get over it." But what I can say to you is this: "Resolve to do everything you need to do to get over it." For the sake of your career, your peace of mind, your relationships, and your life, you deserve to address your triggers through professional healing intervention.

Triggers arise from a wide variety of post-traumatic stress disorders. And they can be mild or overwhelming. No matter where they fall on the continuum, you deserve to have a mental health professional help you neutralize their power. When you take that action for yourself, you become a much more congenial, predictable, collaborative colleague. Until you do, however, you are leaving yourself open to undermining actions by your coworkers who know how to set you off. You become subject to manipulations. And, if your trigger reactions are especially debilitating or emotional, your colleagues may see you as someone who is not easy to work with, a walking-on-eggshells proposition daily.

Claiming mastery over your emotions—especially the most extreme reactions to moments in life—could be the most valuable favor you do for yourself and your career. But don't try to do it on your own. Seek professional help.

8. Forgive yourself and others. We have all things in our life that we regret. We must release ourselves from our own judgment and condemnation. When we carry anger directed at us, we keep ourselves locked in our own prison, even though we have the key to set ourselves free. I used to beat myself up when I would get triggered or feel that I had done something wrong. Each time I beat myself up, I am getting triggered and retriggered all over again. I am in effect torturing myself with self-blame that feels like I am continuously stabbing myself with a sharp knife. When we have deeper levels of self-acceptance, we are called on to practice self-forgiveness. We must intentionally decide to let go.

And when we carry anger, resentment, and judgment towards another person whom we perceived wronged us, we only hurt ourselves. Each time we tap into or experience our hurt we perceive as caused by another, we are also torturing ourselves and pushing self-acceptance further out beyond our reach. Like an oasis in the desert, we never seem capable of finding the peace and relief of discovering greater self-acceptance. Forgiving another isn't about condoning what happened. It is about releasing that person and ourselves from the grip of the past pain.

Practice forgiveness. It's a powerful solution to our pain and suffering.

9. Create Your Own Brand-New Brand You. You're an adult now. You don't need anyone's approval but your own. And you truly can be anyone you want to be. No, I'm not suggesting that you can become a ballerina or astronaut at your current age, lifestyle habits and questionable aptitude at rhythm, math, and science. But then again, who am I to tell you you can't?

My interest here is in helping you determine who you are on the inside—your character, your attributes, yes, even your personality. Those are completely within your control. And maybe there are some aspects of who you are that you really can't accept in our shared journey to self-acceptance. So. Change them. Whose permission are you waiting for? Each one of us can re-write the script of who we want to be. We are not stuck with our childhood reality script. We can redesign how we feel about ourselves, what we say to ourselves, how we react to others, how we show up at work, how we redefine beliefs about ourselves to replace the self-limiting ones. We can write our own script to reconnect to who we really are. And then we just practice that script over and over again.

Assuming you're an ASDP, it's very likely that you were told who you are by parental figures who didn't like themselves very much. And they projected a certain amount of self-loathing onto you—because you were their child, therefore you were a reflection of them in some way.

Now, I was fortunate in that my mother was so supportive and loving. And I saw myself as lovable when I saw myself in her eyes. Even my father, when he wasn't raging, told me that I could be anything I wanted to be. But then he would blow up, and the message he delivered, whether intentionally or not, through his actions was, "You are bad, you are unworthy, your job is to please people who judge you. You don't, so therefore you deserve to be afraid and punished." So I got the debilitating message anyway.

Many ASDPs grow up not having a clue who they are in terms of their innate value just for being alive. They are told by their family, "You are the kind of person who …"

Imagine your family talking to you. How would you fill in the blank? "You're the kind of person who _____."

- "Does everything wrong?"
- "Embarrasses me in public?"

- "Expects too much out of life?"
- "Should be ashamed of the way you look?"
- "Spends all the money?"
- "Is born to fail?"
- "Can't keep me sober long enough to feed you?"
- "Infuriates me to the point I have to hit you?"
- "Can't be trusted?"
- "Always gets in trouble?"
- "Always gets me in trouble?"
- "Can't be counted on for anything?"
- "Will always land on your own feet?"

This is the final step of self-acceptance—but one that will take you on a marvelous, choose-your-own adventure for the rest of your life. You get to be the one who decides what kind of person you are. Damaged is not doomed, my friend!

What will it be? Let's play with the blanks again:

You're the kind of person who:

- "Inspires generations for the life of health, love, ambition and accomplishments you've chosen to live."
- "Greets challenging situations with humor and optimism."
- "Makes everyone in the room feel welcomed and accepted."
- "Stands up for yourself, as well as for 'the little guy,' who needs a champion."
- "Creates value in any organization lucky enough to have you."
- "Is a role model at work whom others look up to and want to be like."
- "Is always up for a laugh and an adventure."
- "Is always encouraging and comforting."
- "Can be counted on to follow through on obligations, promises, and values."

- "Can be trusted with the most precious belongings and secrets."

You can be the person you want to be. And you can demonstrate those attributes at work, building up your personal resume that you can be proud of.

Your family may never agree with you. But that's not their job.

Pleasing them isn't your job either. Self-acceptance is your job. Make a career out of it.

Chapter 7
Joy Is Within Your Reach

ASSUMING YOU GREW up as an ASDP (and that is why you're still with me in the book, right?), you likely grew up to be an adult unconsciously bringing along some beliefs about life, the world, other people, yourself that probably protected you as a child. But they're getting in the way of your experience of a fulfilling life now, aren't they?

Everyone is different, of course. But here's a sampling of beliefs that might be holding you back from a joyful life, causing unnecessary (at the very least, unwelcome) interpersonal drama, disappointments, career setbacks, and unexpected struggles:

- People can't be trusted.
- Any moment now, the other shoe is going to drop on my head.
- People are judging me harshly behind my back.
- My work has to be flawless or people will lose respect for me.
- I can't count on anyone keeping their word.
- Bosses are scary, mean, abusive.
- I am a helpless victim of other people's cruelty, selfishness, ambition.
- I am powerless when other people activate my triggers.
- It's up to me to find a way to belong, make unkind people kind, meet the expectations of people who will never be satisfied.

Those are just samples of some of the thoughts we torment ourselves with. When we achieve greater self-acceptance and move into the next phase of healing, especially at work, the origin of our negative beliefs moves from unconscious to conscious. We're able to spot them as they take hold in the way we experience life moment by moment. And we get better and better at overriding them with healing thoughts and beliefs.

Your work experiences can help you begin—or accelerate—your healing journey, which will benefit all areas of your life. Imagine this scenario:

You're surrounded by a team of people you respect and who respect you in return. Your boss challenges you but in a supportive, constructive way. Communication is clear and trusting. You assume the best in other people's intentions toward you. And they feel the same way about you. So, there's a sense of ease and unself-consciousness. Even when you stumble and fall short of expectations on a goal, you're supported, maybe even celebrated, for taking on the challenge and learning from it. You care about the nature of the work because you know the value and meaning it brings to the world and people you care about. You take observations about your work and suggestions on how things can be improved as constructive contributions about the work itself, not as a reflection of your value as a human being. You can take on most projects or goals with every reasonable expectation that you can see it all the way through. And if a colleague or boss does something that you take to mean something negative about you, you are quickly able to regroup and release the old negative beliefs and responses.

Your work can be your refuge. Here you know what's expected of you (more or less, we're talking a community of people here, and humans are, after all, only human). You're learning new interpersonal skills that you can use not only at work but also at home. And, much to your surprise, you find yourself after work at night with a smile on your face—without thoughts about whether you should make a swing by the wine shop first.

Things are just plain easier. This is joy at work. Can you imagine that as being something within your reach? It is, you know.

Did you ever see the baseball movie, *The Natural*, with Robert Redford? In the novel version, on which the movie is based, author Bernard Malamud had this to say: "We have two lives ... the life we learn with and the life we live after that. Suffering is what brings us toward happiness."

Well, for many of us, our second life begins when we enter the career phase of our lives after a childhood of suffering. Isn't it about time that you had some of that happiness that people talk about?

Happiness and Joy

Philosophers and psychologists like to separate the concepts of happiness and joy. And I can understand why. Happiness is typically regarded as a state of mind that is governed by fleeting, external circumstances. Or external motivations, such as other people's opinions or material rewards—like that car you've been dreaming about. Those moments are like sugar highs. Once they're over, they can leave you feeling crashed and empty. They feel great, don't get me wrong. And they have their purpose and value. But don't count on them to sustain you through challenging times. That's when you need joy.

Joy is more intrinsic. And, weirdly, it isn't even contingent on what's going on in your life from one moment to the next. Even one year to the next. Things around you can actually feel pretty awful, but you can still feel joy. It's about the meaning you assign to the experience that can elevate it from "another day at the mill" to a transcendent moment of radiance that you'll never forget ever. Those moments have nothing to do with the incidentals in motion around you. They are in a context that is much more significant than the moment. Maybe even more significant than you yourself.

In Viktor Frankl's book, *Man's Search for Meaning*, he reflects on his years enduring unspeakable horrors and torment in a series of concentration camps during World War 2, never knowing whether he would make it out (he did) and whether his beloved wife was alive as his thoughts of her kept him going every day, one day at a time (she wasn't). As a Holocaust survivor and a psychologist, he would spend the rest of his life answering questions about what made some people survive and others succumb.

He listed three elements that he found in the hell holes of concentration camp life. But, what's relevant to us now is that we can also find them in benign, modern life with all the usual comforts—and stresses and anxieties. It's about finding meaning, especially in the company of and collaboration with others, which, in turn is where we can always find joy:

> … We can discover this meaning in life in three different ways: (1) by creating a work or doing a deed; (2) by experiencing something or encountering someone; and (3) by the attitude we take toward unavoidable suffering.

Those three elements can be found in any given workday—particularly when you aim high and go for the intrinsic meaning we talked about. We experience joy at work when we're doing work (or, as Frankl put it, a deed) that's important to us in some way; when we have experiences in the company of others we care about; and, in those inevitable times when we are unhappy because of our circumstances, those things that make us suffer are less important than the larger purpose of the thing that we're doing at that moment, with others.

If it worked for thousands of Holocaust survivors, surely we can draw lessons from that model to help us prevail over our pasts and live that second life of happiness and joy that Bernard Malamud talked about.

The bonus that our work environment brings is that people take us at face value, in the context of our second life. When we might have grown up in the harsh light of caregivers who saw us only as reflections of their own dysfunctions, self-hatred, and painful experiences of their own, our coworkers only know us as the people we are today. While we're not exactly starting from scratch with a whole new identity (even Jason Bourne, with his amnesia, couldn't leave his mysterious identity behind him entirely; which, given his mad survival skills, turned out to be a good thing), the person we choose to become in our second life is the person our colleagues will see and know about us. The more consistently we practice the conscious and intentional characteristics we choose for ourselves (stability, optimism, perspective and proportion, calm reassurance, and other hallmarks of self-acceptance), the more they become ingrained in who we are on the most authentic level.

Joy Starts With Your New Identity

As we explored in the last chapter on self-acceptance, the key to unlocking and achieving success at work is creating a loving, accepting, healthy, caring, and positive relationship—with yourself! You then become more grounded, have more clarity about who you are and where you are going. You become less affected by other people's "stuff," like when they are upset, angry, stressed, etc. And you become the driver—the creator—of your own life. You're not constantly in reaction mode.

I can't guarantee that you will no longer have moments of conflict—the Bumper Car Moments we'll talk about in Part 2. But their frequency will dramatically decrease. And you will become far more effective in smoothly managing those unavoidable collisions of yours and your coworkers' pasts and present realities. You will be able to transform those Bumper Car Moments into labs where you can demonstrate how everyone can use each experience to heal their own past wounds. This is the workplace version of turning suffering into joy.

With the self-acceptance we've already discussed as your stable foundation for moving forward, you will demonstrate to yourself and your colleagues that with kindness (for yourself and others), perspective, proportion, a mindset governed by curiosity, and maybe even a sense of humor, your shared working environment is a safe place for everyone to learn, grow, innovate, heal, and take healthy risks. Even, when necessary, successfully stand your ground at the risk of displeasing or disappointing others.

It all starts with how we see ourselves and how willing we are to see ourselves in an even better, more self-loving light. Dr. Maxwell Maltz, author of *Psycho-Cybernetics*, was a plastic surgeon. In his book, he describes his bewilderment when patients, for whom he had made dramatic positive changes to their physical appearance, would leave feeling no differently than before they first walked through his door. As he began to seek to understand this phenomenon, he concluded that people "cannot rise above" how they see themselves. Matt Furey, President of the Psycho-Cybernetics Foundation, who wrote the foreword for Maltz's updated edition, describes a client, named Jack, who expanded on Maltz's belief in this way, "Our future is controlled by a mental blueprint we have inside our subconscious mind, and it dictates where we think we belong."

Furey highlighted how he often felt himself to be a failure in his life, despite many significant accomplishments. He realized later that he felt like a failure because he would constantly think about all the areas in his life where he had not achieved his definition of success. He wrote, "Each day when I would feel badly about myself, it was as if I'd rubbed my face in the manure of bad memories instead of showering my face with clear-water memories of when I had done well." After he read *Psycho-Cybernetics*, he realized he needed to spend more time in a place Maltz called "the Theatre of the Mind," focusing on places in his life when he had experienced positive moments.

As Maltz worked to understand why some of his patients never came to believe they looked more beautiful after surgery, he concluded that "the non-physical face of personality is the real key to personality change … the self-image is the individual's mental and spiritual concept of … self and is the real key to personality and behavior." Self-image, he concluded, is the key to a better life.

The glorious news from Maltz's insights is that power is within us to decide to change our self-image. When we change our core beliefs about who we are, we can change our lives. The self-image is so powerful in determining how our life plays out because it is the determining force of what we believe we can and can't do.

Maltz concluded that developing a realistic self-image will result in our being able to develop new abilities that turn failures into successes. And he said it was possible to do this because we each have a built in "guidance system" that can be reprogrammed. This guidance system capability is the result of the brain and nervous system's ability to redirect a new path for our lives. We can, in effect, reprogram our internal guidance system to create new neural pathways (that *neuroplasticity* we have already talked about). The guidance system, or "goal striving mechanism" as Maltz describes it, is a creative mechanism that we can redirect.

Whatever we believe about ourselves and our life is true. And we are the ones who determine how to direct our brain, either consciously or unconsciously.

We're a work in progress, building ourselves as we go and grow. Maltz reminds us that we will never rise above our self-image. So the challenge and opportunity for us is to decide who we want to be and build up experiences—like a skyscraper under construction, one floor at a time—that will bring us to new heights of our own potential for joy. What better construction site than the workplace where we're known for who we are today and what we can contribute to our workplace community?

Ten Debilitating Beliefs That Get in Joy's Way

Think about the way you talk to yourself all day long. How would you describe the nature of your self-talk and how it makes you feel about yourself? Does your self-talk make you feel good, encouraged, energized, hopeful, and confident? Or do you somehow believe that the only way you can motivate yourself to achieve with excellence is to scold and beat yourself up? Now. Tell me. Would you talk to a child that way? I'm thinking, probably not. In fact, the very idea of being so mean to a tender, young, impressionable spirit probably horrifies you. So why is it okay to talk to yourself that way? If you're an ASDP, whose early caregivers might have believed that harsh words would keep you in line, I'm also betting that you can still hear them in your head. Only this time, the voice is yours.

I'm talking about really mean-spirited self-talk here. These are the familiar self-talk messages that feel like there's an evil imp sitting on your head. The imp just won't shut up; it's reading from a script of debilitating, insulting self-talk. And when it's done, it just starts all over again from the top. Who would *you* talk to the way you allow that imp in your head to talk to you?

Don't you deserve at least some peace of mind in order to become the person you were meant to be? Ralph Waldo Emerson wrote, "The day is always his who works with serenity and great aims." Notice the first necessity is *serenity*. Who can be *serene* when all that noise is going on?

But it's really that imp in your head picking away at you. Pick pick pick. The cumulative result of all this negative chatter? A terrible narrative that you're not good enough, no matter how hard you might try. This turns into a relentless drive at work to constantly prove yourself. And even with outstanding achievements in your career, there is no time for celebration. It's on to the next priority or initiative.

In his book, *Feeling Good: The New Mood Therapy*, cognitive therapist David M. Burns links destructive self-talk to a pervasive sense of unworthiness, which then leads to depression—whether you're an ASDP or not. Likewise, he looks to the way we think, feel, and behave as keys to lifting us up from negative self-beliefs and for many, depression, to get on with the business and joy of being alive. But first we have to learn how to spot those awful messages in our negative self-talk and stop them as instantaneously as we can. Doing so will enable us to experience that workplace serenity.

He lists 10 *cognitive distortions*—ways you might think and look at the world that keep you buried in limiting beliefs about yourself. As you consider these 10 cognitive distortions, don't just ask yourself whether you consciously hold these beliefs. The people who had the most influence on you as a child might have held these beliefs. And they might have passed them on to you to the point where you might be carrying them subconsciously.

You might think, "Well, my parents never said that to *me*." And that's possible. But they might have said those things to themselves, and, just by their role-modeling influence on you, passed their beliefs about their value—and therefore yours, because you belonged to them. You might have watched them fail at prevailing over their own imps. You might have drawn conscious or unconscious assumptions about the world by watching them struggle with their own crippling beliefs. They were likely to have been unequipped to teach you how to master your own mindset and reach for self-acceptance and joy.

Or you might have reached these negative conclusions about yourself all on your own. Children naturally believe that they are responsible for everything good or bad that happens inside their family. In a family setting where so much that's bad happens, children will believe that an adult's violent temper or addiction is caused by their bad behavior or something they did wrongly. Or if they're really, really, really good, maybe Daddy will come home from jail.

You can read about these 10 cognitive distortions in greater detail in Burns's book. But for now, let's visit each one briefly and explore how they might show up at work. It's very likely that if you are an ASDP, one or more of these 10 distorted beliefs may resonate, on a continuum of low to high. If you allow them to run your career, they can hurt you, both professionally and personally. But you can also use the workplace as a way to build up evidence that they're untrue.

1. All or nothing thinking. This cognitive distortion leads you believe that you have to be perfect, all the time. One false move, one missed deadline, one error in a report, and you're doomed. You are nobody. And everyone will see that you're a failure. It's just a matter of time before you're found out and probably fired. Your colleagues may at times find you stressful to work with because they assume that you are just as hard on them in your judgments as you are on yourself.

2. Overgeneralization. You can spot overgeneralization when you hear yourself think or say, "always, never, everyone." One isolated incident causes you to jump to global assumptions about the nature of people, tasks, locations, hopes for a positive outcome on a project. If a coworker acted in such a way that makes you feel betrayed, you might say, "I'll never trust anyone again." And then stick to that resolution, possibly cutting off your chances of fulfilling collaborations in the future—even with that same colleague who inadvertently disappointed you.

3. Mental filter. You might have heard of the *reticular activating system*. It's a bundle of nerves in our brain that allows us to filter out the data that we don't want to see so that we can focus on what we do want. That's why when we're shopping for a red car, we spot red cars all over the place while driving around town. The distorted mental filter allows us to only see the bad side of things. With a negative narrative running non-stop in our heads, the negative mental filter serves up the evidence, causing us to say, "See? What did I tell you? It's always this way." If your father—your first authority figure—was a power-hungry jerk, you might regard all your bosses, or all men, as power-hungry jerks. Even when they're not. You're blind to their kindnesses and those moments of sensitivity and generosity that they show their employees. You can only see those incidents when they don't show up as their best. Burns calls this kind of filtering, *selective abstraction*. You see only the bad and completely disregard the good.

4. Disqualifying the positive. Maybe you don't completely disregard the good, but you lessen its importance or lasting value. Many ASDPs aren't great at recognizing when they have done something well. They are on to the next project lickity split. In a workplace setting where positive morale and a culture of mutual celebration are essential to promote a collaborative atmosphere of teamwork, innovation and accomplishment, the colleague who says, "Yeah, well, it's not that great," is the one who undermines the entire effort. You may have had controlling parents who wanted to make "damn sure" you didn't grow up to be "too big for your britches," or with a "big head." So they diminished your childhood wins with faint praise or just a shrug and a change of subject. That's what feels normal to you now as an adult. You might superstitiously believe that joyfully celebrating a win sets you up for a cosmic comeuppance later. So you downplay your successes. And before long, your colleagues, or worse, your boss, may start agreeing with you. Yeah, you're not that great.

5. Jumping to conclusions. This cognitive distortion comes naturally to ASDPs, especially those of us who were constantly on the lookout for signs that aggression or violence was about to ensue. You look at a set of facts or trends, and then you deduce what is the most likely thing that will happen next. Whatever the circumstance might be, jumping to conclusions might have protected you from actual physical or emotional harm. Likewise, if you had a caregiver who needed to dominate you through blame and accusation, you grew up experiencing someone else jumping to conclusions at your expense. And you might have developed that habit of anticipating what that conclusion might be just to stay one step ahead of your tormentor. To keep from getting hit or screamed at or neglected. To leave the house before all hell broke loose. To hide under the bed if you were too young to run out the front door. You also learned to depend utterly on your gifts of observation and intuition. This habit—which to your coworkers might show up as mind reading or predicting the future, regardless of whether you are correct or not—can be unsettling to others. It signals to them that they may not be able relax and be themselves around you or reveal their most sensitive feelings. Or you will perceive things that they don't want you to know. And it may isolate you as they try to keep their emotional distance and mental privacy.

6. Magnification and minimization. Have you ever known anyone who takes things out of proportion to their actual importance or impact? When the habit is *magnification*, that person will *catastrophize* the smallest issue. There's a tub of yogurt gone bad in the break room fridge? The fridge is ruined forever and must be replaced! A shop has closed downtown and you see a For Lease sign in the window? The whole downtown area is failing and businesses will be closing down right and left! There's a typo in the Investor Relations tab on your company's website? Oh no! The whole world has already seen it and the company will be sued for malfeasance! *Minimization* is the opposite, of course. When ASDPs minimize in this distorted way, they're in denial of a grave situation to the point where it might become too late to rectify easily or inexpensively. This can also look like the person is in denial. Capacity for denial may well be an outcome of being an ASDP because this strategy protected them from the reality of crazy happening at home.

7. Emotional reasoning. ASDPs have already had a long career of relying on their intuition to see through facades in their childhood homes. The ASDP's intuition is a finely calibrated gift, when used appropriately. Over-reliance on intuition, though, puts ASDPs in the trap of depending on their emotions to guide them in making decisions: "This feels right to me." "My gut tells me it's a no-go." "Suddenly I'm in a bad mood. Something is about to hit the fan, I can just feel it." Important decisions—in both work and personal life—require a balance of intuition and evidence-based, data-driven reasoning.

8. Should statements. ASDPs often have parents who overcompensate for the chaos in their childhood homes with strict rules and rigid black-and-white thinking as a power and control play. These kinds of rules often create ASDPs who are constantly judging themselves and others around them for falling short of expectations in some way. Beliefs that include words like *should* or *must*, Burns writes, are actually demotivating, making ASDPs and the people in their lives feel pressured, resentful, even apathetic and unmotivated. Since we're all human and none of us can really measure up to such high expectations consistently, that imp in our heads is many times talking to us about shame, disappointment, self-loathing, and guilt.

"If my boss thinks I'm up to that scary assignment, I really should say yes, even though my workload is already too heavy." "If my admin really cared about his job, he should already be at his desk by the time I arrive in the morning."

9. Labeling and mislabeling. Almost everyone—even people who aren't ASDPs—have a painful memory of being told who they are by someone who might have meant well but got it all wrong. "He's the handsome one; she's the athletic one," parents might say of their children. "She's going to go far in life. My son? I'm not so sure. He's the class clown." ASDPs might have grown up with parents who projected their own self-loathing on them and categorized them in more damaging ways. "You're the kind of person who …" "You are always an embarrassment to the family …" "You're so good at putting other peoples' needs ahead of your own …" A single label may fit, but it never sums up the entirety of anyone. And mislabeling can be as damaging as a curse. A caregiver who labels out of anger or even jealousy can install a piece of code in a child's heart that could drive even the most successful ASDP professional or executive's self-image down a self-destructive, distorted road later. Giving that imp loads of material to work with.

10. Personalization. Burns writes, "This distortion is the mother of guilt!" ASDPs, who grew up tip-toeing on eggshells in their childhood homes as a way to stop parental rage before it builds up steam, take the habit of being personally responsible for negative episodes to work. They naturally assume that if something bad happened, they had a hand in it. Either by something they did. Or something they didn't do. What they said or didn't say. Or how they said it. A day at work is a minefield of opportunities to screw up. And it's up to them to get it right. First time, every time. The impact of personalization of issues happening at work can take a huge toll on us in terms of time spent beating ourselves up and worrying about the consequences of what happened during the workday.

Burns points to these 10 cognitive distortions as being the source of depression.

For some ASDPs, that's a familiar feeling. In ways large and small, our adult caretakers and parents made their problems our problems—never mind the fact that we were still just learning our ABC's and figuring out how to tie our shoes. Our parents' problems were never meant to be ours to fix, far beyond our abilities. By the time we enter our career years, we know our alphabet and reliably have the shoe challenge mastered. Based on our experiences at home, we have developed the habit of believing that whatever challenge is put before us, it's beyond our abilities to control.

Or, conversely, we will overachieve to the point of unhealthy stress, anxiety and worry to master that challenge and save the day for everyone. Whether it's our responsibility or not.

We might be underachievers as a result of our ASDP beginnings. Or, as in my case, super over-achievers, relentlessly and unhealthily hard on ourselves. In either case, these examples of common distorted self-talk make life unnecessarily and often unbearably complicated for us.

Now that we know what's behind that imp's voice in our heads, we can override the messages and start building the self-talk habit of positivity and messages of encouragement.

Take Action to Build the Joy You Deserve

Now that we've talked about some automatic beliefs that might be holding you back from joy in your life, let's talk about active ways you can start building experiences that build joy into your every day. Joy is an extremely personal experience, and you might have a different definition of what it means to you. So I hope you'll just take this section as a starting point for your own unique journey.

If you were to pick a photograph that expresses joy, what image would you look for? You might pick images that evoke a happy celebration, like, say, a birthday cake. But if I were looking for an image that would ignite joy in my own mind, I'd choose a photo of a horse and rider sailing over some kind of fence on a beautiful day. Martha would pick an image of a ballerina performing a *grand jete*, that familiar leap across the stage, where the dancer is performing a full split high up in the air as she surges forward with power, grace, and exuberance.

What do these two images have in common? They are a display of full-out, energized willingness to let go of gravity, even for just a second.

They also depict discipline, skill, practice, and then release! But horses and ballerinas are very specific to just Martha and me. What would be applicable for you?

How about this: A picture of a person (male or female) with arms thrown open wide, face to the sunshine with a broad, open, unself-conscious smile. Can you see the joy in your own mind's eye? You know the theme song for the show, *Friends*, where they sing, "It seems that you're always stuck in second gear?" Well, in this image you're enjoying fourth gear: freewheeling and flying! No sadness. No self-doubt. No friction. You're seeing the joy of freedom, confidence, and exuberance.

You're also seeing two different kinds of energies playing off one another: Release but also embrace. Those wide-open arms are releasing the bad, and they're making space to bring the good into your life. Release and embrace: You can bring those two energies to work with you to begin to experience the kinds of joys that can permeate your entire life.

Here are some examples:

Release the unhealthy compulsion to please. Naturally you want to do well at work. And your boss and team members are counting on you to fulfill your role and obligations. So those are healthy drives to please. Unhealthy compulsions make you miserable; drive you to addictions and destructive behaviors because your self-talk about how you might have disappointed someone won't cut you a minute's break.

Embrace the flawed stream of life. No life is perfect. Even perfect days have bumps and hard stops. That's, well, life. Mishaps and hiccups aren't a reflection of your value as a human. Or even your value as a team member at work. Learn from them, handle them appropriately, apologize where you need to, stop apologizing when you've apologized enough, and get on to the next best thing.

Release the need to fix what's wrong before you give yourself permission to relish what's right. The drive to anticipate what your boss might be dissatisfied with you about could be that habit of hyper-vigilance that you brought with you into your adulthood from your childhood. With your head constantly "on a swivel," looking for what might hurt you or get you in trouble, will keep you from taking in the good of life and work.

Embrace your Kind Inner Career Coach. You might be in the habit of dragging around that Harsh Inner Critic. But you also have a Kind Inner Career Coach who is standing by to celebrate your accomplishments and talents. Since your mind can't hold both competing messages at the same time, try giving your Kind Inner Career Coach the floor more and more. Eventually your Harsh Inner Critic will take a seat in the way back and offer constructive feedback only when it truly helps you.

Release your triggers. Your triggers aren't the boss of you. As you continue doing work on your emotional journey, you'll identify those things that send you into anxiety, judgment, grief or other emotional reactions that threaten to disempower you. Knowledge is power. You know them. You might even be able to see them coming. You're an adult now and you can rise above them.

They are also not the boss of the people you work with. You are the only person who is responsible for your emotional reactions. If your coworkers experience you as emotionally eggshell-delicate in your interactions with them, if you hear yourself say, "You have to understand, that reminds me of the feelings I had when ...", if your rules of engagement with others are more about avoiding drama than creating something wonderful, you're making them responsible for your triggers. Keeping you from getting upset is not their job. In her book, *Forgiving What You Can't Forget,* author Lysa Terkeurst writes, "Unhealed hurt often becomes unleashed hurt spewed out on others." There is no joy in Triggerville.

Triggers are serious business, and you might need professional mental help to address them. Why not take the steps you need to take to get those harmful reactions neutralized and behind you? Respect your need to heal those triggers, treat yourself gently, and then get on with life. There is no need to build a shrine to your wounded past.

Embrace the power of forgiveness in releasing you from past agony and pain. Forgiveness transforms anger and hurt into peace.

I encourage you to seek out ways of letting go of resentment, hurt, anger, hatred you may carry with you because of past experiences with damaged people. This can be done through support groups, like Adult Children of Alcoholics/Abuse, therapy, personal development seminars. When we keep strong negative emotions inside, they eat us up. They make us sick. They hurt us, not the person or persons who hurt us. Forgiveness does not mean you condone anything terrible that ever happened to you. Forgiveness enables you to be able to move forward with your life and begin to take steps to create more joy in your life.

Embrace your own Personal Board of Advisors by identifying people in your life (dead or alive, personally known to you or not) whom you admire, respect, and value that you want to have on your very own "support team". Imagine they are in a room together and are there to fully support and guide you whenever you need to tap into their collective wisdom. When you are feeling alone, sad, scared, or unsure, this is when you can connect with any one or all of your advisors, either in person or by imaging what you think they would say to you if you asked them for advice in handling a particular situation. For those you want to talk with in person, ask them if they would be willing to spare 30 minutes to offer their advice and guidance with you. People love to be sought after for advice. Start a conversation with someone you would like as an advisor by saying, "I greatly respect and admire you and I was wondering if you would be willing to share your thoughts, words of wisdom to a situation I am facing?" Most people are willing to do this, if you are respectful of their time. I also encourage you to share wins with your advisors if you try something they suggest and it works. This not only will enable more joy for you, it will create joy in their lives also!

Embrace your opportunity to contribute to the shared effort of creating a joyful workplace. Consider your colleagues, and remember that statistic that said that at least 67 percent of us have had at least one adverse childhood experience. You're surrounded by ASDPs, most of whom don't even know how their own past is causing them present pain. But now you do. It's your gift to bring a sense of safety and joy into the workplace, and create an emotional space where others can breathe easy. Maybe for the first time.

This is a joyful opportunity to bring healing to the world. Will you embrace it?

Part II
Bumper Car Moments in Action

Chapter 8
What is a Bumper Car Moment?

THE BEAUTY OF the workplace as a laboratory for healing is that we get opportunities daily to practice new ways of responding when we get triggered and have a strong emotional reaction to things that happen to us at work. It happens to all of us. We end up upset and likely experience unwanted stress, anxiety, and worry because an interaction with another went poorly, or completely off the rails. They present themselves all the time in our careers, and frankly in our lives. I call these Bumper Car Moments.

We can all benefit from becoming less triggered at work. When we get triggered, our self-limiting beliefs jump to the forefront of our minds, causing our inner critic to grab control of our thoughts, beliefs and behaviors during and after a negative interaction with another. Something was said or not said, and we take it to mean something negative about ourselves or our relationship with the other person. We personalize what has happened, even if it wasn't intended to be personal or is completely unrelated to us, but to the other person. When these moments occur, we can be instantly launched into reaction mode. And our coping mechanisms and survival strategies take over our thinking.

Some of us try proving ourselves to our bosses or explode in anger wanting to blame, judge or condemn the person who set us off. Some of us run ourselves ragged to be validated by someone else we think has the power to tell us we are "good enough." Instead, we end up feeling alone, frightened, hurt, furious, depressed, betrayed by the very people we must work with every day. Sometimes we even resign only to run into the same issues in different people in our next professional engagement or company.

How to Handle Any Bumper Car Moment

The Rapid Power Reclaim (RPR) is a proprietary process I've designed to help you during workplace Bumper Car Moments to intentionally act in ways consistent with your Conscious Healing Career Path.

- Our greatest breakthroughs come from our most difficult situations.
- Any time you feel stress, anxiety, and worry, recognize these are clues to a healing moment.
- You can step out of the doom and gloom dark places by instead learning how to leverage the workplace as your own laboratory for healing.
- Tough times can be miracles.
- Know that everything that happens is perfect for you at this time in your life.

When we get triggered in a moment of conflict with a colleague, we commonly have a strong negative emotional reaction that can last for days or even longer. This means we are probably currently on the Unconscious Wounded Career Path. Not a good place to be because it is full of stress, anxiety, and worry for us.

What we want our focus on is how to respond, not react, as our functioning professional adult self vs being derailed by the limiting beliefs, we carry about ourselves from our childhoods.

The RPR is a simple framework for handling any workplace conflict that is causing you to feel badly about yourself.

There are three steps:
Step 1: Create Choice
Step 2: Elevate Action
Step 3: Celebrate and Integrate

Step 1: Create Choice

- Master your triggers
  - We have no choices when we get lost in our triggers.
  - Pay attention to your physiological response to what is happening in the moment. Is your heart racing? Does your body get tight? Are you getting warm? Feel like an elephant is sitting on your chest?
  - Feeling the adrenalin beginning to rush in?
  - Do you feel a pit in your stomach?
  - Do you feel anxiety rushing through your veins?
  - A trigger feels like a scab has just been ripped off.
  - Your body tells you to "freeze, fight or flee."
- Pause
  - Tell yourself to stop!
  - Take deep breaths; slow down to let yourself refocus.
  - Talk to yourself as your Inner Adult.
  - Imagine yourself stepping outside of your body and watch yourself beginning to relax.
- Interpret
  - Beware that your childhood past reality may be colliding with your adult professional reality.
    - Are you noticing self-limiting beliefs popping up?
    - Are you noticing how you want to respond to what's happening?
    - Is it possible that you are instinctively responding now because it was how you responded when you were little?
    - Nicole LePera (the Holistic Psychologist and author of *How to Do the Work: Recognize Your Patterns, Heal From Your Past, and Create Yourself*) suggests you thank your ego for protecting you.

Step 2: Elevate Action

- Choose to step onto the Conscious Healing Career Path.
- Be kind to yourself.
  - Know that workplace conflict is natural and happens to everyone.
  - Drop your self-judgment.

- o   Understand how Bumper Car Moments often trigger old self-limiting beliefs making it feel like the moment is life or death. It is not.
- Say goodbye to the Unconscious Wounded Career Path by letting go of:
  - o   Staying stuck to the negative inner critic voice pulling you down.
  - o   Staying unconscious to what is happening.
- Apply body tools.
  - o   Release the feelings you are having about what is happening.
  - o   Write down how you are feeling in the moment of the Bumper Car Moment.
  - o   Let your body get in touch with the feeling as intensely as you can.
  - o   Find a place where you can either scream as loud as you can or scream into a pillow to express that emotion.
- Take conscious steps.
  - o   Realize that you are making assumptions and telling yourself stories about the other person in every Bumper Car Moment that are most likely to be wrong most of the time.
  - o   Practice going from Inner Critic to Inner Coach.
  - o   Remind yourself that there is no need to overreact to old triggers and self-limiting beliefs. Your childhood reality does not need to come crashing into your adult professional reality.
  - o   Build and get support from your Personal Board of Advisors when stuck.
- Be brave.
  - o   Courage isn't about having no fear. It's about stepping into the fear to get to the other side, trusting that the other side is better than staying where you are.
  - o   Every time we step outside our comfort zone, we grow.
- Set boundaries.
  - o   A key in elevating action is to set healthy boundaries.
  - o   A new way of thinking is that others must meet you where you are.
  - o   State what you need from others.
  - o   Energetically own your boundaries.

- Use assessment.
  - In relation to self
    - Be honest about yourself.
    - Be clear about your strengths and weaknesses. Leverage your strengths and mitigate your weaknesses. Good leaders are aware leaders.
    - When you are feeling badly about yourself, focus on what you are good at.
  - In relation to others
    - Become more conscious regarding what may be going on for the other person.
    - Become fixated on what's going on for them rather than consumed with what's going on for you.
    - Be adaptable to what's going on for others.
    - What is the most compassionate way you can interpret the situation rather than through your own self-limiting beliefs?
- Apply new tools.
  - Pay attention to whose property is playing out in the moment.
  - Practice emotionally detaching.
  - Practice compassion.
    - Toward self
    - Toward others

Step 3: Celebrate and Integrate

- Notice successful outcomes.
  - Write down your big and small wins.
- Define how you will acknowledge your wins.
  - Create a list in your 'phone notes' of all of the ways that make you feel happy.
  - Pull out the list when you have elevated your action and practice celebrating.
- Be intentional with how you talk about yourself.
  - "My pattern *was* people pleasing," not "my pattern *is* people pleasing."

- o   I am "learning how to" _____
- o   I'm finding creative ways to _____
- Integrate wins into your evolving identity.
    - o   Celebrating is critical to recalibrating the nervous system and replacing old patterns that no longer serve us by replacing them with new patterns.
    - o   Rewarding ourselves is a key piece of reprogramming and rewiring our brains.
    - o   Celebrating allows us to reprogram our nervous system—we are conditioning our body from being punished to now celebrating.
- Develop deeper self-acceptance.
    - o   See the lessons on self-acceptance in Chapter 6.
- Practice gratitude.
    - o   Each night write five things that you are grateful for that happened to you that day.
    - o   Begin appreciating small moments that are good.
- Find your joy.
    - o   Find small ways to feel joy at work.
    - o   Discover new ways to celebrate.
    - o   Schedule time to celebrate each week.
    - o   Find ways to create joy in other people's lives.

In the following sections, you will find some samples of workplace Bumper Car Moments. Each Bumper Car Moment described helps you to begin seeing the power of using workplace conflict to heal your past.

You may also be dealing with your own Bumper Car Moment right now. I encourage you to apply the Conscious Healing Career Path thinking in your own career, as you learn through these examples how to leverage workplace conflict to overcome your past.

Chapter 9
Bumper Car Moments You Might Run Into

How to Handle 360-Degree Feedback

IMAGINE YOURSELF IN the middle of this scenario. Literally. In the middle.

You're sitting in an uncomfortable, straight-backed, wooden chair in the center of a circle made up of your coworkers. Some of the people are your bosses, maybe bosses of your bosses. Most of them are your peers. And maybe a third of them are your direct reports. They're all staring at you. Some kindly. Some resentfully. Some, you suspect, might actually be angry.

Someone you don't know is walking from one to the next, having quiet conversations about you, writing notes down on a clipboard. Furtive glances are thrown your way. Did you just catch someone rolling their eyes?

And all you can do is simply sit there. You are allowed to say nothing on your own behalf until the interviewer has completed the round of conversations and has processed the results in the form of a report that will be presented to you as a *fait accompli*. This is your reputation set in stone. Anything you say can and will be used against you.

How does this feel in your imagination? If it feels familiar, that's probably because you've been the subject of a 360-degree feedback project.

Naturally, it doesn't happen exactly according to this scenario. It's done discreetly, privately, and confidentially. (You won't know who rolled their eyes.) But when you know that, at the current moment, you're the subject of a 360, you might as well be physically sitting in the center of harsh scrutiny. It feels glaring, exposed, and out of control for you.

This practice, which started out as a well-intentioned development tool, has lost its way in many companies. In a healthy culture, where it's administered by carefully chosen and trained professionals, the opportunity to understand how we are experienced by a wide selection of people we work with truly can help us improve our performance and optimize our careers. We can actually discover positive insights about how well we are respected and valued, as well as kindly shown where we can improve.

That was the original intent, at any rate. But not every company does it that way. In the realities of day-to-day pursuits of efficiencies, short-cuts, and cost savings, decisions on how to administer these reviews often bend to the cheapest, fastest, easiest options. The individuals running the interviews and sharing the results with the subjects may be untrained colleagues from the HR department—people whom you will run into later in the company cafeteria or hallway. The 360-degree instrument that the company chose might have been the cheapest on the market. And if the company has decided to spring for external consultants to conduct the survey, who are these people? What are their credentials and areas of expertise?

The prospects of facing a 360-degree feedback process is uncomfortable for everyone. But if you're an ASDP, you have likely already had the experience of being unfairly judged by people who don't necessarily have your best interests top on their agenda. You know what it's like to sit exposed in the glare of others who might draw their personal power by making you feel small or unworthy. You know what it's like to pay the price of other peoples' lies, fables, and secrets. You are so over being judged and talked about by people who would rather zero in on your flaws as a way of making themselves feel better about their own failings. You know how it feels to be talked about behind your back. And, based on your experiences from your past, you're emotionally braced for more of the same. You believe that anything you might say on your own behalf will just be perceived as being defensive, "uncoachable," "resistant to change." And those notations will also be added to your file.

All you want to do is go to work, be known and respected for the good job you do, and not be secretly scrutinized and talked about by others. The thoughts that cross your mind, based on your past experiences of being judged by untrustworthy people, might include:

- "Oh no, I'm being discovered for the imposter I've always known I was."

- "When all the notes are compiled and compared, my boss will see that I'm damaged goods."

- "The company is going to use the results as an excuse to fire me."

- "So-and-so resents me for getting that plum promotion. Now it's retaliation time."

- "I've worked so hard to have a perfect record and do everything just right. Now they're going to find something wrong and hold it over my head."

- "How can I trust anyone when I can't know who has been saying negative things about me?"

- "I can't stand the scrutiny and criticism. I'm afraid I'm going to get upset and lose my cool when I hear the results."

And yet, here you are, the subject of a company-imposed 360-degree feedback session. There's no getting around it. There are ways to navigate your feelings around it, though, in order to endure the process and emerge from it empowered with new knowledge and understanding.

1. Acknowledge your stressful anticipation and kindly reassure yourself that it's natural for anyone to worry about the process and the outcome. The fact that you're worried about the experience isn't an indication that you're damaged goods carrying anxieties from your past. It just means you're human. Like the rest of us.

2. Try to transform a significant portion of your anxiety into curiosity. You are no longer a powerless child on the receiving end of adults' angry stories about who they believe you are. You are an adult, in full command of your career and reputation. This experience might give you some insights that you will appreciate—for instance, how everyone really likes you and wishes you would be easier on yourself.

3. Check your own distorted thinking, according to the list of 10 distorted thoughts that David Burns describes in his book, *Feeling Good: The New Mood Therapy*. Your automatic negative beliefs might be kicking into gear and leading you down the path of imagining the worst as a protective mechanism.

4. Remember that everyone has strengths to feel proud of and areas of their lives to improve. Some criticisms might emerge from the final report. Welcome them as data points to consider improving. And don't dismiss the positive notes. Allow yourself to feel good and proud of the positive regard that is coming back from your team.

5. Consider the source. Bear in mind that the people giving you feedback have their own filters and agenda. Even some reports that sound negative or critical might have nothing to do with you. They regard you through the lens of their own pasts, triggers, expectations, feelings about their status in the workplace, or that time so long ago when your colleague misinterpreted your distracted glance as a specifically targeted scowl. And they haven't forgotten the hurt feelings that resulted.

6. Ask for clarification when presented with feedback you disagree with or don't understand. Words have different meanings to different people. Maybe someone felt the need to "contribute" a critical observation to balance out a glowing review. Or a benign word that was used by someone in your circle is especially triggering for you personally. Double-checking your interpretation of the ultimate report will help you extract the valuable insight that will support you in the improvements you choose to take on.

7. Bring the results to an outside counselor or coach to help you process them in a way that benefits you. You don't have to take this on by yourself.

It's said that there is no progress in life without a certain amount of suffering. As an ASDP, you've already done your fair share of suffering. As an adult you'll continue to be given these uncomfortable opportunities to "progress." Feedback is a fact of life—especially inside the workplace. As an adult, you can welcome the opportunities to gain insights that will serve you. And you have the right to take a pass on the unhelpful, abusive comments.

Unconscious Wounded Career Path Thinking: "If they're talking about me, they're saying bad things." "I hate the feeling of being ganged up on." "They're a bunch of losers anyway, jealous that I have so much more going for myself than they do." "I feel so vulnerable and exposed. I guess it's time to start looking for a new job."

Conscious Healing Career Path Thinking: "Everyone hates 360-degree feedback. It's normal to feel uncomfortable during this process." "I don't know who this facilitator is. But it can't be an easy job. I wonder what I can do to help make this an easy process for both of us?" "Everyone is going through this same, grueling review. Maybe we should all get together afterward for a fun off-site retreat to blow off steam and renew our bonds. I'll ask around to see who wants to join me in the planning."

Are You Afraid of Your Own Anger?

There's no getting around it: Anger is scary. I'm not talking about moderate-to-severe daily annoyances. I'm talking about white hot rage, the kind where control is balanced at the edge of a cliff—at the base of which lie crashing surf, rocks, bones, and the remnants of careers and reputations.

It's bad enough being on the receiving end of someone else's anger. But it's also horrifying to be the angry person yourself. It's like you have stepped out of your body and are watching this unfamiliar person who is wearing your clothes totally lose any semblance of sanity and civility. Who is that person? And what extreme behavior are you truly capable of?

When you're an ASDP, especially one who grew up in a household where someone in a position of power had severe anger issues, it's even more frightening. You know first-hand what emotional, mental, or physical violence is possible when someone gives into their anger. And you will do almost anything to avoid going there yourself. You deny. You stifle. You rationalize. You stuff. You ignore that building-up feeling. But then one day *boom*!

I'm about to tell a story about myself. And I have to admit right up front, this isn't an easy one to tell. Years after it happened, I'm still ashamed and regretful. My note of sincere apology has gone unanswered. And I can't say that I blame the person who got the blast of my pent-up rage, delivered in an afternoon that I wish I could take back. He has every reason and right to shut me out of his life and ignore my request for forgiveness. Even so, I do wish he'd give me one more chance to make amends.

The details have to be sketchy, to protect everyone involved. So I hope you'll understand. There's a piece of me that's hoping David (let's call him David, shall we?) will read this, recognize himself (even the sketch), and will see that I'm still as freshly regretful as I was the day "it" happened.

I had hired David for a project that he was, and remains, uniquely gifted for. The company, from the CEO on down, was thrilled with the results of his work and talent. And he was so good at the project that soon the project moved into its next phase of maturity, which required new capabilities and skills that were different than David's gifts. And, frankly, he wasn't interested or motivated in going in that fresh direction. But I was blind to that detail. In my loyalty to David, I expected that we could bring him along into the next phase and it would be a natural flow of excellent performance. I thought he would welcome the opportunity to grow the ability that would keep him centrally involved in the project's lifelong journey. And I was wrong.

He started showing signs of disinterest. He wouldn't show up at meetings. He didn't deliver on assignments, and he belittled the need for the deliverables I was requesting. In addition to the frustration I was feeling that the essentials were not being taken care of, I was beginning to feel personally betrayed. Colleagues started to take me aside and warn me that he was taking advantage of me.

Resentment began building up inside me. Then resentment turned into the glimmerings of anger, which culminated behind a full-on rage, closed-door meeting. And then he got angry. And then I got even angrier. The meeting instantly took on the stuff of epic legends. Word traveled fast. And before too long, it seemed that everyone knew about the confrontation.

I had invested my entire life and career in becoming the high-achieving, perfect-performing, people pleaser. So I had zero skills in identifying this strange emotion called *anger*, and learning to control it while it was still manageable from the executive function of my brain. All I knew about anger was that when my father unleashed it on me as a little girl, I was afraid I would die. And whenever someone was mad at me as an adult, it truly felt like my life was at stake. My big coping skill was to avoid anger altogether.

No one likes being angry, right? When you're an ASDP, the experience is even worse. Anger is experienced as a life-threatening event. It feels as if the person who is angry with you can obliterate you with one explosive episode of rage. If you're the one who is angry, you risk first exposing yourself for not being perfect. Maybe out of control. Maybe a little insane. So you stuff it deep down inside. And then it feels like you might self-combust into a small little heap of white ash.

So, yeah, I was afraid of my own anger. And in all my years of avoiding that extreme emotion, I simply didn't have the experience of handling my anger while growing up when the stakes weren't as high as they came to be when I became a corporate executive. And so, naturally, I didn't have the skills to manage the energy behind my scary, negative emotion. I didn't even know what to name it. It all just came flying out of me.

When you're feeling this upsetting emotion that you might later identify as anger, it might initially show up as stress, anxiety or worry. You're feeling the stress of not having your needs met—or objective-critical performance requirements fulfilled by your colleagues. You're worried about the outcome that will result from the performance failure. "Might I lose my job (yes, we are great at catastrophizing)?" You're worried that you don't have the skills or resources to efficiently address this issue as the team member who is responsible for the project's success. And anxiety shows up in the form of vague ghosts of your childhood past where you were made to feel small, helpless, defenseless, and even at risk of your very survival because the person responsible for making sure your childhood needs were met was out of control with rage.

When you're experiencing stress, anxiety, and worry, you are overtaken by emotions that are too large for your inner ASDP self. Your inner child wants to grab your inner adult by the hand and run and hide. But this is the time for your inner adult to take over with calm and compassion, reassuring yourself that you've got what it takes to handle this upsetting situation. These are the moments when our two realities collide—our childhood reality and our adult professional reality.

Settle **yourself down.** When you're feeling stress, anxiety, worry, take time out to truly feel what you're feeling and name it. Is there a trigger kicking in that you can spot because of the emotional work that you've already done? Might you be over-responding in the moment because you have been triggered and you immediately go into automatic pilot mode of fight, flight, or freeze? The settling phase is not about taking action or being right or wrong. It's just removing yourself emotionally from the situation and taking a calm look at the situation from a detached perspective.

Become *aware* of why the situation is particularly upsetting to you. Once you've given yourself the chance to review the situation and why it's triggering you emotionally, you'll likely see that there is some aspect of the past that's colliding with your present—your own personal, internal Bumper Car Moment. Allow yourself to truly understand the connection between what's happening to you now and what happened to you in the past. Don't dismiss or diminish the impact of this collision. And don't try to talk yourself out of it. It's there. It's affecting you. It's just the way it is. And you are okay. You are safe.

Acquire *knowledge* in how to handle the current situation. With this fresh understanding of how the conflict is affecting you emotionally, you're better equipped to rise above it, saying to yourself, "Oh, that's an emotional trigger from my past; it carries with it powerful meanings that have nothing to do with what's in front of me now. I am an adult now and can take steps to address the challenge in a way that protects myself." You know now that the conflict is a business challenge that can likely be addressed in the context of calm and timely communication. You know how to set guidelines and performance expectations inside the appropriate guardrails of your official role in the company. Ask a mentor to help you lay out an appropriate plan of action for addressing the situation with your colleague. Role-play the conversation and the many directions it might end up going, so you're equipped to calmly handle however it will play out.

When I think about how badly I handled the situation with David, I still cringe. I actively wish today that we were still working together. I greatly respect him and his expertise. If it remains his choice to hold that horrible day against me for the rest of our respective careers, I'm sorry about that. But that's still his choice.

As for me, am I still afraid of my own anger? Maybe a little bit. But not as much as I used to be. Thanks to what I'm learning in the workplace, I discover every day that it truly is a lab filled with gifts. The gift in this case is that I know how it feels to be afraid of untapped, unexplored rage. And now I can support my colleagues in identifying and growing beyond their fears to be the fully actualized adults that they deserve to be.

Unconscious Wounded Career Path Thinking: "This person is doing this thing that makes me mad because he knows he can get away with it. He doesn't respect me. He doesn't appreciate all the things I have done for him." "I can read his mind, and I know why he's behaving in this way that makes me so mad. And that makes me even madder." "I'm afraid of anger. It reminds me of my father. It's best that I just not say anything and the whole thing will blow over soon." "Expressing any level of anger is unprofessional, and I'll lose all respect from my colleagues." "Being angry will hurt my career."

Conscious Healing Career Path Thinking: "I'm confused by this person's behavior. It's making me angry, but I don't have to give in to that emotion. I can set it aside long enough to calmly ask for clarification and understanding from his point of view." "I have resources and actions I can take to mentally and emotionally prepare for this difficult conversation. I can speak with my mentor and/or take a walk to clear my head and calm my nerves before my meeting." "I'll first focus on understanding his point of view before expressing my concerns or even displeasure. Maybe there's something I'm not seeing that will help me feel better about the situation." "Okay, so I got angry. It happens. We're all human. If I need to apologize, I will. I can do that and retain my professional dignity."

How to Deal With An Angry, Perfectionistic, Controlling Boss

Wouldn't it be nice if everyone was on the same healing and recovery journey you are? As an ASDP, you likely grew up believing that you're alone in your suffering, lack of confidence, feelings of unworthiness, that sense of being irreparably damaged goods with a past that must be kept hidden. You might have also believed that once you were all grown up, you could leave your nightmarish beginnings, start life fresh, maybe even find a job with happy, normal people. People who will show you what it's like to be treated kindly, respectfully, collegially.

But then you start your working life, and you discover that you're surrounded by people who are on their own journeys to self-acceptance, peace of mind, and that feeling of belonging in a safe environment. You also discover that even your bosses can carry demons with them.

There are hundreds of thousands—if not millions—of bosses out there whose behavior makes their direct reports' lives miserable. They're controlling. They're suffering some kind of deep-seated shame, which they cover up by keeping others at a distance through an explosive temperament. They're perfectionistic and demanding beyond reason. They speak disrespectfully to their staff. They lie. They're jealous or competitive with the people who work for them. They're work-a-holics as a way to avoid intimacy in their private lives—consequently they expect their teams to be available during the weekends and evenings too, or are perfectionists also on a path to constantly prove themselves. Some inexplicably delight in getting the upper hand with their employees by setting them up for humiliating and debilitating "gotcha" moments in front of their team members.

Their behaviors show up in so many different ways. But the impact on you is the same: You're made to believe that nothing is ever good enough, no job completed to the point where you can take a breather before getting started on the next task. You're always on the edge, braced for the next explosion. You feel small, defenseless, your confidence stripped away to reveal the fact that you're damaged goods after all. You feel like a prisoner, trapped in an inescapable prison of this person's unpredictable wrath. You ache in sympathy for your colleague who is currently the recipient of your boss's rage. And you know that it's just a matter of time before your own number is up, and that it's your turn. You are thrown back to your childhood again, feeling small, helpless, afraid.

Wait a minute! That wasn't the way it was supposed to happen! This is exactly the scenario that you dreamed of escaping all those years ago. But instead, here you are again.

Having a powerful role is no guarantee or indicator that peace of mind reigns in the hearts and heads of people who are bosses over others. I've seen evidence in haunted behaviors throughout my career up and down the ranks of companies I've worked for. We have all had bosses who impose their anxieties on their team, making their staff worry about the same things they obsessed about—things they had no control over. We all have known colleagues who had a manager completely lose their cool, to the extreme of yelling, swearing, screaming and maybe even throwing things. There are also bosses who experience some counterproductive sense of satisfaction whenever they are able to one-up their employees in front of others.

This kind of behavior from your bosses would naturally affect anyone at work. If you're an ASDP with a past of trying to thrive under the heavy pressure of a debilitating parent or guardian, abusive bosses can put you into a time machine and send you right back into your childhood. As far as everyone else in the room is concerned, you're still the capable professional with a well-earned track record of success. But I see you. I can see that for just a few moments there, you're a child clomping around playing dress up in adult work clothes. My heart goes out to you.

Your boss is in pain. That's plain to see. But it's not your job to fix it. You are not a mind reader. You're not likely to be a therapist, hypnotist, spiritual healer, or whatever special skill set your boss needs to relieve her or his suffering. That's not your role. Your role is to take care of yourself. And to do your job.

So the question is: How do we minimize the amount of time we're stuck feeling small, unappreciated, judged, criticized, undervalued, braced for the emotional attack that comes from being the Pawn of the Hour, in service of scratching your boss's itchy need to be mean? You can be your own hero when you come face-to-face with this behavior. You just need to know what to do.

- **At every specific incident, step outside your emotional reaction and try to observe in an uninvolved way what's going on, and why it's triggering you so.** The insight won't cure the moment, but it will defang it by helping you arrive at a level of equanimity that will allow you to take the next steps mindfully.

- **Double-check your assumptions that you attach to the episode.** Are you the only one your boss treats this way? Sit back and watch how others interact with your boss. You may discover that you're not the only one who gets the abusive treatment. This revelation will help you keep everything in a healthier perspective.

- **Determine what is your boss's "property" and what is your "property."** What are your boss's issues that have nothing to do with you, but that have unfortunately spilled into your experience of your work? And what are the elements of the conflict that you are responsible for, and that you can take action to mitigate in some way?

- **Determine what this behavior means to you personally.** Do you feel like you've just regressed to the preschool version of you? Does it fill you with rage that alarms you in its ferociousness? What does it make you afraid of? These are valuable insights to bring to your therapist for further exploration. In this way, your boss may be serving as an emotional gift. That doesn't mean your boss is off the hook for his or her own behavior, though.

- **Identify the worst-case scenario that is a possible outcome of your boss's abusive behavior.** And prepare for it. If you're feeling like you might get fired without notice, start laying away additional cash to see you through a period of income insecurity. Cut back on unnecessary expenses and luxuries until you feel as though you're on solid ground again. Make sure you are owning your part in the relationship. Are there things you need to do to uphold your end in the relationship to be more effective? If you don't address areas you need to improve, you will resign and sadly find yourself right back with a boss or colleague with a similar set of issues. If there are things you need to do in the relationship to improve your performance, commit to do that. Once you are sure you have done what you need to in the relationship. Update your resume. Answer recruiters' phone calls, even if they're networking with you to search for someone else. They won't forget you when they receive an order for someone just like you. Expand your professional network at every opportunity. Go to meetings, update your LinkedIn page. Support others in their quests for accomplishment. You will be forging bonds with people who will be so glad to help you should worse come to worst.

- **Escalate your conflict to your boss's boss or HR, if necessary.**

- **If you're feeling abused to the point where you feel powerless, leave the situation.** Maybe it's just a meeting where your boss has singled you out for particularly disrespectful treatment. Or maybe you've discovered that over time your boss's treatment of you has eroded your self-confidence and capacity for peace of mind at home. Leave the room if you can, even if it's just for 10 minutes to take a breather and then return to the conflict. Leave your job, if you must. Take care of yourself every step of the way.

Be as compassionate as you feel that you can afford to be. You may be in the position of being able to help your boss through modeling or mentoring in a way that's appropriate to your role and reporting relationship. Be the "safe" place for your boss to land—without compromising your own interests—and you may find yourself able to take your own healing to the next level by paying it forward. And up.

Unconscious Wounded Career Path Thinking: "When my boss unleashes on me like this, I am powerless to defend myself. I go numb and silent for fear that speaking up for myself will only make matters worse." "This is the only job I can find; I should be grateful that I'm employed at all and just suck it up." "It's unrealistic to expect people to behave kindly and respectfully—at least toward me." "If I was a more perfect employee, this kind of thing would never happen to me. It doesn't happen to anyone else."

Conscious Healing Career Path Thinking: "I may have made a mistake, but this extreme rage that my boss is expressing has nothing to do with me." "I recognize these helpless reactions that this anger is triggering in me. But they are from my past and I am no longer a helpless, defenseless child. I'm an adult and I am empowered to take action to take care of myself." "My boss is responsible for treating me with appropriate, professional respect. I am responsible for my triggers." "I am a valuable employee." "If there are things I need to do in the relationship to improve my performance, I commit to do that." "I can take action to remove myself from an untenable, abusive relationship with this boss—either with a different department in this company, or I can change companies entirely." "There are many companies out there that are committed to emotionally healthy cultures. They will be glad to have me."

When You're the One Who Must Correct an Employee

When we imagine a scenario where someone is being criticized, we naturally picture ourselves as the recipient of the criticism. It really doesn't matter how skilled the other person is in giving us the criticism. None of us are especially skilled at receiving it. And we keep seeing ourselves getting smaller and smaller, while the other person looms larger and larger, as the conversation wears on.

But as you advance in your own career to the point where you're managing the performance of others, you're going to be the one doing the assessing, judging and criticizing. And you may be surprised to discover that this is an agonizing position to be in as well. This is part of your job as a leader. You know intellectually that you're actually helping your direct report improve performance. You're probably doing that person—someone you sincerely value and care about—a career-saving favor. You know the company is counting on you to keep standards high. You know that it's just a matter of focusing on the performance issue that's causing the problem. But you're still dreading the meeting terribly.

All things could go horribly wrong. One or both of you could lose emotional control. The whole conversation could blow up out of proportion to the simple topic of a performance improvement request. In your own emotional insecurity, you could lose your focus and give your employee confusing feedback, unintentionally setting that person up for future failure. All your hard work and professional development to become the highly engaging leader you want to be can explode in your face with one disruptive meeting. Trust in your department destroyed, as word gets out. You lose precious, impossible-to-replace talent. You could lose your own job. At the very least, you could find yourself in front of your own boss, hearing some extremely difficult words criticizing your own performance.

All the skills necessary to be an inspiring leader who ignites quality performance in everyone don't come naturally to most of us. We need specific training, coaching and support as we grow into these new phases of our own careers. This is especially true for ASDPs, whose early role models in criticism and behavior correction might have been parents who themselves didn't know how to kindly correct their direct reports—in this case, you, as a child. Their own parents probably didn't know how to kindly correct their behaviors. As a result, when they tried to guide you, they intentionally—or unintentionally—shamed you, making you feel as if you were *a bad kid*, not just a kid who did a bad thing. You are only the latest generation to have missed the lessons on how to correct someone's behavior while making them feel positive about themselves and supported. The difference here is that you know it. And you don't want to do to your direct reports what your parents did to you.

This process of replacing old punishing behaviors from your parents' example with inspiring leadership skills is not a DIY project. Too many careers and objectives are at stake. If criticizing others in the appropriate context of your role is an area that challenges you specifically and repeatedly, seek out the support of a training program, mentor or executive coach to give the essential (and learnable) skills that will serve both you and your team to manifest the performance standards that everyone wants.

As much as you might be focused on mastering the art of correcting, leading, and inspiring your team members to perform at their highest levels, this is also a healing opportunity for you as well. You are building your own personal narrative proving that leadership doesn't have to be a frightening, punishing experience. Being an inspiring, high-performing leader—even one with rigorous, exacting, strict standards—is a learnable skill that builds up your own personal history of kindness, positivity, and quality.

Look back at your earliest role models in criticism and behavior correction. What did you learn from the way they made you feel when correcting you? Did they make you feel that all you needed to understand was just how to improve this isolated issue? Or did they make you feel as though you were fundamentally bad and unworthy of their love or loyalty? Imagine how you felt back then when they were correcting you. Are you worried that you might make your direct reports feel the same way?

Focus only on the performance issue at hand. Depending on what role modeling you had while growing up, you might be tempted to read your employee's mind, or unconsciously assign greater meaning to the nature of the performance issue that needs to be corrected. You will be able to tell that you're doing this if you find yourself thinking or saying out loud, "If you _____then you would _____." For instance: "If you really cared about this company, then you would come in on time." Or, "Your repeated pattern of delivering work half-completed tells me that you really don't care about customer satisfaction."

As an ASDP you likely have relied on mind-reading from your earliest years as a survival or coping mechanism. And harshly judging parents likely used mind-reading as a controlling mechanism against you. So mind-reading might feel automatic, second-nature to you. You might not even know you're doing it. But in the complex, adult life of the workplace, you're likely to be wrong anyway. As much as you depended on this skill when you were a child to determine whether your parents or guardians were in unsafe moods that might ultimately endanger you, that sixth sense might not serve your best interests at work now that you're an adult. While we tend to appreciate empathic colleagues who make us feel safe, known, and accepted for who we are, we perceive mind-reading colleagues as invasive, judging, moralistic. And very unsafe.

Establish a partnership rapport with your direct report so that your mutual focus is on improving outcomes—ideally in measurable, identifiable ways. As a direct report's manager, your role is to inspire quality performance that can be measured in some way. Collaborate with your team member to identify goals and objectives for performance improvement that you both can readily measure and acknowledge. Find out what that person needs from you to help achieve those improvement goals.

Be emotionally safe. You may not be the only ASDP in the room. Yes, it's inappropriate for you to read your employee's mind, as we've already discussed. But it's entirely likely that your employee is trying to sustain dignity and composure during this high-stakes conversation, rising above emotional turmoil. Keep your demeanor calm, curious, kind, and collaborative. You are the leader. As much as it's up to you to create an environment where everyone in your team can feel safe as they focus on working together toward mutual goals, it's also in your power to keep this specific, difficult, encounter safe and focused. Even if your employee tries to emotionally hijack the meeting, you're still the leader. And you can control the climate of the conversation.

Give yourself what you need to create the encounter that gets the results you desire. If you grew up with judging, negative, moralistic, competitive or unpredictable role models who caused you to believe that corrective conversations are naturally high-stress and frightening, acknowledge that the right teachers can show you a better way through role modeling and role playing. Find a compassionate counselor or coach with a track record of inspiring confidence in high-performing teams. And ask that person to help you learn and build a skill set that helps you get the same results.

Unconscious Wounded Career Path Thinking: "I can't seem to be able to lead my team without hurting their feelings or offending them in some way. I'm just not cut out to be a leader." "If my people can't cut it on my team, they can just find another team, or better yet, another company to work for." "I'm not going to be one of those namby pamby managers. They work for me. I don't work for them."

Conscious Healing Career Path Thinking: "This is a skill set I need to acquire. It's a good thing that it's learnable." "It's a good thing that it's teachable, too. If I approach this challenge with openness and willingness to learn, I can demonstrate to my team through my example that the learning never stops." "I wasn't corrected in a helpful way while I was growing up. But I can take these skills I'm learning at work home with me and show my children how to do it right. And future generations will learn this valuable skill that will continue to inspire children coming up behind them. My job is helping me touch the future in ways I never dreamed."

When People Try to Give You Boundary Busting Advice

One of the fundamental responsibilities of parents (human and otherwise) is to teach their children how to thrive in life. In the savannah, among lions, it's called survival. In human society, it's called success.

But when you're an Adult Survivor of a Damaged Past (ASDP), you likely learned success and survival secrets from parents and other influential adults who were from damaged pasts themselves. Some of their advice was probably faulty, at least in some areas. So you grew up with some flawed ideas about being an adult that you are now discovering might be counter-productive to your own success. Now that you're an adult, you welcome other people's advice and feedback to replace some of the dysfunctional lessons you received as a child.

The healthier we become as we build a life of our own, the more receptive we are for healthier advice on how we can fulfill our own potential for career performance, success, and happiness. As we seek out new opinions and insights, we eventually find that we have to learn yet another new skill—how to be open to other people's opinions, while keeping our boundaries intact.

Why? Some people subconsciously—or even consciously—conclude that if we are asking them for their advice, feedback, opinions, they get to boss us around in any and all other aspects of our lives. The price of their wisdom, they believe, is our complete, abject obedience. And before we know it, we find ourselves in another relationship where we are under the control of someone else. Not everyone is going to be like this, but you will run into this dynamic at least once. And it can be confusing, disappointing, and, in some cases, downright infuriating.

The giving and taking of advice can be a tricky thing—a delicate dance where both partners are always seeking balance and solid footing. And now and then, a boundary gets stepped on. It happens to everyone, not just ASDPs.

If you're tired of experiencing various forms of this control cycle, you might be open to this advice:

Ask yourself, "Whose property is this?" If any form of advice from anyone—no matter how respectfully offered—ruffles your feathers, the problem might be the subconscious meaning you attach to the experience of being given advice. This experience may invoke an emotional trigger. If you grew up in a childhood where an influential adult delivered life lessons in such a way that you were made to feel bad, unworthy, or stupid, today you might have a strong negative reaction to a suggestion as benign as, "Hey, there's a parking spot right over there."

Knowledge is power, and now you have the power to neutralize this reaction. Maybe through therapy. Maybe through mindfulness practice. Maybe just practicing the conscious habit of saying to yourself, "Oh hello, Gut Reaction From the Past. This has nothing to do with the moment at hand. Thanks for your input, but I've got this now."

Ask yourself: Do I feel that I have the freedom to say, "No, thanks" to the boundary buster? We all have the freedom to say, "No thanks," to any unwanted advice. The question here is whether you feel you have the freedom to say no without suffering some emotional punishment?

You've done your honest gut check, and, yup, you've correctly concluded that it's the other person's property. Okay. How bad is it? How bad is it likely to become? Under the best of circumstances, you can say to the other person exactly what you might say to yourself. "Thanks for your input, but I've got this now." And then the two of you move on to focus on something else.

Under the worst of circumstances, you might have to call the relationship to an end. You will know that time has probably come when your advisor repeatedly tries to make you feel bad, stupid, or crazy (or even disobedient) for reserving the right to make up your own mind for the final decision.

Otherwise, assume the boundary buster means well. Most people really do mean well. They want the best for you, and they can see where their insight or experience might support you in making a wise choice. They respect the fact that it's up to you to decide whether or not to take their input.

Still, they have a clunky way of offering suggestions. Maybe they forget to ask for permission to weigh in with their opinion, and they just deliver it on your head like dropping heavy cargo on a dock. Or their advice is just plain wrong for you. Or you welcome their advice on one particular subject, but that subject only. And they forget that.

You like and care about them as true friends, despite this annoying trait (hey, who's perfect?). You don't want to hurt their feelings. "Thanks for your input, but I've got this," spoken gently should send them the signal to back off. To soften the sting of embarrassment or rejection, you might quickly change the subject back to a topic that's really their special expertise and ask them for their thoughts on that. This sends them the reassuring signal that you value and respect them and their Zone of Genius.

Use your work-related advisors exclusively for work-related mentoring needs. Ask your personal friends for advice on personal matters. You're wise to reserve your professional questions and uncertainties for mentors who have achieved their own success in specifically those areas. On the other hand, you may have personal friends with great furniture-arranging skills. But if they're consistently struggling financially, they're not the ones to talk with about salary negotiations.

Don't burden your professional mentors with your personal problems. Likewise, they don't need to hear about your ASDP past to give you great advice on how to perform at your best at work. You will be left feeling over-exposed in the workplace, where you want to be respected as competent. Not only are you signaling that your own boundaries are porous, but you're also invading theirs.

The giving and taking of advice can be a tricky thing—a delicate dance where both partners are always seeking balance and solid footing. And now and then, a boundary gets stepped on. It happens to everyone, not just ASDPs.

Just remember, you're not alone in this feeling. That's my last piece of advice for you here. I hope you'll take it. But it's okay if you don't.

Unconscious Wounded Career Path Thinking: "Everyone knows better than I do how to live happy, flourishing, joyful life." "They grew up normal while I grew up nuts. They are wiser than I am. Every time." "If I don't listen patiently and follow all their advice to the letter—even advice I didn't ask for—they'll get mad and won't be available to give me valuable advice when I really want it."

Conscious Healing Career Path Thinking: "Respectful friends and colleagues understand boundaries. I can tell them nicely that I value their advice and opinions for specific areas, in such a way that they'll feel valued and appreciated. Not offended." "Healthy friendships aren't controlling relationships. We all have the right to decide what we want to do after we have considered all the possible approaches." "If an advisor insists that I follow his or her advice and gets offended when I don't, that's a sign that I will probably want to seek out other advisors in the future." "I'm the only one who can live my life. I have confidence in the decisions that I make—with or without other people's advice."

How to Cope with Criticism

"Close the door and have a seat. We need to talk."

How does it feel when you read these words? I'm thinking your stom-ach might have just fallen to your knees in dreadful anticipation—even if it's just in your imagination. I'm also pretty sure you didn't go in the direc-tion of planning a team celebration party. No. You went to, "Uh oh, I'm in trouble." That imaginary seat that you were just invited to take is the hot seat. And you know you're going to be rattled to the core, once you're al-lowed to open that door again and escape the scene of the confrontation.

You're just about to be criticized. Naturally, no one likes criticism. But for you, maybe it holds an extra powerful sting. As an ASDP—maybe one who grew up with an unpredictable, punishing adult in the household, someone who liked to control you by keeping you on high alert, uncertain about your standing or even physical safety—criticism can feel like a direct attack on your sense of security and self-worth. And now that you're all grown up, someone who has a different kind of power over you is about to tell you that you're not perfect.

ASDPs commonly start their careers believing that perfect perfor-mance is their ticket for not only job security but also the ability to hide their darkest sets of self-doubts and debilitating memories. When their per-formance is criticized to be below expectations, their confidence and peace of mind plummet. If they're being blamed for something, they often feel as though they're about to be physically attacked. Even when they know they're physically safe, a voice deep down inside is screaming, "*Run!*" It's more than just an uncomfortable half hour during which everyone involved wishes they could be somewhere else. It can feel truly earth-shaking and devastating.

Now here *you* are. The time has come when some hard truth must be said to you in the privacy of a closed-door meeting. All sorts of thoughts run through your mind. Maybe one or more of these might sound familiar:

- "I thought my performance has been flawless. I really must be crazy to be so self-delusional. And now I've been found out."
- "I thought my coworkers all liked me. But clearly someone has been talking about me behind my back. I feel so betrayed, alone and angry. I can never trust anyone again. I can't even trust my own instincts and judgment again."
- "I'm about to lose my job. If I do, I'll lose my house."
- "This means they see that I have no value to the company."
- "I'm powerless to help myself."
- "I did something wrong. Therefore, I'm fundamentally wrong. Or crazy. Or bad."
- "Why do I feel like I'm 10 years old again?"
- "All the valuable contributions I have made are wiped out by this ding on my performance record."
- "Here I thought I was doing everything right. I'm doomed to getting everything wrong for the rest of my life."
- "Everybody knows. I'm so ashamed, embarrassed, humiliated to be the last to know."

Unless you have an ego of galvanized steel, criticism is just going to feel bad, no matter how you grew up. There's comfort in knowing that everyone feels upset when blindsided by unexpected criticism. So you're not "crazy" or "bad" for feeling any of the thoughts above.

But you can learn how to master your emotions and rise above the immediate urge to freeze, fight, or flee that comes with knowing that someone is about to drop some criticism on you. How you handle criticism is likely to be more about mindset and sense of proportion than your inherent value to the company or as a human being. Your feeling of upset and confusion is within your ability to control and prevent from doing further damage to your career, your reputation, your relationship with your manager. Here's how you can rise above the moment:

Don't believe everything you're thinking. Let's assume that the meeting is respectful. If you're feeling emotional whiplash or a flashback to the time you were a child and an enraged adult got in your face, try to mentally remind yourself that you're now an adult, seated in a safe office, hearing difficult words from someone who fundamentally respects you and values your contributions to the company. Keep telling yourself, "This is just an isolated moment in time. It feels bad but it has no greater impact on my life than this one thing that needs to be fixed."

Feel compassion for the person giving you the hard news. This is a classic Bumper Car Moment. Both of you are bringing your past realities to the conversation, and they're about to collide with your present realities. Especially if you disagree with the basic premise that the criticism is appropriate. You're not the only person in the room who would give anything to be somewhere—anywhere—else. The person giving you the criticism is probably worried about saying the wrong thing in the wrong way, unnecessarily upsetting you and making matters worse. If you can sustain your equanimity as the other person is clumsily doling out criticism, it's possible that you can transform this confrontation into a bonding experience for the two of you. The way you handle this can add trust to your relationship that you can both draw on in the future when you're shoulder-to-shoulder on a high-stakes project. When you walk back out of the office, you will want to hear the person exhale relief. And you'll want to be able to stand in line together in the company cafeteria in an authentic spirit of friendliness and mutual respect. You have the power to drive the conversation to that eventual outcome by sustaining your composure and professionalism. And actually, feeling a little sorry for the person sitting across the desk from you.

Focus on the performance, not the personal. If the criticism is a request for professional improvement, remind yourself that you're not being judged as a person—even if you do privately wrap up your self-identity with your professional reputation. Ask for insights into how the improved performance can be identified and measured. What action steps can you take to quickly make positive changes in this performance issue? Collaborate with the other person to agree to deadlines for evidence of improvements. Brainstorm together on how the improvement can be made visible. Pretend, if you must, that the performance improvement request is simply another department project. It's not an indictment on your right to exist—which is how your emotions might want to lead you if you gave them full rein to take over your mind.

If your manager is too emotional, self-conscious, or confused to part-ner with you on a rational approach to the conversation, take the lead in the conversation. You can be the one to describe what a successful improve-ment would look like. You can be the one in control.

Search for the emotional meaning that's hiding behind the noise of the upset. What meanings get triggered for you personally by this meeting? Does, in your eyes, the other person weirdly take on the persona of the abusive adult from your past because it feels like a surprise attack? Are you reacting like the defenseless, 10-year-old child you once were? If you're feeling betrayed because others' opinions of you influenced this criti-cism, does that remind you of adults who outnumbered you and made you feel ganged up on when you were small? Do you feel powerless to speak up on your own behalf because the adults from the past kept saying, "Children should be seen and not heard?"

Likewise, can you determine what meanings *your manager* might have attached to this performance issue that you're being criticized for? Are those meanings just, fair and wise? Or can you see a connection between this confrontation and some other kind of political situation that might be in play? Maybe you are being ganged up on as part of some kind of political power game that others have operationalized. If you keep a cool head, you will be able to more easily see what might be behind this uncomfortable conversation beyond any legitimate request for a performance improvement.

Give yourself time to calm down and see things clearly before taking any action or making any commitment that feels like a pressure tactic to you. On rare occasions, that "close the door and have a seat" meeting may conclude with a document you're expected to sign. Sign nothing under duress, under threat, or if you're being made to feel un-worthy in any way. Ask for a 24-hour breather so that you can consider the situation with a clear head, and ideally with the counseling of a trusted, but independent, colleague who believes in you. Or call your mentor, coach, or therapist for support as you sort out what might be the components of this challenge.

Have a Personal Board of Advisors already in place so that you have someone you can turn to for rational feedback and advice. Create this group as soon as you can. Don't wait until you're in a five-alarm career emergency and you need trusted people to talk to. You want a group of accomplished career men and women who can help you see upsetting situations through a rational perspective. They can introduce you to others who will expand your network in valuable ways. And they can help you see your own value.

Finally, remind yourself that everyone involved—including you—means well. If you grew up constantly braced for an attack without warning, it's understandable that you might habitually stay on high alert for unexpected—even unfair—attacks from someone who has power over your career. Survival mechanisms are deeply encoded into your mind. And without intentional effort to write over that coding with filling your life with positive experiences, it's natural to expect to live with hypervigilance and the need to anticipate worst-case scenarios wherever you turn. It's an exhausting way to live and work, isn't it?

The whole affair might be handled poorly, and you might have every reason to feel betrayed by one or more people you have to work with on a daily basis. But you have the power to set the tone of positivity, trust and safe, open communication where feedback is given and received with equanimity. You are no longer a victim. You are now a partner. The power is in your hands, no matter how everyone else behaves.

Unconscious Wounded Career Path Thinking: "I'll never get anything right." "It's only a matter of time before people discover the real me and I'll have to start looking for a new job." "Everyone in power positions let their power go to their heads and they start to lord it over everyone else." "I've known for days that he was mad at me about something. Why didn't he just come right out with it before now?" "She may be focusing on some isolated problem, but what she's really telling me is that I don't fit in here because I'm unlikeable. It doesn't take much to read between the lines."

Conscious Healing Career Path Thinking: "I can feel myself getting upset and insecure. But I have always trusted my boss's judgment and advice. I know he's only trying to help me." "This is just a moment in time. This conversation is only about this one isolated issue. It has nothing to do with my value as a human being." "See, he just mentioned that time when I helped the team meet that impossible deadline under budget. He hasn't forgotten how important I am to the organization." "My boss is looking really uncomfortable with this conversation. I wonder how I can make it easier for her."

When Other People Treat You Like An Emotional Dumping Ground

One of our common experiences as adult survivors of a damaged past (ASDPs) is that, when it comes to friendships and work relationships, we often find ourselves in the "helper" role. Which can be a familiar place for us to be in emotionally. We unconsciously bring that role into our adult lives, especially at work, because commonly our adult caretakers inappropriately put us in that role to support *them* while growing up. It can become a point of pride for us to be a source of emotional support for our coworkers, because we commonly grew up hearing, "You're so easy to talk to; nobody understands me like you do." Sound familiar?

Which is okay … until it stops being okay. When does it stop being okay? When you can't get your work done because there is always someone in your work area wanting to unload their worries or latest drama. Or when coworkers only seek you out for personal advice but they don't invite you to fun after-work get-togethers. Or when you go home emotionally drained and lonely because your hours have been soaked up by other people's negativity. Or they call you at home "just to talk." You've become your company's in-house social worker. Your colleagues aren't your work friends. They're your case files. I'm not talking about colleagues coming to you for professional advice, insights, and as a sounding board, especially if you are in a position for which this is a role requirement, like Human Resources.

"I feel like I've become the emotional pack mule for my coworkers," says an ASDP I know. "I'm the one they pile their problems on. I'm carrying around the weight of other people's issues. The load keeps getting heavier and heavier. My gift of being a good listener (which I am and I'm proud of it) is turning into a career liability. I can't concentrate on my own work. Someone else's emotional emergency always seems to be more important than the project in front of me. I don't know how to say 'no' to them without being mean and selfish."

This dynamic happens so gradually that often ASDPs don't even know it's costing them until it feels like it's too late to reverse the trend. We blame ourselves for letting it go on too long. And we don't know how to back out of the role of amateur therapist without putting relationships at risk. But one day it gets to the point where there's no denying the toll. And something must be done. Now.

My ASDP friend says, "It got to the point where I felt like my future was just draining away out of an open vein. And I even stopped caring about my own needs and interests because others were filling my head with their big troubles. I was being squeezed out of my own life. That's when I knew I had to save myself. But how?"

I'm not here to tell you that reversing course is going to be easy. You will probably inadvertently hurt some feelings. Maybe some people will take your new boundaries personally and react in an over-the-top kind of way. But here is some advice from my own personal journey that might help you feel supported as you take your first steps in the direction of being your own champion:

Know what's your "property" and what belongs to your coworkers. This is the foundation of everything else you do to reclaim your focus, time and emotional energy. When a coworker is taking up your time with personal or work problems, are you somehow absorbing the negative feelings that come from those problems? Do you find yourself demoralized and it's hard to return to a sense of positivity and equanimity around your day and projects? *Your* property is giving yourself what you need to focus on your responsibilities and career with confidence, creativity, and peace of mind. Your coworkers' problems and challenges are *their* property. Don't try to take their property away from them, even if it feels like you're helping them. If you want to start building up your understanding of the "property" concept, a great place to start is the May 13 entry in Melody Beattie's book, *The Language of Letting Go*. It's one of my favorite days of her year. I refer to it frequently.

Have scripted responses ready to deploy when people want to interrupt your day with their problems. "I'm under a deadline right now and need to stay focused on my work." "This sounds like a perfect concern to bring to your boss." "Did you know the company has an employee assistance program?" "I've got five minutes, what's up?" Or use humor: "This one is above my paygrade. I'd be practicing without a license if I advised you on this issue."

Use body language to signal your unavailability. My ASDP friend found that wearing noise-cancelling headphones and keeping her back to her cubicle opening sends the "do not disturb" message. Now with many of us working remotely due to Coronavirus, this could be that you set your computer schedule to "busy."

If you have to specifically express your new boundaries, focus only on needed behavior changes. "I need to work uninterrupted from 8:30 to noon." Or, "I know we've gotten into the habit of just dropping by (which could be in person or remotely), but I'm building a new work discipline to help me be more productive. Let's text each other first to be sure it's a good time for a chat." And then cut down on your availability for those chats.

Prepare for potential drama. If emotionally needy coworkers have latched onto you, they might resent your new ground rules. They may take them as a personal rejection or criticism. They may try to re-recruit you into the role of therapist by playing on your own emotional triggers. Stay calm, stay focused on your requested behavior changes.

Find non-coworkers to confide in. If you have workplace confidants yourself—people you turn to for personal, emotional support—find people outside of work to take on that role instead. You'll be demonstrating through your own actions that your boundaries are clear, consistent and easy to understand. They can't use the excuse, "But you're doing it too," to rationalize their intrusive behaviors on your workday.

Above all: Be your own hero, taking care of your own property. You may feel like you're being selfish to make yourself unavailable to coworkers who just need someone to talk to. And old voices in your head might try to shame you into dropping your early boundary-setting attempts. You can prevail.

You're not being selfish. You're doing your job. Unless your title is Company Chaplain or Company Therapist, every workplace minute you spend acting as your coworkers' chaplain or therapist is a minute you're not doing the job you're being paid to do.

Demonstrate to your colleagues through your actions what it looks like to set expectations and uphold high-performance behaviors. That actually might be the biggest favor you can do for them.

Unconscious Wounded Career Path Thinking: "I'm an empath and it makes me feel good about myself to be a caring ear for my coworkers. I can make up on my own work at night and on the weekend." "People come to me because I am the only one at work who will listen and care about them. Everyone else is too busy to take the time to help them feel supported." "I come home at night emotionally drained from other people's problems. I know there are healthier ways to relieve these negative feelings. After I finish this wine, I'll make a list of better things to do." "I can't turn away troubled people in pain. They need my emotional support. Putting myself and my job first would be just wrong."

Conscious Healing Career Path Thinking: "I'm being paid to do a job for this company. I owe it to my boss to keep focused on my workplace responsibilities." "I like the way it feels when people trust me with their sensitive, private concerns. But I don't like the way it feels to always be working during off-hours when everyone else is recharging themselves with their families. I owe it to myself to have a more balanced life." "It's emotionally safe to draw boundaries with these people and redirect them to others who are better equipped to help them anyway, unless, of course, they are coming to me in for professional advice, given my role in the company. If they react negatively, that's their problem, not mine."

Office Politics Will Always Be With Us

"Hey, Susan! Got a minute?"

I turned away from my computer screen, and smiled at Bruce, who had just popped his head in my office door. "Sure, what's up?"

"It's probably nothing, but I thought I should tell you that Carol has been telling the team that she has serious doubts about your judgment."

Well, that was a bit of unexpected intelligence. I liked Carol, and all this time I thought she liked me too. We'd been friends ever since we started with the company at the same time. And we routinely turned to each other for brainstorming career advice. We trusted and respected each other as we built our careers over the years. Maybe Bruce was mistaken; maybe he had misinterpreted something she had said. Maybe this was just a one-off bad moment for Carol.

"Thanks for the heads up, Bruce, I'll check it out," I said, and returned my focus to the spreadsheet on my screen. Before long, though, more people came to me confidentially to let me know that Carol had started some kind of whisper campaign against me. Different people, different teams. Same theme: My judgment was in question. I clearly couldn't ignore this anymore.

What had happened? I thought Carol was my friend. My trusted colleague. Did I say something to her to ruin our friendship? What have I done to bring this on? My go-to self-talk immediately sent me to, "This must be my fault. Why does this kind of thing always happen to me? What did I do to make her hate me? I would never in a million years do this to her. What is it about me that makes it okay for her to do this to me? I'm never going to trust anyone again."

After I cycled through my automatic, emotional catastrophic self-talk, I sat back and coolly considered the situation. Yes, Carol and I started our careers with the company at the same time, and at the same level. And we advanced together, pretty much keeping pace with one another as we climbed the ranks. We were "classmates," so to speak. And because we started out together at the lower level of the company, we had plenty of other classmates. As the years had gone by, our other classmates peeled away—some to new divisions, some to different business units, others to new careers with entirely different companies. That's how it goes. Carol and I were still in the same unit. Our opportunities for advancement became fewer and fewer as we climbed the ranks. This meant, of course, that we were increasingly competitive with each other.

I hadn't really paid any attention to this fact of organizational life. But she sure had. And now she was working it. The fact that I was blind to what was going on was her potential competitive advantage. And now I was grateful that a few of our teammates were kind enough to tell me what was going on behind my back.

It was still up to me to do something about it though. As much as I felt hurt and betrayed by her behavior, I still had my own career and reputation to protect. I had to set my emotions aside, and address this issue head on. So. I invited her to lunch.

Once we ordered and we were alone to chat, I got straight to the point.

"Carol, I have heard from multiple coworkers that you have expressed doubts about my judgment. I respect your opinion, so I'd like to know what you've seen that would cause you to feel this way."

Carol's reply was predictable—she denied everything. "That's not true," she said, "Who told you this?"

"It doesn't matter. I didn't want to believe it, because we've been friends for such a long time. But since I heard about this from multiple people, I thought it was only fair to you to check it out directly. So you don't have any issues with me, right? And if you did, you would come to me directly, right? No talking about each other behind our backs?"

Carol wordlessly nodded. And our salads arrived. No need to say anything more about it. I didn't need her confession. I just needed her to know that I knew. And the reports of her betrayal stopped.

Office politics. There's no avoiding them. Even in the best of company cultures, there is internal competition. Some people play more aggressively than others, engaging in ruthlessly self-serving behaviors, often at the expense of others, depending on their personal philosophies about what *winning* means. And how "all's fair in love and war." Even the company's best interests can take a direct hit when the political game is vicious enough.

For ASDPs, though, to be on the receiving/losing end of someone else's political strategies can feel like deep betrayal. Maybe our parents told us that outsiders can't be trusted, and episodes of office politics just prove them right. Maybe the experience of being victimized by someone else's selfish behavior triggers those old feelings of being helpless when up against confusion and lies. Maybe you feel that somehow you deserve the mistreatment. You're not sure why, but the voice in your head tells you, "This is what you get for letting your guard down." The debilitating messages your parents told you about your place in the world echo in the way you interpret your experiences in office politics.

It's tempting to stay on the Unconcious Wounded Career Path, with thoughts like, "Office politics means you have to fight dirty. That's not me. I'm just not a dog-eat-dog kind of person." Earlier in my career, I would overthink and worry about what others might think about me. "Did they believe her?" But office politics can also be an invitation to hop on the Conscious Healing Career Path because these episodes give you a chance to reframe your experience as a success story in an environment where competition is real but healthy, relationships are mainly collaborative and positive. And where you are totally equipped to take care of yourself.

Have a platform. In the political world, politicians develop a platform—beliefs, goals, values, a vision for the future that they stand by and that others can dependably rally around. Even though you might not be a professional politician, you can have a platform too. In the business world, it's often called *a personal brand.* Those attributes and qualities that people know you for. What are your values? What are your standards of excellence? In what ways can your colleagues trust you to protect their interests? I had demonstrated through my behaviors throughout the years that I was trustworthy with my colleagues' confidences and secrets. So they felt safe to tell me that Carol was actively hurting my reputation, and possibly career prospects.

Know your competitive position. I have always operated on a day-to-day basis that the quality of my work speaks for itself, and that my reputation for performance excellence is my best defense. This way I can concentrate on my work and not always look over my shoulder. But it's not enough to just focus on your work and pour all your energies into doing a good job. The more successful you are inside the organization, the more likely it is that someone wants to knock you off your career path and take your place. This is almost always the case. And it becomes even more so as you move up in your organization and opportunities at your level become fewer and fewer. Somebody is likely to want what you have. That's the law of the jungle. This doesn't mean that they're bad to want it, or that you're selfish to want to keep it. It just is. Know where you are in the hierarchy of advancement opportunities. And know who might be angling to take your place.

Develop alliances up, down, and laterally. Those people you have identified as possible competitors don't necessarily represent enemies. They may be people you can groom to, yes, one day replace you ... as *you* advance up the ranks. Positive relationships will protect you. People who admire, respect and believe in you will give you insights that you might miss in your day-to-day focus on your work responsibilities. Colleagues above you can mentor you not only in your everyday work and career challenges, but also during excruciatingly sensitive times when office politics threaten to overwhelm you. They can help you find stable, unemotional strategies for handling those experiences of betrayal.

Own the feedback if it's legitimate. If not, don't take it personally. When you hear feedback you don't like, it's still important to investigate it. Is there some truth to it that needs looking at? Take a look at ways you may need to modify your behavior to have different outcomes in the future. Then do so. If, though, after an honest self-assessment, the feedback does not "stick" to you, let it roll off your shoulders. When this happens, likely the feedback belongs to the other person and their unconscious past relationships.

Looking back, I don't think of Carol as an enemy, even though it felt like she actively set about to sabotage my career and betray our mutual trust. Her behavior had nothing to do with me personally. She was just looking out for Number One. And, to her credit, her own career has done very nicely in the years since our lunch date. I'm glad for her.

But looking back at particular moment in time, I mostly feel sorry for the person she was back then. She saw where we were on the corporate career ladder and looked at our shared situation through the lens of lack, rather than abundance. The beliefs she brought with her to her career made her believe that the dog-eat-dog approach was the way to get things done. Her behaviors really had nothing to do with me and what I was doing in my work.

What I do take personally, though, is the joy I have remembering those colleagues who cared enough about my well-being to take a personal risk in their own careers and tell me what I needed to know to protect myself. They remain my friends to this day, and I will always be grateful to them. That is the story I choose to focus on when I think about internal politics and personal power that comes from cultivating trusting relationships. Yes, each of us still looks out for Number One. But we also look out for each other.

Unconscious Wounded Career Path Thinking: "I am powerless when it comes to office politics." "My family was right when they told me to trust no one. Ever." "I will always be played for the sucker. That's my destiny." "No matter where I go, there always seems to be a 'kick me' sign on my back." "The rules of the game are always changing. I'm set up to fail from the get-go." "If I'm outsmarted, out-maneuvered, I get what I deserve." "The only way to win in the corporate world is to leave your ethics at the door." "If someone is saying negative things about me behind my back, will others believe them? Will it hurt me?"

Conscious Healing Career Path Thinking: "My focus is consistently on taking action and making decisions that benefit the company. My track record of loyal performance will be my best defense." "I'm so grateful that I have a team of loyal coworkers looking out for me, and that I can do the same for them." "There are plenty of opportunities to go around." "Who can I help develop now to be ready to take my place when I get my next promotion?" "Yes, that was a betrayal, and it hurt my feelings. But that person's behavior has nothing to do with me." "Some people just think of office politics as a winner-takes-all game. That doesn't have to be my style." "What can I take away from this experience that will help me strengthen the valuable relationships I have in place?"

Don't Be a Slave to Anyone's Triggers

We all have emotional buttons—those areas of sensitivity that, when touched, set our teeth on edge, make us bite our tongue before we say something that we can't take back, force us to count to 5 or 10 or 75 ... whatever it takes to make sure our response is measured and reasonable.

I'm not talking about those. What I'm talking about here are *triggers*—ignition points that, if we ASDPs aren't in total control of them, could derail our careers. What's the difference? Buttons keep us in the here and now. But triggers ... well, it's like they're one of those circus cannons, and we're the human cannonball. The trigger ignition sends us soaring high over the present moment and straight into our damaged past, often without us even being aware of it. If we don't know how to manage them, they put us at risk of damaging our present and our future at work. And ruining relationships.

One of my triggers has been being yelled at. Before I got on top of this trigger, whenever I was yelled at as an adult, I would go right back there to my defenseless childhood when my father raged at me. It was like I was falling down a dark well, getting smaller and smaller as I went, completely powerless. It was like emotional obliteration. There would suddenly be a pit in my stomach; my heart would start to beat fast (getting me all pumped up and ready to run—the classic fight or flight reaction). And I would immediately lock into stress, anxiety, and worry, which would freeze up my ability to offer creative solutions to whatever the problem might have been. Not an effective stress response for an executive in the C-Suite, or for any person at work for that matter.

The other day I asked my coauthor, Martha Finney, whose mother was an alcoholic, what one of her triggers might be. She said, "That moment when I hand in a finished project, and my client immediately asks me what the status is of an unfinished project. It makes my elbows get hot. In my family, the only source of selfhood was pride in accomplishment. So, whenever a boss or client takes my finished work and then asks me about work still in progress, it makes me feel like I'm back to nothing again, never ever making it above the zero line. Now, intellectually, I know that it's reasonable for someone to inquire about work in progress. But because of the meaning I've attached to the question, that question deeply demoralizes me."

Another ASDP says that she hates to hear the sound of her own name. The reason: Her mother was so neglectful and abusive that the only time she heard her name as a child was when her mother was loudly scolding her in a hateful way and telling her she was bad.

She says, "Today, I tense up even when I hear my name called at Starbucks. I know it's irrational. My best hope is that no one can see the fear in my eyes."

I know my reaction to being yelled at was irrational. Martha knows that clients have every reasonable right to respectfully ask the status of pending work. Our ASDP friend knows that the sound of her name is just that—the sound of her name. In a work setting, who doesn't hear their name now and then? Get asked the status of a project? Or even hear raised voices on rare occasion?

A Vast Array of Triggers at Our Fingertips

Likewise, consider the triggers you might be inadvertently firing off in your coworkers:

- Feeling out of control when someone else makes decisions that affect them without their input.
- Being accused of something that's untrue.
- Feeling disrespected or undervalued.
- Being interrupted.
- Being misunderstood.
- Being left out of an important meeting or valuable social event among colleagues.
- Being caught up in someone else's political agenda.

- Being told to back off an initiative that's personally and professionally important to them.

- Having their ideas overlooked—or worse, credited to someone else.

"Well, yeah," you might be thinking. "No one would like those feelings. And they happen all the time to all of us." Granted. But for some of us, our reaction is so over the top that we act out in such a way that we might as well throw a lit match on our career right then and there. You've probably witnessed a trigger in action and were left wondering, "What on earth just happened here?"

It's the *meaning* that ASDPs uniquely attach to those experiences—often unconsciously—that make them triggers. But we can take steps to defang those meanings so we can get on with our workdays without losing our sense of calm and stability.

Be the Master of Your Triggers

You don't have to have these triggered responses to ordinary events and annoyances that everyone has to deal with. There are things you can do to be the boss of those bossy emotional reactions. Remember you can practice the Rapid Power Reclaim, step one to help you become the master of your triggers.

Susan David, PhD, author of *Emotional Agility: Get Unstuck, Embrace Change, and Thrive in Work and Life*, tells us, "Emotions are just data points, not directives."

- **Resolve to not believe everything you think and feel.** Recognize that a triggered reaction is just your past reality colliding with your present one. The result is a combination that has very little to do with what's happening at the moment. And your colleagues are likely innocent bystanders.

- **Know what your triggers are.** List them. They might be one of the triggers I listed above. Or they might be something as seemingly benign as the sound of a coworker chewing ice or clicking a pen constantly. Or the smell of fishsticks in the break-room microwave. Don't judge the relative legitimacy of your triggers. Just write them down.

- **Identify the meaning you attach to each trigger that fires up your emotional reaction.** Does the trigger violate your sense of fairness? Make you feel obliterated? Worthless? Powerless? Does the trigger somehow validate your belief that everyone (by which I mean, everyone) is fundamentally selfish, irresponsible, mean, untrustworthy, unsafe? Does it make you want to run? Cry? Quit? Fire someone?

- **Recognize that your triggers are just artifacts from the past.** They are left over from the time when you needed survival mechanisms to cope with circumstances far beyond your childhood ability to control.

- **Select the ones that threaten your present-day effectiveness.** And gently dismiss the others, sincerely thanking them for the role they played in helping you become an adult.

- **Put a plan in place for neutralizing those triggers when they crop up.** Go for a walk. Get those endorphins pumping. Take a break to give yourself a gentle talking to in the restroom mirror. Even a few sips of fresh, cold water can disrupt the trigger.

- **Question your own beliefs attached to the meaning that is associated with the trigger.** For instance, are you really going to lose your job because your boss is yelling? Is the fact that you weren't invited to attend that golf outing really indicative of your peers' lack of respect for you? When your direct report blew off that important assignment, does that really mean that your request was unreasonable to the extreme?

- **Learn to apologize and accept apologies.** We're human, and we all lose our cool at times. That's the way it is. A sincere apology—either given or received—can wipe the slate clean and save an important relationship in your career.

Understanding Others' Triggers Will Help You Effectively Work With Them

It's first essential to acknowledge that only we are responsible for our feelings, reactions, and triggers. No one else. However, when we have the extremely valuable opportunity to understand what might be our colleagues' triggers, we can use that insight to boost our effectiveness with them.

For instance, remember how Martha's elbows get hot when she is asked the status of work in progress? Well, the flipside of that trigger is how much she values praise and acknowledgement. I make a point of sincerely expressing to her how much I appreciate our partnership in developing our *Healing at Work* material together. She has shared with me that appreciation helps her stay focused, motivated, respected, and inspired.

Likewise, Martha knows to ratchet back her energy when expressing to me her passionate opinions. She learned this way to communicate from her, let's just say, *emphatic* family of origin. For her, it's normal. For me, it can feel like yelling at times. And she knows that the force behind her enthusiasm—even when it's with my best interests in mind—can be counterproductive.

We don't change our behaviors to manipulate each other into doing things we wouldn't otherwise do. We have each others' best interests and our passion for *Healing at Work* always in the foreground. We just know how to use our knowledge of each other's sensitivities as a tool to get the best from each other. In a way that feels really good.

Workplace teams give us the opportunity to experience healthy growth and successful collaboration in an atmosphere of mutual respect, trust, and self-esteem. Isn't that ultimately what healing at work is all about?

Unconscious Wounded Career Path Thinking: "I am in danger all the time. The world is a frightening place and I'm not equipped to protect myself." "I have strong intuitive reactions to events, and I know that I'm right to react this way every time." "If I don't take extreme action to protect myself, no one will respect me." "No one else feels the way I do. I'm the only one who is vulnerable to triggers like this. I'm all alone in these vulnerable feelings." "I will do anything and everything to avoid these triggers, even if it means compromising my personal power or effectiveness on the job."

"Having triggers is a sickness. I have to hide them from everyone. There is no hope or help for me."

Conscious Healing Career Path Thinking: "Triggers are nothing to be ashamed of. ASDPs have them as a natural part of surviving a threatening childhood. And everyone—even non-ASDPs—have sensitive buttons that get pushed every now and then." "I don't have to be a victim of other people responding to their own triggers. I have what it takes to stand up for myself appropriately, calmly, and with dignity." "There is help available to me when I have to cope with triggers that are too powerful for me to handle alone. I can go to the company's employee assistance program, or find a coach or therapist who specialized in cognitive behavior therapy, to help me reframe the meanings behind my triggers."

Epilogue:
The Rest of Your Life is Yours

When suffering falls away, what is revealed is not a big blank, but a
natural sense of gratitude, good wishes for others, freedom, and ease.

Rick Hanson

AS WE WRAPPED up the research and writing of *Healing at Work* this Christmas season, we can't escape the fact that 2020 has been an unprecedented year in the world's history. The COVID crisis descended upon us all and changed everything about our lives. But even in the book's earliest days of development, way before COVID, Martha and I were each undergoing multiple life changes and challenges that are significant in the most ordinary of days: multiple cross-country moves; major job changes; global travel; a new marriage; surgery; relationship upheavals; etc. And that tells us that no one can say to Life, "Everything stop! People are healing here!" Emotional healing must run concurrent with everyday life.

The beauty of the workplace as a laboratory for healing is that we get opportunities daily to practice new ways of responding when we get triggered and have a strong emotional reaction to things that happen to us at work. It happens to all of us. We end up upset and likely experience unwanted stress, anxiety and worry because an interaction with another that went poorly, or completely off the rails. These Bumper Car Moments present themselves all the time in our careers, and frankly in our lives.

You get to decide if you stay stuck on this Unconscious Wounded Career Path—the path of suffering—or decide to step onto the Conscious Healing Career Path—the path of self-acceptance, growth, and joy.

You will experience an easier, more smooth professional existence once you understand that your ASDP childhood does not doom you to a life of struggle forever. You will realize you are not alone in your career experiences which have been influenced by your earliest beliefs about yourself, other people and the world.

My purpose in writing *Healing at Work* is to show you how your unconscious self is showing up with you each day in your career and is affecting you in countless negative ways. You have the right and deserve to take back the steering wheel of your career experience by stepping into your "functioning professional adult self" on the Conscious Healing Career Path. This is your higher self and the version of you who should be in the driver's seat as much as possible! And as you do this, you will become aware of your ability to make different, healthier present moment interpretations, decisions, and choices, which will absolutely influence how you feel about yourself in your professional world. You will also reduce the number of times you let other people's behaviors and words influence how you feel about yourself.

My wish for you is to take back your power to determine your worth and stop delegating it to others, assigning them the right to influence how you see and feel about yourself.

Healing is a never-ending process of growth. And there is never a sense of having arrived. However, there will come a time when you are able to turn around and extend the healing understandings to colleagues and family members who are inspired by you. The entire circle of your influence will feel and see the positive shifts you are making. As this happens, you play a role in a much bigger way. You might even be able to create a healthier organizational culture where you work. And as more people become aware of the Conscious Healing Career Path, companies will stand to make collectively healthier choices and decisions, have more positive work environments, and their impact on their people and ultimately society will be profound. Yes, you can teach others through your actions deeper levels of self-acceptance which will, in turn, create a more joyful world.

Each day at work, we face healing at work "pop quizzes" when Bumper Car Moments happen that challenge us to see if we are practicing the healing path or are still letting our pasts influence us. In some high stakes Bumper Car Moments, we are facing "final exams" if our unconscious choices and responses end an important professional relationship or end a career with a company and we decide to leave altogether.

I invite you to gently begin taking steps to live an awake Conscious Healing Career Path by practicing the lessons in *Healing at Work*. The gifts you receive over time will feel like opening a lifetime of treasure chests full of precious surprises. You will experience less time beating yourself up, stuck in the cloud of stress, anxiety, and worry, and more time celebrating your successes, setting healthier boundaries and agreements in relationship to work and colleagues, and making decisions coming from growth, not suffering. Ultimately, you discover deeper levels of self-acceptance. When this happens, you will have more joy at work and in life.

The choice is yours.

I hope you choose the Conscious Healing Career Path.

The rest of your life is yours.

Susan Schmitt Winchester
Oconomowoc, WI
Christmas, 2020

Dedication

TO MY SWEET sister Nancy, born on Easter morning 1965. She was an amazing spirit who lives on in my heart. Our shared childhood and the traumatic night she died are what inspired *Healing at Work*. Nancy was a light to all who knew her. She was wise beyond her years and cared deeply for those in her inner circle. Her entire essence was about taking care of and serving others. I have a feeling she is smiling down from heaven seeing how our story may help you.

To Charles, my Love and partner, who inspires and partners with me to make a difference for others. Charles and our marriage are a huge joy in my life!

To my sons Joe and Sam for the immense joy they also bring to my life every day with their quick wits, intelligent insights, laughter, questions, love and passion for life.

My Mom is my greatest role model. She is an amazing woman who lives her life to the fullest in service to others all day, every day. She taught me that all things are possible and that making the world a better place is key to a joyful life. She did all that she could to ensure my sister and I had a loving childhood. She is brave and bold. She taught me that if you set your mind to a goal, you will achieve it, with God's help.

Thank you to Jerry Schmitt, great dad to our sons, who supported my independence, including time to work on this book. I am grateful for our time together and our life role as co-parents to our sons.

And to each of you who showed up to learn about healing at work principles seeking a more enlightened and positive career experience. It is my greatest hope that you will find comfort, success and possibility for your own workplace experience by stepping onto the Conscious Healing Career Path.

Acknowledgements

MY GIFTED CO-AUTHOR, Martha Finney, was fundamentally instrumental to bringing this book to life. Without her, *Healing at Work* would not be. Martha took my original manuscript, *Dark Storms-Great Gifts,* which had been written over 13 years, and created a vision for it. She could see past my amateur writing efforts to the possibility of a powerful book that could teach readers how to use the workplace as a place for emotional healing. She conceptualized *Healing at Work* by seeing the power of integrating my challenging childhood experiences, my 30+ year corporate career in Human Resources, my Personal Board of Advisors' lessons, plus many stories of leaders and professionals from my own career.

I am grateful to Martha for her creative genius, guidance, advice, expertise, curiosity, divergent and conceptual thinking, vision and partnership. She opened many doors that will enable my work to go from "Success to Significance," which is Martha's tagline. Martha was instrumental in my own continued healing journey because of the insights I had about myself during our work together. We developed many of the lessons we share inside as we strived to find more clarity regarding how to truly use the workplace as a laboratory for healing. It has been an amazing and epic journey with Martha as my guide and partner.

Chiquita Jones was my super talented virtual assistant for a good part of the writing of the book. She has been the strong force behind and played a key role in the work we have done over the past year to build a community of professionals and executives who want to have careers with much less stress, anxiety and worry. With her expertise, I have built a following of thousands of people through social media. Her ability to stay calm in any situation and take care of countless complicated things, handle complex technology enabled services and manage many technology providers, and find talented virtual team members were all catalysts for the creation of the *Healing at Work* strategic platform. She always brought positivity and joy to every moment enabling Martha and me to bring this book and global community to life. She is a precious treasure in managing multiple aspects of a digital movement and business operation.

My Personal Board of Advisors

Healing at Work is a tribute and thank you to my personal board of advisors, without whom, I'd be still unconsciously on the wounded career path. Some I know and some I don't know. Some are alive, and others are not. Each play or played a key role on my professional and life journey. I highly recommend creating a support net of your own by intentionally surrounding yourself with people who make you better.

***

Sue Paige is love. Sue taught me what it feels like to have complete love with unconditional support with no judgment. She empowers people to lead more enriched, successful and fulfilled lives so our world is a better place for the children of today and for a thousand generations to come. I discovered my life purpose to teach self-acceptance to create a more joyful world in her Pathways to Successful Living Leadership seminar in 2003. This book is a manifestation of that purpose.

Ken Wright, leadership and organization expert and dear friend, was the first one to wake me up to how much perfectionism and people pleasing were affecting the quality of my professional and personal life. The lessons he taught me have been and continue to be fundamental to how I think about the workplace, leaders and Human Resources.

Keith Nosbusch is the boss of lifetime for whom I would take a bullet any day. He taught me about unconditional professional support, leadership and guidance. It was the privilege of a career to have worked with him for 9.5 years.

Gary Dickerson is a visionary and strategic relationship builder and my current boss. I have learned countless lessons about leadership, culture and myself serving as his HR leader.

Chris Lapak, formerly of Pathways, made me set agreements, kept me accountable and saved my life. He continues to hold me accountable to this day not to use alcohol to numb feelings of not being good enough. He was one of my first teachers to show me how people pleasing is a total waste of my time.

Nancy Lee is a wise mentor. She offers insights that challenge conventional human resources practices for far more powerful and fundamental concepts that drive leadership and organizational effectiveness. Her gentle guidance has enabled me to find new ways to make a difference for leaders, as well as myself.

Mara Swan, Tracy Keogh, Perry Stuckey and Kevin Cox are Chief HR Officers (CHRO) *extraordinaires*. Mara took me under her wing when I stepped into my first CHRO role in 2007. I called her many times for advice in navigating the complexities of being in the CHRO role. I learned many lessons from her that I use regularly. Tracy, my HR inspiration, is always willing to share her ideas, thoughts and advice. Whenever I am unsure what I should do as the HR leader of my employer, I imagine what Mara and Tracy would do and I emulate them. Perry has the gift of discernment and clarity. His wise counsel is priceless. Kevin is like a lighthouse in a stormy sea. His thoughtful leadership and compass to always do the right things for his companies inspire me. All three of these amazing leaders share their knowledge openly and willingly in their desire to support other CHROs.

Celinne Da Costa guided me to discover my "why" buried deep inside and clarify my life purpose: *To teach executives and professionals (from dysfunctional pasts) living unconscious careers to find greater self-acceptance, fulfillment and joy at work and in life.* Her process is powerful, highly intuitive, and life changing. She is masterful in teaching me how to overcome fears that get in the way of living a joyful life.

Gary Goberville was an HR and leadership role model and led me to Pathways to Successful Living by how he showed up every day. I learned more from him in the short 7 months I knew him than I did from many of my other HR bosses.

Dr. Elliott Jaques massively shaped my views of what levers to pull to enable more effective organizations and leaders—the most under-appreciated organization thought leader I think in the world.

***

A Special Thank You

Toni Lynn Chinoy, of Harlan Evans, taught me many leadership and organizational lessons through many of my own career and life Bumper Car Moments and supported me to help colleagues work through their career conflicts. Her executive coaching gets at fundamental "felt-shift" insights that help her clients, including me, reach new levels of performance and self-understanding.

Kathy-Sue V. has been my closest friend as we have known each other since we were three years old. She has been with me for a lifetime of ups and downs and is always there for me with kindness and support.

Kathleen Caya is by far the best equestrian trainer/rider and dear friend anyone could ever dream of. She guided me to believe in my capabilities to compete successfully—something I had been seeking since I was 10 years old.

Carolyn Rose is a consistent force of friendship, mentorship, and is a brilliant joy in my life. She is a role model for courage and always speaking her truth.

Big thank you to Becky, Jennifer C., Roberta, Barbara, Jennifer, Sandy, Anne, Cindy, Jessie, Shane, Kristin, Bahr, May, Sujeet, Bela, Craig, Rebekah, Matt, Sue, for your friendship, support, encouragement, and love.

I'm incredibly grateful for the amazing Kostis Pavlou, artist for our book cover bumper cars.

And a sincere thank you to Molly Fabiano for creating the entire look of *Healing at Work*, both the book and my website.

Finally, a special thank you to Jen and John Purcell for saying to me, "Say, I know this guy ..."

Leaders and Experts Who Made a Difference In My Life

Betty Alewine, Becky Bruns, Artie Byrd, Janet Langford Carrig, John Cohn, Bob Creviston, Jill Ebeling, Betsi English, Jill Edelen, Jack French, Kyle Gray, Allea Grummert, John Harper, Jake Jacobs, Barry Johnson, Laura King, Jim Larson, Chuck Mazza, John McCloud, Jeff Montie, Don Parfet, Jen Peck, Bill Proudman, John W. Quinn, Norm Smallwood, Mike Smith, Leigh Weinraub, Dave Ulrich, Mark Van Clieaf, Dr. Robert Young, The Applied Materials Executive and HR Leadership Teams, The Rockwell Automation Executive and HR Leadership Teams

One Final Acknowledgement

My dad, who died in 2002, gets a note of appreciation. I know my Dad did his best to be loving and giving father. And I know he had a difficult and damaged past too. As challenging as he was for me when I was growing up, I know deep in my heart that he loved me and wanted only the best for me. I can now see that he was a tremendous gift giver to me, and I am thankful he was my dad. I felt great pain for years of my life from the beliefs I took away about myself in my relationship with him, but in the end, he may have been the greatest teacher of learning that it is my job to approve of me and no one else's. While you read about some of the difficulties I experienced as a little girl and as an adult because of him, I honor him and thank him. I learned along the way, that holding resentment and anger towards others who hurt us only hurts us and keeps us stuck. Resentment is the insidious weapon that viciously only hurts the one carrying it. We have a choice and can decide to release the resentment or allow it to continue to cause pain.

Most importantly, I acknowledge the powerful impact of God in my life. I am grateful every day for the amazing journey I am on and for all the gifts He gives me, both in warm loving moments and in the most difficult and challenging times of my life.

Books That Inspired Our Thinking

Just as emotional healing is a lifelong process for ASDPs, so is learning. When Martha and I were growing up thousands of miles apart from each other in our own separate trauma worlds, no one knew what the long-term impacts of our experiences would be on us and the millions of children like us hiding under beds all around the world. We all did the best we could with the limited understanding of what unconscious beliefs about ourselves and the world we would be bringing into our adult lives.

Luckily for us, and happily for you as well, there is now a wealth of research and literature around neuroplasticity, positive psychology, happiness, emotional mastery, joy, common adult characteristics of ASDPs, and the physical ramifications of growing up having had one or more adverse childhood experiences.

We had a tremendous amount of joy doing the research and understanding ourselves better. But we also know that *Healing at Work* is just a humble offering in the vast array of life-changing insights that can be had out there for all of us. We hope that what you have read in this book will inspire you to do your own deep dives into some of the areas the pique your interest the most.

Here are some of the books that especially influenced our own thinking. You'll love the learning!

Broadcasting Happiness: The Science of Igniting and Sustaining Positive Change, Michelle Gielan

Childhood Disrupted: How Your Biography Becomes Your Biology, and How You Can Heal, Donna Jackson Nakazawa

Complex PTSD: From Surviving to Thriving, Peter Walker

The Deepest Well: Healing the Long-Term Effects of Childhood Adversity, Nadine Burke Harris

Emotional Agility: Get Unstuck, Embrace Change and Thrive in Work and Life, Susan David

Feeling Good: The New Mood Therapy, David Burns

Flourish: A Visionary New Understanding of Happiness and Well-being, by Martin Seligman

Forgiving What You Can't Forget, Lysa Terkeurst

Gifts of Imperfection: Let Go of Who You Think You're Supposed to Be and Embrace Who You Are, Brene Brown

The Happiness Advantage: How a Positive Brain Fuels Success in Work and Life, Shawn Achor

The Happiness Hypothesis: Finding Modern Truth in Ancient Wisdom, Jonathan Haidt

Hardwiring Happiness: The New Brain Science of Contentment, Calm, and Confidence, Rick Hanson

Healing the Shame That Binds You, John Bradshaw

Honoring the Self: Self-Esteem and Personal Transformation, Nathaniel Branden

Joyful: The Surprising Power of Ordinary Things To Create Extraordinary Happiness, Ingrid Fetell Lee

The Language of Letting Go, Melody Beattie

Man's Search for Meaning, Viktor Frankl

Positivity: Discover the Upward Spiral that Will Change Your Life, Barbara Fredrickson

The Power of Neuroplasticity, Shad Helmstetter

Psycho-cybernetics, Maxwell Maltz

Radical Acceptance: Embracing Your Life With the Heart of a Buddha, Tara Brach

Resilient: How to Grow an Unshakable Core of Calm, Strength, and Happiness, Rick Hanson

Sacred Contracts: Awakening Your Divine Potential, Caroline Myss

Self-Compassion: The Proven Power of Being Kind to Yourself, Kristin Neff

Self-Sabotage Syndrome: Adult Children in the Workplace, Janet Woititz

Thinking Into Results, Bob Proctor

Your Brain at Work: Strategies for Overcoming Distraction, Regaining Focus, and Working Smarter All Day Long, David Rock

More Praise for *Healing at Work*!

Vulnerability, humanity and healing all balled up into one. Workplaces can be boundless healers to the suffering, many of whom go undetected for decades. Susan and Martha help give hope and health to the people of our modern-day workplace.

Greg Brenner, "HR Dad"
Assistant VP of Talent and Organizational Development, University of Miami

With an awesome combination of candor and insight, Susan and Martha share the steps you can take to move from the cocoon of victimhood, anger and depression into the butterfly mode who can survive life's many slings and arrows, traumas, and dysfunctions. The impact on your physical and emotional health, relationships both at home and at work and your sense of mission and purpose in a life well lived can be one of the best gifts you give yourself.

Ken Wright, President, Ken Wright & Associates

There is tremendous healing power in story—not only the stories we tell others but also the stories we tell ourselves. They can empower and inspire. Or they can debilitate. Adult Survivors of Damaged Pasts commonly grow up with negative narratives that get in the way of fulfilling their potential and achieving the success they deserve. *Healing at Work* shows you a better way—how to use your on-the-job experiences to evolve in your relationships (with others and with yourself), get back into the driver's seat of your life, and become the author of your own story.

Celinne Da Costa, Brand Story Expert and Master Mindset Coach

We in corporate leadership have known for decades that our people do their best work when they know that they can bring their whole selves to work every day. That they don't feel like they have to leave any part of their identity in the proverbial "parking lot" when they start their workday. We're usually talking about family concerns—kids and aging parents, for instance. But we're just coming to grips with the fact that a high percentage of our best talent is also haunted by devastating pasts that drain their energy, compromise their focus, and destroy their confidence. If you are a team leader, chances are that two out of every three of your precious people are suffering from secret pasts. This book will help you understand their struggle.

Keith Nosbusch, Retired CEO and Chairman of the Board, Rockwell Automation

Authors Schmitt Winchester and Finney have written a book showing how unresolved childhood trauma plays out in our daily work lives. Until we recognize the power these traumas have over us, we can't achieve our full potential. *Healing at Work* provides us with a roadmap to navigate our emotional triggers with eyes wide open. Read it and re-claim the rest of your life as your own.

Robert W. "Jake" Jacobs, Author, *Leverage Change* and *Real Time Strategic Change*

With vulnerability, passion, and commitment Susan and Martha provide a resource for those seeking to create more in their life, by understanding how unconscious beliefs inhibit self-acceptance and greater success. It's been a privilege to watch Susan go from corporate dynamo to an absolute force in the corporate world, standing taller and prouder than ever before. If you're looking to elevate your success, I strongly recommend reading *Healing at Work* from start to finish.

Chris La Pak, President and COO, Mini Graphics

Millions of adults from dysfunctional childhoods (Adult Survivors of a Damaged Past) grow up embattled, overwhelmed, abused, and ill-equipped to defend themselves against being victimized. That's how they learn to relate to the world, because they expect the world to relate that way to them. That's their normal. The workplace is a brand-new chance to learn new skills, new ways of building relationships, new ways of discovering your place in the world where you are welcomed and supported. *Healing at Work* shows you how to use your professional life as a laboratory for learning how to live the joyful life of self-acceptance.

Shay Rowbottom
Marketing Guru and Social Media Influencer

With her gripping, and sometimes harrowing, stories, Susan courageously opens her soul to the vivid and life-damaging events that would have derailed anyone. Her journey of reflection and healing is a great reminder of the secret all great leaders know: Understanding and investing in yourself must come before you can truly help others.

Jay Kerley, SVP, Enterprise Enablement Group and CIO, Applied Materials

We often carry baggage from adverse childhood events in our past. As adults we trip over them at home and work. In *Healing at Work*, authors Schmitt Winchester and Finney deal with how these events complicate our work life and show us the way to liberate ourselves from the bondage of our past. This book is a must read when you are ready to embrace a new way of looking at your life.

Bruce D. Silverstein, MD, University Professor and Corporate CEO Coach

As an executive coach working with senior-level leaders, I often see executives unwittingly allow stories from their past to negatively impact their current workplace behavior. Now, with *Healing at Work* as a guidebook for identifying and overcoming past adversities, I have a powerful resource to help my clients reframe those challenges and move forward with heightened self-awareness and strategic coping mechanisms.

Libby Gill, Author of *You Unstuck* and *The Hope-Driven Leader*
Executive Coach, Libby Gill & Company

As CEO of WD-40 Company, my personal purpose in life is inspired by the words of the Dalai Lama: "The purpose of life is to make people happy. And if you can't make them happy, at least don't hurt them." Upon reading *Healing at Work*, I've come to realize in a fresh new way how many people all over the world come to work already in pain as a result of extremely harmful childhood experiences. I can also fully appreciate what a precious opportunity I have to help my tribe members fill their lives with new, positive experiences that can actually heal their wounds.

Garry Ridge, CEO, WD-40 Company

I strongly recommend this book for CEOs and leaders who want to understand why workplace conflicts can quickly escalate, disrupting the organization from achieving its most desired goals. Susan and Martha teach universal lessons that unlock insight about our most important asset—our people—that every leader must have. As I highlighted almost every page, the thought kept coming to me: Everyone in HR definitely must read this book!

Mendy Erad, former CEO, Chairman of multi-national, multi-segment companies

As a corporate wellness professional, I know that our job is to do more than provide fitness centers and smoking or weight-loss programs. Our people's emotional life is as crucial to their wellbeing as how many steps they manage to get into their day. Even more so, in many cases. This book is an eye-opener for those of us in the wellness fields. I especially point out the sections about the lasting health impacts that traumatic experiences can have on people. Be sure to read the chapter that helps us understand how the workplace can be an actively healing place! This book will resonate for most everyone. I have a fresh depth of understanding of wellness needs—for myself, as well as many of my team members and colleagues.

Cynthia Radovich, Managing Director, Global Benefits, Applied Materials

In 2020, our personal and professional lives have become more intertwined than at any point in modern history. What a timely and insightful treatment of the interplay between these two worlds to deliver profoundly powerful advice on how to harness our individual life experiences to create a framework for healing as well as a platform for both personal and professional growth. Sincere gratitude to Susan and Martha for their masterful treatment of this difficult topic for many people!

Dan Durn, SVP and Chief Financial Officer, Applied Materials

Healing at Work is intense: Intensely moving and intensely hopeful. Don't race through it, just savor it page by page.

Ken Siegel, PhD, President/Owner, The Impact Group, Inc.

Healing at Work beautifully unveils the unspoken reality for many in the workplace—that many professional difficulties, challenges, frustrations, fears, worry, and clashes originate from our pasts, most of the time without us even knowing it. You will see yourself in the stories that Susan and Martha passionately share. And you will receive the rare gift of feeling unconditionally understood, heard, connected and accepted, while also learning practical solutions for what to do when things at work aren't working.

Praburam Raja, PhD, Senior Vice President, Semi-Products Group, Applied Materials

About the Authors

Susan Schmitt Winchester is the Senior Vice President, Chief Human Resources Officer for Applied Materials and its more than 23,000 global employees. She has more than 30 years of experience in HR providing executive leadership most recently at Rockwell Automation and the Kellogg Company. She continually looks to meet today's global business challenges with creative HR strategies that engage people, support a dynamic, inclusive corporate culture, and enable company exceptional performance. Her passion is teaching executives and professionals how to succeed by discovering greater self-acceptance, fulfillment and joy at work and in life.

She has lived, studied and worked in the United States, France and England. She earned her master's degree in Industrial/Organizational Psychology from Illinois State University, and her double bachelor's degrees from Albion College in Michigan. She also attended the University of Grenoble, France.

Susan is a fellow of the National Academy of Human Resources—the highest professional honor for individuals in HR. She is also Vice Chair, Leadership Advisory Board to the Dean of Engineering, College of Engineering, University of Michigan. And she is a member of the Forbes HR Council.

She and her husband Charles live in southeastern Wisconsin, near Susan's sons Joseph and Sam.

To follow her online, learn more about her programs, courses and other opportunities to learn, or contact her directly, go here:

https://www.linkedin.com/in/sjschmitt/

www.susanjschmitt.com

Martha I. Finney is the author, ghostwriter, and co-author of 27 books on HR, leadership, employee engagement, and career management. Her best-sellers include HR *From the Heart: Inspiring Stories and Strategies for Building the People Side of Great Business*, which she wrote with Libby Sartain, former CHRO of Southwest Airlines and Yahoo.

She is also a publishing and platform consultant and coach, helping an exclusive clientele expand their professional thought leadership brand by leveraging publishing and social media. Her clients and interviewees come from such companies as Intuit, JetBlue, Avery Dennison, WD-40 Company, Marriott, Caterpillar, Sears Holdings, the U.S. Marine Corps, H-P, and SAS Institute.

Her own original research into employee engagement has been featured in *The Wall Street Journal, The New York Times, The Washington Post, Miami Herald, The San Francisco Chronicle, The San Jose Mercury News, Time Magazine, The Huffington Post*, CNN, NPR, among other business media outlets.

To learn more about Martha and to contact her directly, visit
www.marthafinney.global

Follow her on LinkedIn via
https://www.linkedin.com/in/marthaingramfinney

Printed in the USA
CPSIA information can be obtained
at www.ICGtesting.com
JSHW050220231023
50616JS00005B/11

9 781951 744526